BACKSTORIES IN THE LAW:
TALES OF VICTORS, VILLAINS AND VICTIMS

ALAN M. WEINBERGER
PROFESSOR OF LAW
SAINT LOUIS UNIVERSITY SCHOOL OF LAW

BACKSTORIES IN THE LAW:
TALES OF VICTORS, VILLAINS AND VICTIMS

ALAN M. WEINBERGER
PROFESSOR OF LAW
SAINT LOUIS UNIVERSITY SCHOOL OF LAW

ACADEMICA PRESS
WASHINGTON~LONDON

Library of Congress Cataloging-in-Publication Data

Names: Weinberger, Alan M. (author)
Title: Backstories in the law : tales of victors, villains, and victims |
Weinberger, Alan M.
Description: Washington : Academica Press, 2021. | Includes references.
Identifiers: LCCN 2021940237 | ISBN 9781680538021 (hardcover) |
ISBN 9781680538038 (paperback) | 9781680538045 (e-book)

To

Robin and Noah and Lee

Contents

Acknowledgments

The Author is grateful to the staff in the Manuscript Department of the Library of Congress for their assistance during his visit in August 2017 to inspect The James Couzens Papers. Much appreciation to Karen Bachmann, curator of the Timmons Museum: National Exhibition Centre, for her research assistance and hospitality, and David Yaschyshyn, environmental and sustainability assurance manager for Glencore PLC, for his time, assistance and conversation during the Author's visit to the Kidd Creek Mine in Timmons, Ontario in 2016.

Previous versions of these chapters appeared in the NYU Journal of Law & Business, the Washington and Lee Law Review, the Securities Regulation Law Journal, Texas A&M Law Review, Hofstra Law Review, Mississippi Law Journal, and the Saint Louis University Law Journal. The Author acknowledges the helpful comments and suggestions provided by the editors of these journals.

The Author is grateful to Saint Louis University School of Law for generously supporting his research. He thanks Professor J. Scott Colesanti at the Maurice A. Deane School of Law at Hofstra University for assistance with research, and encouragement. He thanks Michael Brain, Doug Giles, Amy Harms, Megan Murphy, Jordan Taylor and Elizabeth Tucker for their valuable research assistance in the development of these chapters, and especially August Bonacci for his timely and tireless research and editorial assistance. The mistakes that remain are the fault of the Author. Additional thanks to Professors Marc Steinberg, David Lipton and Jules Janick, and Stephen Cousley, for their support and encouragement. Finally, the Author wishes to thank his students at Saint Louis University School of Law, and the students at Washington University School of Law, the University of Iowa College of Law, Hebrew University in Jerusalem, the University of Osnabrück, and Ruhr

University in Bochum, Germany who first listened patiently to these stories.

Introduction

Legendary trial lawyer Edward Bennett Williams observed that a third of all cases can never be won, a third can never be lost, and the battle over the remaining third is what makes or breaks a trial lawyer's reputation. In the third category of cases, beyond the facts of the dispute or relevant legal doctrine, something else is crucial to the result: Dimensions of time and space not only influence, but ultimately govern the outcome of close cases. Each chapter that follows is a compelling drama, complete with victors, victims and villains, that explores the historical and social moment, and often the physical place, in which seven iconic corporate law cases arose.

Why would someone choose to name a Thoroughbred racehorse "Affirmed" after his criminal conviction for federal securities law violations had been affirmed on appeal? This inquiry is the basis for the first chapter, which explores the enigmatic life and spectacular career of Louis E. Wolfson, owner and breeder of the longest-reigning winner of horse racing's Triple Crown.

Perhaps best known as the central figure in the scandal that resulted in the forced resignation of Supreme Court Justice Abe Fortas, Wolfson left a sizable footprint on corporate legal history. He has been described as the original corporate raider, the inventor of the market for corporate control through the hostile tender offer, and the founder of the first modern conglomerate. Principal cases involving Wolfson appear in all Corporations and Securities Regulation casebooks. Long the subject of academic study, commentary, and controversy, these decisions continue to be cited as authority for the indemnification of officers and directors, and the proposition that controlling persons expose themselves to criminal liability for effecting a distribution of unregistered shares of stock. Interviews with attorneys on both sides of litigation involving Wolfson enhance his story through the lens of first-person observation.

During his company's most profitable year ever, Henry Ford suspended the payment of dividends to shareholders. In *Dodge v. Ford*, the Dodge brothers, minority shareholders, challenged Ford's decision in court. Had Ford simply been willing to testify that he suspended dividends with a view toward maximizing long-term profitability, the court likely would have deferred to his business judgment. Instead, Ford boldly, if not recklessly, asserted that he turned off the dividend spigot because his company made too much money! Ford explained his goal was to increase wages and decrease the price of cars, prioritizing workers' and customers' interests over the interests of shareholders. The court rendered an enduring decision, establishing the primacy of maximizing shareholder profit above all other concerns.

Focusing on the pivotal role played by James Couzens, Ford's wingman at the Ford Motor Company, the second chapter explores the backstory of *Dodge v. Ford*. Previously unreported information contained in Couzens' personal and official papers, including his correspondence with the Dodges and other shareholders, suggests that tax avoidance was Ford's actual motivation for suspending dividends at a time of confiscatory income tax rates in the run-up to the First World War.

"Come hell or high water" describes a tenant's unqualified common law obligation to pay rent in full on the first of the month. A long-standing principle of Anglo-American law, this rule persisted for centuries until recognition of an implied warranty of habitability in 1970 in the groundbreaking case of *Javins v. First National Realty Corporation*, the subject of the third chapter.

Javins recognized that legal principles developed in agrarian societies where the land itself was the subject matter of the lease were no longer adequate to protect the interests of modern tenants who expect habitable improvements on the land. Judge Skelly Wright substituted modern contract law principles for centuries-old property law doctrine. The Clifton Terrace Apartments, infamous for giving the District of Columbia its designation as "murder capital," is the principal character in the third chapter, which features graphic descriptions of life at Clifton Terrace drawn from former resident Molly McCardle's chapbook. The complex symbolized the frustration of inner-city black tenants living in substandard housing owned by white landlords. The discrimination minority tenants continue to face fifty years after *Javins* demonstrates that legal rights are meaningless without access to affordable legal services.

It does not happen often. But sometimes, while writing an opinion, a judge has an inkling, or perhaps an intention, that it is destined for law school casebooks — not merely as a note case but as a principal decision, and not just for a couple of editions but for a half-century or more. Whether or not Judge Sterry Robinson Waterman had that idea or purpose in mind in 1968, his opinion in the landmark insider trading case of *SEC v. Texas Gulf Sulphur* certainly had that effect. *Texas Gulf Sulphur*, the subject of the fourth chapter, promulgated the evergreen rule that a purchaser of securities is required to disclose material information unknown to the seller, or otherwise abstain from trading. Opponents of insider trading regulation question why it is both lawful and considered prudent business conduct to profit from informational advantages in the real estate market but it is unlawful to do so in the stock market. This chapter suggests that differences in the duty to disclose in the real estate and securities markets may be exaggerated. Loss of the right to remain silent may be a natural byproduct of natural resources extraction because — according to a former principal at the mining company Texas Gulf — trespass and or deception are often prerequisites or antecedents to natural resource extraction.

At the confluence of three major rivers, Madison County, Illinois was the intersection of the nation's struggle for a free press and the right of access to appellate review in the historic case of the *Alton Telegraph*, the subject of the fifth chapter. The newspaper, which perpetuates the memory of Elijah Lovejoy, the first martyr to the cause of a free press, found itself on the losing side of the largest judgment for defamation in U.S. history as a result of a story that was never published in the paper — a case of immaculate defamation. Because it could not afford to post an appeal bond of that magnitude, one of the oldest family-owned newspapers in the country was forced to file for bankruptcy to protect its viability as a going concern. Attention must be paid to a case in which plaintiff's counsel earned a place in the Guinness Book of World Records, and his adversary was honored for distinction in the defense of a free press and the people's right to know. The Author's correspondence with plaintiff's counsel sheds light on a jury verdict, arguably influenced by prejudicial pre-trial and evidentiary rulings, that was never subject to appellate review. The chapter also contemplates implications of the reality that trial judges experience the drama of the courtroom in a way that appellate judges do not.

For its central role in Penthouse's financial collapse, its links to the FBI's tragicomic ABSCAM sting operation and the epic historo-pornographic film *Caligula*, and with cameo appearances by real estate magnates Harry Helmsley and Donald Trump (not to mention former Miss America Vanessa Williams), the case of the Penthouse casino is a very good story. On another level, *Penthouse v. Dominion Federal Savings & Loan*, the subject of the sixth chapter, dramatically illustrates the role and function of lawyers in sophisticated transactional practice. It exposes the risks an attorney incurs in zealously promoting a client's strategic business objectives: practicing the art of breaking the deal.

While achieving success as a five-time Golden Glove-winning major league catcher, Mike Matheny was preparing for a post-baseball career in real estate development. He could not have picked a worse time. Matheny lost his accumulated savings and his family's home after being held personally liable for a $4.2 million deficiency judgment following foreclosure of property he was unable to develop or market during the Great Recession. Matheny's failure to succeed in real estate was the proximate cause of his return to baseball as manager of the St. Louis Cardinals and later the Kansas City Royals.

Yet sometimes a story is not just a story. A detailed account from a human perspective, Matheny's story provides a compelling narrative and framework for examining a persistent problem in land finance law: calculating deficiency judgements. The seventh and final chapter proposes a re-imagination of the method of calculating deficiency judgments. It seeks to accommodate the interests of borrowers and lenders, and the public interest in judicial efficiency and access to affordable credit.

The focus of these chapters is on the backstories — the invisible part of judicial decision-making that is not expressed in published opinions but nevertheless controls the outcome. The lesson of these law stories is that, ultimately, what lies behind the curtain determines whether justice was done or denied.

I

What's in a Name? — The Tale of Louis Wolfson's Affirmed

I. Introduction

On the first Saturday in May of each year upwards of 150,000 people converge on Churchill Downs in Louisville for the Kentucky Derby. Because Churchill Downs has a seating capacity of 50,000, the overwhelming majority of them are packed in the infield and lucky to catch a glimpse of the race, known as "the fastest two minutes in sports." Churchill Downs perpetuates this slogan in its marketing although it has not been true since the advent of motor sport. An audience of 16 million watches the Run for the Roses on television. They are hoping to witness the next three-year old Thoroughbred who, in five weeks' time, will achieve one of sport's greatest accomplishments: the Triple Crown. The Kentucky Derby, run over 1-1/4 miles, is the first jewel in the Triple Crown, the other two being the Preakness Stakes ran two weeks later over a 1-3/16 mile course at Pimlico Race Track in Baltimore, and the Belmont Stakes ran three weeks thereafter over a 1-1/2 mile course at Belmont Park in New York. In 1978, Louis E. Wolfson's Affirmed became the eleventh and longest-reigning winner of the Triple Crown. It would be nearly four decades until American Pharaoh won the Triple Crown in 2015.

By the time Affirmed won the Triple Crown, his owner had won and lost fights for corporate control of such household names as Montgomery Ward and American Motors, established the first modern conglomerate, been convicted twice of, and served time in prison for, securities law violations, caused a justice of the Supreme Court of the United States to resign in disgrace for the only time in history (not to mention the arrest of television personality Larry King), and enriched a legion of corporate and white collar criminal defense lawyers. Yale law professor Alexander Bickel described Justice Abe Fortas' acceptance of money from Wolfson, then under investigation for securities fraud, as "very probably the gravest known lapse in the personal ethics of a Justice of the Supreme Court in the history of the institution."[1] Wolfson may also have been responsible for President Lyndon B. Johnson's firing of Attorney General Nicholas Katzenbach in 1966 for refusing to block Wolfson's indictment and subsequent conviction.

Wolfson is said to have invented the hostile tender offer and activated the modern market for corporate control. Henry Manne, former Dean of George Mason University School of Law and the founder of the law and economics discipline, credits Wolfson's invention as a "contribution to human welfare far exceed[ing] the total value of all private philanthropy in history." The modern hostile tender offer, according to Professor Manne, "activated and energized the market for corporate control, was the primary cause of the revolutionary restructuring of American industry in the 1970s and 1980s, and the ensuing economic boom."[2]

In race-track parlance, a horse's "connections" consist of the principal humans involved in its ownership and training, and its jockey. This chapter explores the meaning behind the name of Louis Wolfson's most successful racehorse, Affirmed, and his connections to 20th century American corporate legal history.

Louis Wolfson's complex life and spectacular career are described in Part II of this chapter. Part III examines Wolfson's sizable footprint in American corporate legal history. In almost every corporations and securities regulation casebook, principal cases bear Wolfson's name. He is the subject of leading cases on the indemnification of officers and directors, and the requirement that controlling persons in a corporation cannot dispose of their shares without registration. Wolfson's central role in the resignation of Justice Abe Fortas is discussed in Part IV. Fascinating new details continue to emerge more than four decades after the scandal. Part V describes the life and extraordinary career of Affirmed. He is arguably the best of the 13 winners of the Triple Crown because he thrice defeated a horse that was almost his equal while the other winners were clearly the overwhelmingly dominant members of their generations. Part VI explores various theories for the name, Affirmed. It includes explanations not previously offered based on conversations and correspondence with attorneys who litigated on behalf of and in opposition to Wolfson, and with equine historians who knew the principals.

II. The Original Corporate Raider

Perhaps the result of his capacity for litigiousness during the first half of his life, and publicity shyness to the point of reclusiveness thereafter, no biography of Louis Wolfson was written during his lifetime or since his death in 2007. Potential biographers would have been aware, for example, that Wolfson sued the *Washington Post* for $30 million for defamation after the paper criticized his chairmanship of the Washington, D.C. public transportation system. Perhaps ironically for a corporate raider, Wolfson was described by friends as "a quiet man, a private man, one who avoids the limelight of public appearance."[3] Known to refuse the numerous social invitations that came his way, he once remarked to guests at a celebration for Affirmed in Florida in 1978 that he had recently turned down an invitation to a private gathering hosted by one of the nation's governors where the President of the United States was to be among the guests.

The story of Wolfson's rags-to-riches (and back again) life and career may be pieced together through a combination of published opinions, media accounts and sources about his contemporaries. New information has emerged within the past few years as a result of the principals becoming more reflective, candid, or both in their retirement. Interviews with attorneys on both sides of litigation involving Wolfson enhance the legal archeology.

Louis Elwood Wolfson was born in St. Louis, Missouri on January 28, 1912. The following year the family moved to Jacksonville, Florida, where his father went into the salvage business. Wolfson very likely inherited his instinctive entrepreneurship, capacity for hard work and determination to succeed from his father. Morris D. Wolfson was a Lithuanian Jewish immigrant who escaped to the United States in 1896 at the age of 17 to avoid conscription in the Russian army. Before moving his family to Jacksonville, he worked in St. Louis as an iceman, clothes presser and fruit peddler.

An indifferent student but four-sport star athlete in high school, Wolfson was an All-Southern end in football, and lettered in basketball, baseball and track. He also boxed professionally in his teens under the ring name "Kid Wolf," earning up to $100 per fight. Wolfson attended the University of Georgia on a football scholarship and, according to one source that described him as a "salaried football player," Wolfson demanded and received $100 a month to play for Georgia.[4] A starting right end as a sophomore, he suffered a career-ending shoulder injury in the Yale Bowl in Fall 1931 tackling Yale football legend Albie Booth while returning the second-half kick-off. The injury, which left Wolfson with a steel plate in his shoulder, ended his ambition to pursue a career as a professional football player and coach, and made him ineligible for service in World War II. Wolfson would remain at Georgia another year, playing basketball and wrestling, before dropping out of college to help his father rebuild the family scrap metal business, M. Wolfson & Co., in Jacksonville that had been crippled by the Great Depression. Taunted by classmates for being "all muscle, no brains," Wolfson confided to a friend, "Those guys think they're pretty smart, but let me tell you — one of these days I'm going to make a lot of money and make them eat those words."[5]

In 1932, with $10,000 (half borrowed from a wealthy Georgia football booster, Harold Hirsch, and the rest a loan against the family's life insurance policies), Louis, his father and older brother, Sam, invested in a construction supply firm, Florida Pipe and Supply Company. Younger brothers Sol, Cecil and Nathan later joined the business as partners. Working 18 to 20 hour days loading trucks and selling pipe, their sales grew from $100,000 in the first year to $4.5 million per year. "In those days, there were no hours," recalled brother Saul. "You worked morning to night, Saturday, Sunday, until you got the job done."[6] According to family legend, Wolfson made his first "killing" when he bought plumbing supplies and fixtures for $275 from the son of department store magnate J.C. Penney. Intended for Penney Farms, a retirement community for clergy whose construction was temporarily placed on hold by the Depression, the supplies were hauled by Wolfson to the family scrap metal yard, held until the price rose, and sold piecemeal for $100,000. When World War II broke out, brothers Sam, Saul and Cecil enlisted but Louis Wolfson was turned down because of his shoulder injury, which had never healed properly, and a bad kidney.

Having discovered how under-valued scrap metal and building supplies could be bought and sold for a substantial profit, Wolfson realized that the skills developed in the junkyard might be transferable to something more lucrative and less strenuous. "Wolfson soon perceived that the junkyard, with its mounds of twisted scrap iron, old tires and skeletons of wrecked automobiles, offered little more than back breaking toil and a bare hand to mouth living."[7] He taught himself to scan corporate balance sheets and recognize under-performing assets. Wolfson became known as the "Junkman" for his aptitude for identifying, acquiring and liquidating undervalued businesses.

Wolfson played the game of business as aggressively as he had once played football, earning the reputation for being a "raider" decades before the term became commonplace in the corporate lexicon. Wolfson was the successful bidder in 1946 for St. John's Shipbuilding Company, a government-owned war-surplus shipyard in Jacksonville, which he liquidated at a considerable profit. In what became a recurring pattern, his St. John's success was clouded by allegations of bribery, a congressional probe and grand jury investigation. Wolfson took advantage of a mistake by the government, which inadvertently omitted a requirement that the winning bidder operate the shipyard and not merely dismantle it. Wolfson parlayed the proceeds from the St. John's liquidation into the purchase in 1947 of a chain of movie theaters, and a second Florida surplus shipyard, Tampa Shipbuilding Co., which he also liquidated for a considerable profit. Wolfson's total profit on the two shipyards was $10 million.

In 1949, Wolfson gained control of Capital Transit Company, the District of Columbia's public transportation service, in what has been described as the first hostile tender offer. Capital Transit at the time held $6.7 million in cash and securities. Wolfson and his three brothers acquired 46% of the shares for $20 per share, a total of $2.2 million. Soon after taking control Wolfson replaced almost all of senior management and the board, installing himself as chairman.

Wolfson's management of Capital Transit was seen as a classic case of "milking" by an absentee owner, a characterization that Wolfson did not dispute. At a 1954 press conference announcing his plans to seek control of Montgomery Ward & Company, Wolfson admitted to milking Capital Transit, justifying his conduct on the basis of its being in a regulated industry. Instead of investing money in needed new equipment, he caused the company's surplus cash and subsequent earnings to be paid in dividends. Capital Transit made multiple requests for fare increases while bus and streetcar ridership declined, and costs for labor and fuel climbed. According to one newspaper editorial, "His tactics, indeed the whole Wolfson operation of a once-sound company have been a hark-back to the robber baron days of the last century."[8]

A midsummer bus strike that started on July 1, 1955 immobilized the capital for seven weeks in the heat of summer. Capital Transit workers went out on strike after management refused to negotiate a new labor contract until Congress approved yet another fare increase. As chairman of the Capital Transit board, Wolfson's presence was requested before a Senate subcommittee. He could not be located. In response to a subpoena, he sent a telegram. Pandemonium erupted when Wolfson finally appeared on July 12. In the course of his testimony, he engaged in a shouting match with committee members. Wolfson expressed his philosophy that stockholders came first: "I believe in being liberal in dividends. I expect always to be."[9] After the strike ended on July 30, Congress passed legislation making Capital Transit a public utility. Although Wolfson got the last laugh, selling the company in 1956 for $13.5 million, his turbulent tenure as head of Capital Transit made Wolfson a high-visibility figure, and the subject of considerable animosity among official Washington.

The year 1949 also saw Wolfson engineer the successful acquisition of Merritt- Chapman & Scott Corporation (MCS), then a small marine salvage company, through one of the first proxy contests of the post-war period. Ripe for take-over, MCS suffered from stodgy, internally divided management. The common stock had a value below $6 million at a time when the firm's net worth was at least $8 million, including $3.4 million in cash. "Management was old, weak, and unable to adjust to the postwar environment. Like many other men of their generation, they were unassertive, psychologically scarred by the Great Depression."[10] Together with his brothers, Wolfson accumulated more than 35% of MCS shares. He formed an alliance with Hirsch and Company, a New York brokerage firm whose customers owned a large number of MCS shares. By the end of the contest, Wolfson and his associates held 13 of the 21 seats on the board of directors.

As chairman of the board and chief executive officer from 1951 through 1969, Wolfson transformed MCS into the first modern conglomerate, acquiring businesses in such diverse industries as paint production, steel manufacturing, and money lending. Although it may have seemed like a lack of coherent agenda to be randomly assembling businesses without regard to synergy, Wolfson was decades ahead of his time in conglomerating companies based solely on the rationale of their having unrealized values. An MCS subsidiary, New York Shipbuilding Corporation, built the *Savannah,* the first nuclear-powered cargo ship, and the aircraft carrier *Kitty Hawk.* Within six years under Wolfson's management, the value of MCS increased from $8 million to $132 million. By the mid-1960's MCS was 210 on the Fortune 500.

In 1954 Wolfson announced his plan to seek control of Chicago-based Montgomery Ward & Company, the nation's oldest catalog retailer, by means of a proxy contest.

> It was the business story of the year. Newspaper readers who earlier had no interest in such matters wondered just what it was Wolfson was attempting, why he was going about it in that way, and what it had to do with them. People who previously demonstrated little or no interest in the subject started reading the financial pages.[11]

Like MCS, Ward's management strategy appeared to Wolfson as overly conservative to its stockholders' detriment. Challenged by rival Sears, Roebuck and Company, Ward was closing stores and cutting inventory. "By 1955, as Fortune magazine later put it, 'Montgomery Ward was a very sick cat.'"[12] Like Capital Transit, Ward was hoarding $300 million in cash and debt-free in anticipation of the next Great Depression, which octogenarian chairman Sewell Lee Avery feared was around the corner. "Avery awoke in the morning of postwar America on the wrong side of the bed,"[13] but was hardly alone in his belief in a strategy of accumulating cash reserves with a view to expansion if real estate and construction prices fell in a repeat of the Great Depression.

The struggle for control of Montgomery Ward was, according to the *New York Times*, "one of the fiercest battles in the history of corporate finance."[14] A proxy contest for control of a public corporation was largely unregulated, dangerous and difficult in the 1950's. "Wolfson was subjected to anonymous telephone calls threatening kidnapping, which were reported to federal authorities. For a while, FBI agents traveled with the Wolfson party."[15] By the 1980's, however, the greater availability of credit including junk bond financing caused the hostile tender offer to almost completely replace the proxy contest as the preferred means of acquiring corporate control. Wolfson clearly perceived a proxy contest to be a campaign for the hearts and minds of its shareholders. According to Wolfson,

> Proxy contests are wholesome because similar to public elections they serve to focus attention on the stewardship of those holding and aspiring to office. They are a form of surgery sometimes necessary to effect the cure of corporate ills. Just as the cure for any physical condition must start with the patient himself, the cure for corporate ills must start with management.[16]

Ward's 2,000 employees were enlisted to contact stockholders asking them to vote with management. Invoking his Capital Transit and Florida shipyards track record, Ward management attacked Wolfson personally, describing him as an irresponsible raider seeking to loot the company.

Wolfson sought to portray himself as a strong voice for stockholders, and the Daytona Beach Morning Journal portrayed him as "a modern St. George: out to slay the dragons of entrenched business greed for the protection of thousands of small stockholders."[17] He traveled to shareholders' meetings in Florida, California, New York, Chicago, and Detroit. Convinced that the low level of stock ownership in America was the product of a lack of confidence in corporate management, he claimed to be on a mission to restore U.S. companies to their rightful owners, and thereby inspire more Americans to become stockholders.

Notwithstanding a public persona of somewhat humorless intensity, Wolfson became a media celebrity. “Tall, strikingly handsome, with piercing eyes and a slow drawl,” Wolfson, together with his photogenic wife and children, attracted the attention of *Time, Look, Life*, the *Saturday Evening Post, Forbes* and other mainstream publications. Wolfson’s is believed to be the first photograph ever published in the *Wall Street Journal*. Images of the Wolfson family can be found on the website of Post Time USA.[18]

Because of staggered terms, only three of Ward’s nine directors were up for election each year. Using cumulative voting, Wolfson might hope to achieve at most a minority voice on the board. His solution to this problem was an audacious lawsuit challenging the constitutionality of the staggered board of directors. A week before the annual meeting of stockholders, the Illinois Supreme Court held for Wolfson, ordering that all nine directors’ seats be placed on the ballot for election. Wolfson hailed the decision as “a tremendous victory for corporate democracy,” and Ward’s stock rose on the news.

> The showdown took place on April 22 at the Medinah Temple, a Shrine auditorium on Chicago’s North Side. The meeting was well attended and covered in detail by the press. The board tried to restrain the elderly Avery, but he would have none of it, insisting on personally answering questions. He appeared weary and confused, rambling at times, rarely responding directly. Wolfson was courteous, content to permit Avery to damage his credibility with this kind of performance. No one there could have failed to conclude that the chairman was ill-equipped to continue in office.[19]

Avery’s daughter, a spectator to her father’s alarming performance at the meeting, wept as a *Life* photographer captured dramatic images of the proceedings.[20]

Avery allowed the rumor to spread that, regardless of the outcome, he would resign as chairman following the election. A few days after the meeting, Avery resigned, although he remained on the board until his death in 1960. The day he announced his resignation, Montgomery Ward was the most active issue traded on the New York Stock Exchange. As buy orders flooded in, trading in Ward stock was suspended for an hour until the balance between buy and sell orders could be restored. The retirement rumor may have reassured enough stockholders that Wolfson received just 30% of the votes, entitling him to only three seats using cumulative voting. However, Avery's successor, Vice President John Barr, instituted most of the changes urged by Wolfson in his proxy fight. The battle for control of Montgomery Ward cost Wolfson $500,000 in proxy solicitation expenses, but Ward's stock price rose, and Wolfson's profits more than covered his costs by the time he and his associates resigned from the board in January 1956.

Wolfson followed his bid for Montgomery Ward by targeting American Motors Corporation (AMC). This effort likewise was unsuccessful. Wolfson also failed in efforts to buy the Brooklyn Dodgers, Washington Senators, Baltimore Colts and Churchill Downs, for which he reportedly offered to pay $46 million in 1985. Targeting AMC, Wolfson shorted its stock by 137,000 shares, betting that the price would fall. As the price rose under the leadership of George Romney, Wolfson faced the prospect of considerable losses covering his short position.

In June 1958 Wolfson's long-time confidante and investment adviser, Alexander Rittmaster, planted a false story with the *New York Times* that Wolfson was selling AMC shares, believing the stock to be fully valued. (Wolfson had already sold his shares and was in fact short in the stock.) By this time, Wolfson had attracted the attention of government investigators by reason of the public fascination surrounding him during the D.C. transit strike and struggle for control of Montgomery Ward. The Securities and Exchange Commission (SEC) accused Wolfson of using false information to drive down the price of AMC stock. However, Wolfson claimed that, after deciding to abandon his bid for AMC, he put an associate in charge of selling the 400,000 shares of AMC that he owned. This associate, without Wolfson's knowledge, not only sold all of the shares but left Wolfson short. Wolfson settled the case without admitting wrongdoing, entering into a consent decree not to make any fraudulent statements about AMC stock or his holdings.

III. When You Soar Like An Eagle, You Attract The Hunters

Louis Wolfson's downfall was being plotted even as the wealth was piling up and his long-term success seemed assured, not unlike the tragic and untimely end that awaits a great Thoroughbred pushed to exceed his levels of endurance and talent, whose destruction is sowed by his success.

High-profile battles in the 1950's for control of AMC, Montgomery Ward and MCS had made Wolfson "something of a folk hero, a sort of Robin Hood," according to Paul Windels, a former federal prosecutor involved in the AMC case who was interviewed two years before his death in 2009.[21] Along with great wealth and celebrity status, however, Wolfson's spectacular career trajectory earned him a reputation for sharp dealing and widespread distrust in the business community. He was reputed to have been "a known friend and business associate of various members of the Florida criminal underworld."[22] Having challenged the leadership of large corporations, Wolfson made powerful enemies. Unproven charges of skillful opportunism dogged Wolfson in the 1950's. More serious accusations of criminal misconduct in the 1960's would haunt Wolfson for the rest of his life.

Two indictments were returned against Wolfson by the same federal grand jury on September 19 and October 18, 1966, respectively, for unrelated violations of the federal securities laws in connection with trading in the shares of MCS and Continental Enterprises, Inc., a Jacksonville theater-management company. The indictments presented novel legal and complex factual problems. Securities and corporate law issues raised by Wolfson's vigorous and persistent defense against these charges have since been the subject of academic study, commentary and controversy. Wolfson was not alone in his belief that he was the target of over-zealous prosecution in both cases.

While investigating a suspicious pattern of trading in MCS stock, the SEC staff probed into Wolfson's financial affairs more generally, and became interested in Continental Enterprises. Its stock price had increased dramatically after Wolfson had licensed the rights to Propel-Pak, an aerosol device for dispensing soft drinks, to Continental Enterprises. From

1960 to 1962 Wolfson and Elkin ("Buddy") Gerbert, a close Wolfson associate and director of MCS and Continental Enterprises, sold 690,000 unregistered shares through six brokerage houses as the price rose from $2.75 to $8.50, for a profit of $1.6 million. The government charged Wolfson and Gerbert with hyping publicity about the stock to increase its price while they sold shares at a substantial profit without first registering with the SEC as required under Section 5 of the Securities Act of 1933 (the "33 Act").

The SEC referred the Continental Enterprises case to the Department of Justice for criminal prosecution in March 1966. The case was assigned to the office of Robert M. Morgenthau, who served as U.S. Attorney for the Southern District of New York for 35 years until his retirement in 2010 at the age of 90. The fiercely independent Morgenthau inspired the original district attorney character, Adam Schiff, on the television drama "Law and Order." Critics have accused Morgenthau, who once left his position as prosecutor to run unsuccessfully against Nelson Rockefeller for governor of New York in 1962, of putting too much emphasis on white collar crime and targeting prominent persons to further his own political ambition. The experience of Morgenthau's office in dealing with complex white collar crime surely influenced the Justice Department's choice of where to assign the Wolfson cases. Wolfson's lawyers argued, unsuccessfully, that the cases should have been transferred to Florida. Florida was not only closer to Continental Enterprises' office and Wolfson's home, where he would have been on friendlier ground, but by 1967 Wolfson had suffered a heart attack and first wife, Florence Monsky Wolfson, was dying from cancer.

Under the government's theory, Wolfson's position as the largest individual stockholder in Continental Enterprises and its guiding spirit made him a "control person." Together with immediate family members and the Wolfson Family Foundation, Wolfson and Gerbert directly and indirectly owned more than 40% of the Continental Enterprises stock then outstanding. In a somewhat novel interpretation of several complex provisions of the '33 Act, the government argued that the sale of stock on behalf of a control person makes the broker an outlet for the distribution of securities to the public and the transaction not exempt from registration.

The considerable uncertainty as to the rules governing sales of securities by controlling persons in brokers' transactions was largely resolved by *In re Ira Haupt & Co.*, 23 S.E.C. 589 (1946), but that proceeding involved a broker. The Continental Enterprises case was the first time the government brought criminal proceedings against a control person. At the time, it could still be argued that, if the broker sold for the controlling person without knowledge that it was participating in a distribution of securities, no specific provision of the '33 Act imposed liability on the control person either.

Wolfson believed he was being victimized for his celebrity, and by those who felt threatened by his challenge to the entrenched leadership of large corporations. Henry Manne characterized the Continental Enterprises case as "a completely trumped up securities violation case heralded by the managerial establishment" to extract revenge against the inventor of the hostile takeover.[23] Robert Sobel, Professor of History at Hofstra University, added that "From the vantage point of a quarter of a century later, it seems clear that Wolfson had no criminal intent, that the government had come after him with guns blazing, determined to rid the business scene of a dangerous raider. There are no subtle shadings here; Wolfson was the victim of a zealous prosecutor."[24] Indeed, Wolfson testified at trial that he had no idea there was any law requiring registration of a security before its distribution by a controlling person to the public, that he operated at a level of corporate finance far above the details of the securities laws, and that he relied upon others in matters of regulatory compliance. Wolfson pointed the finger at his stockbrokers for willfully neglecting to call his attention to the registration requirements for fear of aborting the transactions and losing substantial commissions. Wolfson later filed suit against the broker who handled the largest number of sell orders claiming the broker had fraudulently misrepresented that Wolfson would be able to dispose of his Continental Enterprises stock without registering with the SEC. Joe DiMaggio and Ed Sullivan were among the many celebrities who testified as character witnesses to Wolfson's reputation in the community for truth and veracity.

Wolfson had reported the stock sales on his tax returns and paid income taxes on the profit. He claimed he would not have done so had he known that what he was doing was unlawful. The weak-link in Wolfson's inner circle, financial advisor Rittmaster agreed to cooperate with the government to avoid indictment as a co-conspirator. Rittmaster testified that he had placed sales orders for Continental Enterprises stock as a nominee, suggesting that the defendants were aware of the illegality of their conduct.

Following a three-week trial, on September 29, 1967 the jury convicted Wolfson and Gerbert of 19 counts of violating and conspiring to violate the securities laws in selling unregistered stock in Continental Enterprises. Assured by his attorneys that, at worst, he might be subject to civil penalties but not criminal prosecution for what amounted to minor, technical offenses, Wolfson now faced a possible 95 years in prison. On November 28, 1967, Judge Edmund L. Palmieri sentenced Wolfson to one year on each count, to run concurrently, assessed a fine of $100,000, and ordered Wolfson to pay the costs of the prosecution.

According to one account, while awaiting sentencing, Wolfson claimed he was approached by Dr. Samuel Belkin, President of Yeshiva University, who purported to be acting as intermediary for Francis Cardinal Spellman of New York. If Wolfson contributed heavily to Catholic Charities, "my legal problems would be over," Wolfson is said to have reported. Wolfson did not recall that a price had been set, but an associate put the figure at $1 million. After considering the offer Wolfson became furious. "I refused to buy any political influence or any other type of influence," he is said to have decided. "I spent in excess of two million [dollars] fighting this injustice." According to this account, Judge Palmieri was a friend of Cardinal Spellman who, at the time, was trying to finance a lobbying effort to secure an amendment to the New York state constitution to permit state aid for parochial schools and presumably needed funds for that purpose.[25]

Wolfson moved for a new trial a year later on the basis of newly discovered evidence. To refute Wolfson's claim that he was unaware of the registration requirements of the '33 Act, the government had called as a rebuttal witness James Duncan, a retired SEC attorney present during an interview SEC staff members conducted with Wolfson in 1950 on the specific subject of the registration requirements of Section 5. The government introduced a damaging piece of rebuttal evidence consisting of an eight-page internal memorandum from the SEC files, dated in 1950, purporting to contemporaneously memorialize the interview. After reviewing the memorandum to refresh his recollection, Duncan testified as to who was present and what had occurred. Wolfson claimed the watermarks on the paper did not come into existence until 1952 and the document had been fabricated by the government. Following a six-day evidentiary hearing, including reports of ink, signature and neutron activation analysis (a method for determining the elemental composition of matter by placing samples in a nuclear reactor and measuring the emitted radioactivity), Judge Palmieri found that Wolfson had not proven the document was spurious and denied his motion for a new trial.

Wolfson's conviction was affirmed on appeal. The opinion of the United States Court of Appeals for the Second Circuit is still studied in Securities Regulation courses and cited as the leading case establishing the criminal liability of a control person for making an unregistered distribution of stock. Through a curious method of drafting, the '33 Act does not explicitly hold the conduct of controlling persons illegal when they effect a distribution of unregistered securities through brokers. To reach this result, Senior Circuit Judge Peter Woodbury skillfully weaved his way through several provisions of the statute.

Section 5 makes it unlawful to use means of interstate commerce to sell a security unless a registration statement is in effect. However, Section 4(1) exempts "[t]ransactions by any person other than an issuer, underwriter, or dealer." Wolfson and Gerbert claimed they fell within this exemption because they were not issuers, underwriters or dealers. The difficulty with this argument, according to the court, is that it ignores Section 2(a)(11) which broadly defines "underwriter" to include both traditional underwriters and any person who has purchased from an issuer with a view to the distribution of any security. The definition goes on to define "issuer" for purposes of Section 2(a)(11) to include any person directly or indirectly controlling the issuer. As a result, the first sentence of Section 2(a)(11) reads, "The term underwriter means any person who has purchased from a control person with a view to, or any person who offers or sells for a control person in connection with the distribution of any security." When a control person sells securities, the broker who assists in the sale is deemed to be selling for an issuer, which makes the broker an underwriter. In other words, a control person is not himself an underwriter; control persons taint brokers by turning brokers into underwriters. If the broker is an underwriter, the transaction is not exempt under Section 4(1).

As Johnny Carson, former host of the Tonight Show, would say, "If you buy the premise, you buy the bit." The intellectual honesty of the interpretation may be challenged by noting that the next time someone is in Wolfson's position, he could avoid prison by selling the securities without involving brokers. By effecting the distribution himself, the control person would not be deemed an issuer, underwriter or dealer and would fall within the Section 4(1) exemption. However, as a practical matter, control persons cannot dispose of large blocks of securities to the public without involving the securities industry. They need a broker.

"The 'deemed issuer' provision of section 2(a)(11)," wrote University of Michigan Law Professor Alfred Conard, "is a curious piece of draftsmanship, by any standard."[26] "The one clear lesson . . . is that section 2(a)(11)'s definition of underwriter is a trap for both the careless and unwary."[27] When the dust settles on this exercise in complex statutory construction, the brokers who provide outlets for the sale of large blocks of securities by control persons are thus underwriters. Securities sold in transactions by underwriters are not exempt under Section 4(1).

But, appellants argued, there is yet another exemption available under Section 4(4) for brokers' transactions executed upon customers' orders. Wolfson and Gerbert ingeniously tried to piggy-back along with the brokers in claiming entitlement to the Section 4(4) exemption. Because none of the brokers had solicited the sales and Wolfson had kept them in the dark as to the scope of his sales, they were innocent parties entitled to the exemption for brokers' transactions. Unfortunately, Section 4(4) was intended only to exempt the brokers. As Judge Woodbury famously wrote, "Control persons must find their own exemptions." This statutory interpretation, although tortuous, is entirely consistent with the legislative intent. If a control person who has access to material nonpublic information about the company is unloading shares, the public ought to be informed. Also, like any other change in the company's business, the influx of shares in large volumes is a significant event that ought to be known by other traders in the market.

The court rejected appellants' assertion that Judge Palmieri committed reversible error by allowing the prosecutor to cross the line in closing argument to the jury, although Judge Woodbury did acknowledge that allusions to violent crimes, specifically bank robbery, murder and Jack Ruby's shooting of Lee Harvey Oswald, "were somewhat extreme." *United States v. Wolfson*, 405 F.2d 779, 785 (2d Cir. 1968), *cert. denied*, 394 U.S. 946 (1969). "But," Judge Woodbury observed, "counsel for appellants went to the other extreme of likening their clients' purported offense to parking too close to a hydrant." In response to appellants' argument that Sections 4 and 5 of the '33 Act are unconstitutionally vague, the court noted that Wolfson and Gerbert were not claiming to have misunderstood or misinterpreted the statute, but rather to have been unaware of it because it was beneath their notice. "There will be time enough to consider that question when raised by someone whom it concerns.," scolded Judge Woodbury. *Id.* at 783. Professor Conard observed that

> The government's successful contention that Wolfson should be deemed an issuer and his brokers deemed underwriters reminds one of an anecdote about a Canadian judge who held that an equestrian who shot his horse when it went lame should be convicted under a law against feather merchants who shoot songbirds. In either case, the conduct was outrageous, and had escaped a more specific prohibition.[28]

In 1979, after serving his prison sentence, Wolfson filed a civil suit to recover actual and punitive damages from the stockbroker who handled the largest number of sell orders, alleging the broker had fraudulently misrepresented that Wolfson could sell his Continental Enterprises stock without violating the securities laws. In granting defendant's motion to dismiss and for summary judgment, the court held that, as a result of his conviction, Wolfson was collaterally estopped from claiming he was unaware of the registration requirements at the time of the sales.

In 1964 the SEC commenced an investigation of irregularities in trading in MCS stock. On June 10, 1966, the Department of Justice received a referral of the MCS case from the SEC with a recommendation for criminal prosecution. Morgenthau's office secured an indictment charging Wolfson, Gerbert, Joseph Kosow, MCS President Marshal Staub and Rittmaster with conspiracy to violate the securities laws, obstruction of justice and perjury.

In summer 1968, a year after being convicted in the Continental Enterprises case, Wolfson was back in Judge Palmieri's courtroom facing trial in the MCS case. Wolfson unsuccessfully sought recusal of Judge Palmieri, himself a former federal prosecutor, on the grounds of his having presided over the Continental Enterprises case and bias. Before and during the trial, Judge Palmieri denied motions by various defendants for severances, including Kosow's motion for a severance based on the conviction of Wolfson and Gerbert the previous year in the Continental Enterprises case.

After accepting a plea bargain, Rittmaster provided information that formed the basis for the government's prosecution, and testified as its star witness. Rittmaster had pled guilty in 1964 of conspiring to bribe a New York City official to obtain a parking meter contract and probably believed that he would face a severe sentence upon a second conviction. Wolfson had tried to discourage Rittmaster from cooperating with the government in February 1966 by hinting of access to friends in high places who would intervene on their behalf if necessary. After connecting the dots and deducing that Wolfson had been referring to Justice Abe Fortas, Rittmaster revealed this information, together with the fact that Fortas had become a consultant to the Wolfson Family Foundation, to Morgenthau's office (which was initially incredulous). According to Morgenthau, he asked Attorney General Ramsey Clark to pass the information along to Chief Justice Earl Warren. After waiting a couple of weeks for Clark to act, Morgenthau decided to take the bull by the horns and called Justice Byron White, a law school classmate. Justice White reported that he spoke to the Chief Justice who told him that Clark had not spoken to him, but that the Chief Justice had spoken with Fortas who denied taking money from Wolfson.

The indictment in the MCS case charged defendants with hatching and carrying out a scheme beginning in 1961 by which Kosow, not himself an officer or director of MCS, purchased 700,000 shares of MCS on the open market while the stock was trading at artificially low prices of $8–12 per share, considerably below book value. The artificially low share price reflected losses suffered as a result of MCS having expanded beyond its capacity, undertaking vast construction projects in the mid-1950's including dams, power plants and sections of the Mackinac and Throgs Neck bridges. New York Shipbuilding Corporation, an MCS subsidiary, was engaged in a bitter dispute with the Navy in connection with the construction of the super-carrier Kitty Hawk. MCS was forced to borrow from lenders under terms that prevented MCS from using its cash to make stock purchases. The stock repurchase deal was designed to circumvent these terms.

Simultaneously, defendants caused MCS to enter into a secret binding agreement to repurchase Kosow's stock at $18.75 per share, thus assuring a substantial profit, while concealing the arrangement from stockholders and the SEC. The government claimed this constituted a conspiracy to violate SEC Rule 10b-5, which prohibits the use of deception in the purchase of securities, because MCS stockholders without knowledge of the secret repurchase agreement were deceived into selling their shares to Kosow at low prices. To prevent discovery, defendants had conspired to destroy all copies of the repurchase agreement, file false documents with the SEC and the New York Stock Exchange, testify falsely under oath that no such repurchase agreement ever existed, and influence witnesses to do likewise. Although the government conceded there was nothing wrong with MCS contracting with Kosow to purchase his stock, prosecutors believed it was a fraud upon stockholders who sold their shares to Kosow not to be told about the repurchase agreement, and therefore a violation of Rule 10b-5. The perjury, subornation of perjury and obstruction of justice through destruction of documents and filing of false reports were clearly criminal violations.

At the end of the government's case, Judge Palmieri dismissed the portion of the conspiracy count dealing with violation of the securities laws, there being no basis for the jury to find that the defendants had violated Rule 10b-5 on these facts. According to Judge Palmieri, the defendants' conduct might well have constituted a civil violation of the securities laws, but not criminal fraud because it could not be said that a person of ordinary intelligence would understand that the conduct delineated by the government's evidence was forbidden by the terms of Rule 10b-5. As ultimately submitted to the jury, the case thus would be limited to perjury, subornation of perjury, obstruction of justice, and conspiracy to do so.

The seven-week trial ended on August 8, 1968 with the conviction of all defendants on all counts. In December 1968, Judge Palmieri, for the second time in 12 months, pronounced sentence on Wolfson, this time to imprisonment for 18 months (to follow his sentence in the Continental Enterprises case) and a $32,000 fine. Judge Palmieri refused to postpone the sentencing date despite the fact that Wolfson's wife was fatally ill at the time. Florence Monsky Wolfson died the day after sentencing. Wolfson sent a telegram to the judge a few days later pledging "to do everything to have you removed from the bench."

On appeal, the Second Circuit reversed defendants' convictions in the MCS case on all counts. The court agreed with their argument that deletion of the securities fraud portion of the conspiracy count constituted a material alteration of the indictment as returned by the grand jury. The court did not think the amendment of the indictment constituted grounds for a mistrial. However, because four weeks of evidence concerning defendants' alleged stock fraud and $3 million profit had been offered in proof of a portion of a count that had been dismissed, Judge Palmieri committed reversible error by waiting until his instructions to inform the jury of the amendment, not striking the evidence introduced in proof of the deleted portion of the count, and not adequately explaining the effect of its elimination to the jury.

A separate basis for reversal was Judge Palmieri's curtailment of defense counsel's effort to challenge Rittmaster's credibility on cross-examination. On the grounds that it would "unduly prolong this trial" and "complicate the already complicated issues with a peripheral and complex question," Judge Palmieri refused to permit defense attorneys to impeach Rittmaster based upon the fact that he had lied before under oath in the parking meter case, and had a specific motivation to testify favorably for the government in this case. Rittmaster owned $500,000 worth of unregistered shares of MCS stock for which he needed the SEC's permission to sell publicly. SEC approval, granted almost immediately following Rittmaster's grand jury testimony in the MCS case, was clearly part and parcel of his plea bargain.

Although Rittmaster died in 1969 and Kosow was not retried, the government retried Wolfson twice, resulting in hung juries in favor of acquittal by 11-1 and 10-2. Famed criminal defense attorney Edward Bennett Williams represented Wolfson in both retrials. The decision to retry Wolfson for a third time following a previous trial in which the jury was hung 11-1 for acquittal is evidence of over-zealous prosecution. Other evidence includes the decision to pursue the MCS case at all, given the lack of proof that Wolfson profited personally, and the decision to retry the case once it was determined at the first trial that the underlying subject of the cover-up was not itself securities fraud.

A fourth trial was avoided when Wolfson agreed to plead *nolo contendere* to one felony count of filing a false corporate statement in return for the government dropping the rest of the charges. It has been speculated that the Nixon administration may have intervened on Wolfson's behalf in 1972, and that being allowed to plead no contest to the charges in the MCS case may have been his reward for making himself available to the government in 1969 to answer questions about his involvement with Fortas. Although John Mitchell had resigned as Attorney General in 1972, his successor, Richard Kleindienst, had been in the Justice Department in 1969 and surely knew about the discussions with William O. Bittman, Wolfson's attorney at the time. "Significantly, although Edward Bennett Williams had replaced Bittman as Wolfson's attorney, Bittman was brought in to negotiate with the Department of Justice."[29] Wolfson received a suspended 18-month sentence and a $10,000 fine.

Wolfson's long legal battle with the government cost him an estimated $10 million, and he had fallen upon hard times. Wolfson was named as a defendant in multiple civil suits by stockholders in Continental Enterprises and MCS. A derivative suit filed by MCS stockholders seeking disgorgement of compensation paid to Wolfson since 1961 was dismissed. In 1972 Wolfson agreed to pay $250,000 to settle a similar suit. Following the reversal of his conviction in the MCS case and two inconclusive retrials, Wolfson sought reimbursement from MCS, which had begun the process of liquidation, for legal fees incurred in defending against the multiple counts dropped by the government as part of his agreement to plead *nolo contendere*.

Wolfson claimed he was entitled under the language of the Delaware indemnification statute to reimbursement for legal expenses attributable to this part of his defense on the basis of being "successful on the merits or otherwise." Because only a portion of the conspiracy count had been dismissed, and defendants ultimately were found guilty of conspiracy, MCS argued that partial indemnification would be diametrically opposed to the spirit and purpose of the statute and sound public policy. The 1974 opinion by the Superior Court of Delaware granting partial indemnification of Wolfson's expenses in the MCS case has been cited extensively, and is studied in Corporations and Business Associations courses. The opinion is controversial in requiring indemnification of a convicted felon for expenses incurred in connection with each charge that was not proven.

The Delaware statute in effect at the time provided as follows: "To the extent that a director, officer or agent of a corporation has been successful on the merits *or otherwise* in defense of any action suit or proceeding . . . he shall be indemnified against expenses (including attorneys' fees) actually and reasonably incurred by him in connection therewith." In ruling on cross-motions for summary judgment, the court rejected MCS's argument that the public policy underlying the statute required vindication by a finding of innocence, not the dropping of charges for pragmatic reasons.

The opinion in *Merritt-Chapman & Scott Corp. v. Wolfson* established several important points. Its broad interpretation of Delaware law governing the indemnification of corporate managers is one of the reasons Delaware is so often chosen as the jurisdiction of incorporation by U.S. businesses. First, the statute does not require complete success. Each count of an indictment is an independent criminal charge. A corporate manager is entitled to partial indemnification if successful on any count of a multi-count indictment, even if unsuccessful on other counts. Second, the language of the statute limits judicial inquiry into the reason charges may have been dropped or claims not pursued. The definition of "successful" is not limited to securing a judgment of acquittal. In a criminal case, any result other than conviction must be considered success. Third, the statutory policy of indemnification is designed in part to induce capable persons to serve as corporate officers and directors. Accordingly, in assessing the reasonableness of expenses incurred by managers facing criminal charges in successfully defending themselves, the court should consider their position at the time they incurred the expenses, when they assumed the risk of not being indemnified.

The court rejected MCS's contention that attorneys' fees incurred by Wolfson were unreasonable because the Williams, Connolly & Califano law firm charged a flat fee of $250,000 for each trial rather than an hourly rate. Wolfson retained the Williams firm after having been convicted of all counts and faced with the possibility of a prison sentence, not to mention other consequences of a criminal conviction. The indictment against Wolfson, which presented novel legal and complex factual problems, was vigorously and persistently prosecuted. Edward Bennett Williams had acquired a national reputation based upon twenty-eight years of experience in trial practice, often in major criminal cases. He personally spent about 1600 of his firm's 2633 hours in preparation for and in two long trials, while he had to lay all other work aside. The court specifically observed that Edward Bennett Williams did not charge by the hour.

IV. The First Cover-Up

To the extent Louis Wolfson's name registers with most Americans, it is likely for his role in the scandal involving Supreme Court Justice Abe Fortas. According to wordsmith William Safire, the term "cover-up" first entered the political lexicon in a 1968 telephone conversation Wolfson recorded on tape in which Fortas can be heard describing with prophetic accuracy the inevitable perception that would result when the consultancy arrangement between Fortas and the Wolfson Family Foundation became public knowledge.

> Your letter and the subsequent acceptance of the foundation post will be put together and will be construed as follows: That you giving me and my accepting the foundation post was nothing but a cover-up and that what was really happening was that I was taking a gratuity from you in terms of . . . supplementing my salary. You see? And that is very bad.[30]

Wolfson had retained the law firm of Arnold, Fortas and Porter in June 1965 to try and settle a $65 million claim against the Navy on behalf of New York Shipbuilding Corporation arising from construction of the *Kitty Hawk*, and in connection with the SEC investigation into trading irregularities in MCS stock. Paul Porter was placed in charge of the SEC matter. But Fortas met with Wolfson in his capacity as managing partner, and later when Porter had a scheduling conflict that prevented him from attending an MCS board meeting.

President Lyndon Johnson offered Fortas a seat on the Supreme Court in July 1965, replacing Justice Arthur Goldberg who resigned to become ambassador to the United Nations. Aware of Fortas' reluctance to give up his lucrative law practice, Wolfson helped persuade Fortas to accept the nomination. Fortas made it clear to Wolfson that the financial sacrifice involved weighed heavily on his mind. A child of the Depression, Fortas was concerned about financial security. A Justice of the Supreme Court in 1965 earned $39,500. Fortas earned $200,000 a year before joining the Court. Fortas did not want to alter the Georgetown lifestyle to which he and his wife, tax attorney Carolyn Agger, had become accustomed.

It was characteristic of Wolfson, a multi-millionaire at the time, to support friends, and countless philanthropic and political causes. Wolfson donated a share of MCS stock each June to every graduate of the University of Georgia, his alma mater. He was the major contributor to

George McGovern's unsuccessful presidential campaign. He tried to persuade Edward Bennett Williams to run for president, offering to raise money and pay for a national poll to prove that Williams had high name recognition. He encouraged former Oklahoma football coach Bud Wilkinson to run for Senate, promising a $30,000-a-year job if he was defeated. He helped finance Mel Brooks' first film, "The Producers." The Wolfson Family Foundation supported medical, educational and religious charitable entities in Jacksonville, including the Wolfson Student Center at Jacksonville University, the River Garden/Wolfson Health and Aging Center, and the Louis E. Wolfson Wellness Center at Baptist Medical Center. In 1968 Wolfson agreed to contribute $25,000 toward the investigation by New Orleans district attorney Jim Garrison of President John F. Kennedy's assassination. It was arranged that Wolfson would deliver checks in increments of $5,000 to Larry King, then a radio talk show host in Miami, who would pass them along to Garrison through an intermediary. Before reporting to prison in 1969, Wolfson fulfilled his pledge, giving King five checks for $5,000. Garrison never received the full amount. King admitted he failed to deliver $5,000. King was not arrested until December 20, 1971, at which time he was charged with grand larceny. Because the two-year statute of limitations had expired, the charge was dropped, but King was off the air for three years after being fired by the station as a result of the incident.

Wolfson previously attempted to offer financial assistance to Justice Arthur Goldberg, who refused to accept. "It was always nice to have friends in high places," Wolfson believed.[31] The funneling of money to politicians was commonplace in Wolfson's era. Wolfson's bother, Cecil, for example, was among the many people who flew to Tennessee from all over the country to pay top dollar for purebred Angus cattle at auctions conducted by Albert Gore, Sr., former senator and father of the former vice president. Although he had known Fortas less than two months at the time of his nomination, by letter dated July 22, 1965 Wolfson offered Fortas "any financial assistance that he felt necessary."[32]

A New Deal liberal, Fortas likely was attracted to Wolfson in part by his charitable foundation's focus on civil rights, race relations and juvenile justice. Wolfson established the Wolfson Family Foundation in

1951. Financing for the construction of The Wolfson Memorial Children's Hospital, the pediatric wing of Baptist Memorial Hospital in Jacksonville, was provided in memory of Morris Wolfson. Fortas was reported to have been impressed by a plaque indicating that the facility was for the healing of the sick and the afflicted irrespective of race, color or creed. Perhaps to relieve the suffocating sense of isolation that the energetic Fortas experienced upon joining the Court, he agreed to consult with the foundation on matters of mutual interest, attend one meeting per year, and prepare pamphlets and brochures. The agreement called for Fortas to receive half again his salary for consulting work from a source he knew to be under investigation by the SEC. The Wolfson Family Foundation gave away $77,680 in 1965, a quarter of which was to Fortas. Fortas would later insist that he had agreed to the arrangement "simply to prevent dying on the bench, to get away from that isolation. . . . It wasn't anything financial."[33] Had altruism been Fortas' motivation, he could have accepted $1 per year plus expenses. "Money *was* important to him and, as he had made manifestly clear to the White House, to his wife as well."[34]

On October 22, 1965, the Wolfsons attended a reception in Fortas' honor at the Supreme Court. They dined together afterwards. During a visit to Fortas' home in Georgetown the next day to discuss the foundation, Wolfson mentioned the SEC investigation into trading in MCS. Fortas purportedly reassured Wolfson that this appeared to involve nothing more than technical violations. Wolfson exchanged correspondence with Fortas about the investigation, receiving a hand-written letter from Fortas urging him not to resign the chairmanship of MCS. Wolfson remained confident in the outcome, secure in the knowledge that his contact on the Court would intercede if it became necessary. After all, Wolfson knew that Fortas had been responsible for the Johnson administration's appointment of SEC Chairman Manuel F. Cohen.

Wolfson sent a $20,000 check to Fortas in January 1966 to cover services to the foundation for 1966. An exchange of correspondence and formal letter agreement followed in February. Two weeks after receiving Wolfson's check, Fortas wrote to Johnson suggesting the President might "get some pleasure" from an "excellent" resolution adopted by the board of directors of MCS as a "policy of non-discrimination."

On June 14, four days after the MCS case had been referred to the Justice Department, Fortas flew to Jacksonville for a meeting of the foundation's trustees concerning the juvenile justice system. After the meeting Fortas traveled with Wolfson to Ocala, where Wolfson's stable was located, and stayed overnight. Wolfson expressed concern to Fortas about his legal troubles and recalled being assured by Fortas that they were technicalities. Wolfson discussed his legal problems with Fortas again after he was indicted. "There seems little doubt that Louis Wolfson believed that he was getting important advice about his growing legal troubles from a sitting member of the United States Supreme Court."[35]

President Johnson tried to reach Fortas during his trip to Florida. Unable to locate him, a persistent White House operator called the home of his law clerk, Daniel Levitt, who knew Fortas was visiting Louis Wolfson in Florida. When Levitt mentioned the call to Fortas' secretary the next day, she told him the Justice had recently received a substantial check from the Wolfson Family Foundation. Levitt knew about Wolfson's problems with the SEC. He asked Fortas' secretary to convey his concerns about the appearance of impropriety. The secretary relayed Fortas' response: "He said you should mind your own business."[36]

Fortas followed his law clerk's advice. On June 21 he wrote to Wolfson to terminate their arrangement. However, he did not return the money until December 15, 1966, eleven months after its receipt and three months after Wolfson's indictment in the MCS case. Porter claims Fortas' motivation for not returning the money immediately was humanitarian, citing the fact that Wolfson's wife was dying from cancer and that Wolfson himself had a heart condition. Others point to his returning the money near the end of the calendar year in which it was received as evidence that Fortas was motivated by tax considerations.

Richard Nixon took office in January 1969 after campaigning for President in part by promising to nominate strict constructionist Justices to replace the liberal majority on the Supreme Court. Nixon and Attorney General John Mitchell were particularly eager to replace Fortas and William O. Douglas with more conservative Justices. Until the Wolfson scandal unexpectedly fell into the Nixon administration's lap, Douglas seemed the most vulnerable among the Justices. Nixon lost no time putting various federal agencies to work, including the Internal Revenue Service that began an audit of Douglas' tax returns five days after Nixon's inauguration. Quoting a memoir by Nixon aide John Ehrlichman, former White House counsel John Dean wrote, "Nixon cleared his desk of other work to focus on getting Fortas off the Court."[37] Woodward and Armstrong share Dean's belief that Nixon took great interest in the Wolfson affair. "The Fortas investigation became one of [Attorney General] Mitchell's first action projects, and Nixon demanded almost minute-by-minute reports, personally calling the shots from the Oval Office."[38] Sensitive to judicial independence, Mitchell enlisted the intellectually adroit William Rehnquist, then Assistant Attorney General, for help in navigating the constitutionality of the executive branch investigating a Supreme Court Justice.

On April 1, 1969, the Supreme Court denied Wolfson's petition for a writ of *certiorari* in the Continental Enterprises case. On April 11, 1969, Wolfson wrote to Fortas: "Abe, I want you to do something for me. I cannot go to prison right now; if you could do anything to get me a presidential pardon — have President Johnson call Mr. Nixon."[39] In his last days of freedom, Wolfson wrote letters to legislators, including Senator Spessard Holland of Florida, asking them to personally appeal to the President to delay his imprisonment until he could file more appeals. Holland did so on April 22, asking for an appointment with Nixon. After checking with Mitchell, Nixon instructed an aide to turn down the request.

Wolfson, who had been released on bail pending the determination of his appeals, finally entered the prison camp at Eglin Air Force Base near Pensacola on April 25, 1969. Nicknamed "Club Fed," the Eglin Air Force Base prison camp was long a minimum-security facility for non-violent offenders before being closed as a cost-cutting measure in 2006. Other notable inmates included Watergate conspirator E. Howard Hunt and former Maryland Governor Marvin Mandel.

A six-page story by reporter William Lambert describing Fortas' connection to the Wolfson Family Foundation appeared in *Life* magazine on May 4, 1969. The source for Life's story may have been a mid-level official of the IRS (the federal agency responsible for monitoring how foundations spend their money) motivated not by politics but simply offended by the impropriety of the transaction. Then Commissioner of Revenue Sheldon Cohen, a Johnson appointee himself, would not have approved the leak. Alternatively, the Department of Justice may have passed along the information received by Morgenthau's office from Rittmaster.

On May 6 Wolfson surrendered to the Justice Department the agreement showing that the $20,000 fee was not a one-time payment, but rather the first installment of an annual retainer for the rest of Fortas' life, or to his widow as long as she lived. Mitchell's aides showed him the papers. "Mitchell was incredulous. He thought they might be phony."[40] The otherwise brilliant Fortas somehow failed to appreciate the perception created by the "tail" for Carolyn Agger. Why continue payments for work no longer being performed? Perhaps the pension to which a Justice is entitled seemed small to Fortas. "Obviously, Fortas viewed his contract with Wolfson as an annuity."[41]

On the weekend of May 9, FBI agents traveled to Eglin Air Force Base with a subpoena for Wolfson. Asked what Fortas had done for him, Wolfson emphatically exonerated Fortas of complicity, telling the agents Fortas had not lifted a finger to help him, but only gave Wolfson hand-holding assurances that his problems were of a technical nature. Some, like Justice Douglas, believe that Fortas had offered no assistance, or even hinted that he might. Justice Douglas sat up with Fortas for two nights during this period. In response to Douglas' questions, Fortas denied intervening on Wolfson's behalf with Johnson or any SEC official. "He apparently had held Wolfson's hand, so to speak, but had never undertaken to give legal advice or acted as counsel after coming on the Court."[42] Morgenthau believes otherwise. In a recent interview he recalled receiving weekly calls during the Wolfson investigation from Fred Vinson Jr., head of the Justice Department's criminal division. "He'd say, 'You're being abusive and unfair to Wolfson.' And I'd say to my assistants, 'Let's not waste any time and move this case along.'"[43] Morgenthau believes Fortas contacted President Johnson who got the Justice Department to pressure Morgenthau to drop the investigations, and that Fortas later asked Johnson to pardon Wolfson.

Although Wolfson's statement was not the smoking gun for which he had hoped, Mitchell decided to go to the Supreme Court to meet with Chief Justice Earl Warren and use the mere fact that the government had a statement from Wolfson to create the impression that the Attorney General was on top of a rapidly unfolding investigation in which far more serious evidence against Fortas would come out unless he resigned. Mitchell's bluff succeeded. Having lost the support of his fellow Justices, and amid growing calls for his impeachment, Fortas resigned on May 15, 1969.

Although Douglas was the only one to overtly resist Earl Warren's campaign to secure the support of the Justices to ask Fortas resign, even Douglas was surprised, wondering at one point, "God, how did Abe do such a stupid thing?"[44] If Douglas was unaware before, the Fortas scandal clearly served to focus his attention on the danger of being in Nixon's cross-hairs. "Having disposed of Fortas, Nixon turned loose on me," wrote Douglas.[45] Douglas soon resigned as a $12,000 a year director of the Albert Parvin Foundation. Douglas believed Nixon was trolling for adverse information about Douglas from Wolfson. According to Douglas, a lawyer in private practice hired by a Louisiana congressman contacted William O. Bittman, an attorney for Wolfson, seeking an interview with Wolfson, and offering assistance in return for Wolfson's cooperation. Wolfson replied that he had no information adverse to Douglas.

Disclosure of his association with Wolfson was the final straw for Fortas, whose reputation was already tainted by his having continued to serve as adviser to Johnson after joining the Court. During an unsuccessful 1968 struggle in the Senate over his nomination to replace Warren as Chief Justice, it had been disclosed that Fortas had received a $15,000 fee, solicited from wealthy businessmen, to conduct seminars at American University. Former White House counsel John Dean believes Fortas broke no law, or did anything that other Justices had not done, citing Douglas' relationship with the Parvin Foundation and Chief Justice William Burger's service as a board member of the Mayo Clinic for which he received remuneration. According to Fortas' biographer, even Mitchell would later admit that Fortas had committed no crime. Others disagreed. Gerald Ford, for example, wrote that, "The statutes were clear that members of the federal judiciary could not earn income from sources outside the government."[46] Comparing Fortas and Johnson, it has been suggested that "Wolfson was Fortas' Vietnam war."[47]

Wolfson's relationship with Fortas remained cordial. In 1973 Wolfson again offered Fortas $20,000 annually to consult with the Wolfson Family Foundation, an offer Fortas declined in a letter stating that he was too busy.

With time off for good behavior, Wolfson was released after serving nine months and one day in federal custody. He would later recall watching the 1969 Triple Crown races on a black-and-white prison television with an assortment of con artists, thieves, bootleggers and draft-dodgers.

V. Affirmed

Louis Wolfson bought his first racehorses in 1958 as a hobby undertaken on the advice of his doctor to find some relaxation. He had previously been an occasional visitor and heavy bettor at the race track. In 1960 he established Harbor View Farm on 500 acres near Ocala, and turned his attention and considerable ambition to breeding champion thoroughbreds. By 1964 Harbor View Farm, identified by flamingo pink, black and white silks, was the second highest money-winning stable. The Harbor View Farm colors were once as famous in racing circles as the New York Yankee pinstripes are to baseball fans.

Harbor View Farm was nearly crippled in the wake of Wolfson's conviction and imprisonment. The issuance and renewal of horse racing licenses to convicted felons is restricted by New York and other states. Forced to sell most of its horses to pay Wolfson's debts, Harbor View Farm's purses dried up and earnings dwindled to virtually nothing. Wolfson resumed racing in 1971, a year after his release from prison. In 1972 he married Patrice Jacobs, daughter of training legend Hirsch Jacobs. At the time of his death in 1970 Hirsch Jacobs had won 3,596 races, more than any other trainer in horse racing history. Harbor View Farm was restored to fourth place in winnings by 1977.

Conceived in Kentucky and born in Florida, Affirmed was one of 28,271 Thoroughbred foals in the class of 1975. Blessed with extraordinary agility, grace, speed, stamina and courage, the Thoroughbred is a distinct, created breed of horse that evolved from mixing the bloodlines of three Arabian stallions in the early 18th century. It is very rare to find two Thoroughbreds without at least one recent common ancestor. For example, Affirmed and archrival Alydar were blood relatives. Alydar's sire, Raise a Native, was Affirmed's paternal grandsire. Alydar's name is itself the subject of dispute among racing historians. The explanation most frequently offered is that the name is a contraction for "Aly, darling," intended by owners Gene and Lucille Markey as a sentimental homage to their dear personal friend, Prince Ali Solomone Aga Khan (known informally as Aly Khan), a former Vice President of the United Nations General Assembly.

Affirmed was the great-great-grandson of War Admiral, winner of the Triple Crown in 1937, whose legendary rivalry with Seabiscuit was the subject of Laura Hillenbrand's best-seller and 2003 Oscar-winning film. Affirmed bore a resemblance to Seabiscuit both in physical appearance and personality. Like Seabiscuit, Affirmed was relatively small in stature, and laid-back in demeanor. Archrival Alydar of Calumet Farm was more physically-imposing, muscular and powerful looking. Affirmed was more relaxed and sociable around people. Alydar was more popular among racing fans, but Affirmed reportedly ran with the precision of a timepiece. American Thoroughbred horse racing historian Edward Bowen wrote that, "Affirmed had a heart of steel and a reservoir of class that, combined with dashing speed and classic stamina, made him a racehorse of engulfing style and efficiency."[48]

The 1978 Triple Crown has the distinction of being the only time in history when the same horses finished first and runner-up in all three legs. Affirmed was ridden during the Triple Crown by 19-year old jockey Steve Cauthen and trained by Lazaro "Laz" Barrera. Video of the three races may be viewed online.[49] Affirmed's margin of victory over Alydar in the three races was a combined total of less than two lengths. Affirmed beat Alydar in the Kentucky Derby, Preakness and Belmont Stakes by 1-1/2 lengths, a neck and a head, respectively. Their duel in the 1978 Belmont is considered one of the greatest horse races ever run. They would race against each other ten times, with Affirmed winning seven by a combined total of ten lengths. Only once, in their first meeting at age two, were they separated by other horses. Theirs has been described as the most celebrated rivalry in American racing history.

Over the course of his career, Affirmed won 22 of the 29 races he entered. He finished out of the money only once. In 1979 Affirmed became the first Thoroughbred racehorse in history to win $2 million. In 1978 and 1979 Affirmed was named Horse of the Year, the highest honor in Thoroughbred racing. After the Belmont, Affirmed was syndicated into 36 shares (of which Harbor View Farm retained 15) for a total of $14.4 million. Affirmed's lifetime progeny earned $43,618,008, well above average for a stallion, but exceeded by Alydar's who earned $60,604,510.

Following a bout of laminitis, a circulatory hoof disease, Affirmed was euthanized on January 12, 2001 at the age of 26. In the ultimate tribute to a champion Thoroughbred, Affirmed was buried intact, in the flamingo pink, black and white silks of Harbor View Farm, at Jonabell Farm in Lexington, Kentucky.

VI. The Naming of a Thoroughbred

The meaning of Affirmed's name has long been the subject of speculation among equine historians and journalists. None have considered why Louis Wolfson would think to name a race horse "Affirmed" after his conviction for securities law violations had been affirmed on appeal. As the final word of an appellate opinion which Wolfson understood would likely end his freedom, "Affirmed" could not possibly have held a positive connotation.

Responding to questions about Affirmed's name, Wolfson gave a pat answer. At a press conference following the 1978 Kentucky Derby, Wolfson said, "My wife likes 'Aff' on account of Affectionately and we've had some good luck with these kinds of names – so far." Affectionately was a champion mare trained by Hirsch Jacobs in the 1960's and the mother of Personality, winner of the 1970 Preakness. Wolfson's horse Affiliate finished ninth in the 1969 Derby won by Seattle Slew.

To take Wolfson's explanation at face value would ignore the fact that there is nothing casual about the naming of a racehorse. Strict rules, including The American Stud Book Principal Rules and Requirements, govern the naming of Thoroughbreds. Names cannot be more than 18 characters in length, including spaces and punctuation. A Thoroughbred cannot be named after a person without permission. It is not by random coincidence, but after much serious thought, that a Thoroughbred's name is bestowed. Proud owners typically want their horses to have meaningful names, appropriate for what they hope will be a champion. Having bred the horse through three generations, the Wolfsons, and especially Patrice whose understanding of breeding was equal if not superior to her husband's, may have had an inkling that Affirmed had the bloodlines to develop into something special. Equestrian John Williams observed that, "In Affirmed, the Wolfsons had the phenotype of the bench mark Thoroughbred. . . . [I]t was almost assured that Affirmed would become legendary."[50]

"The name Affirmed sounds like a statement, not a name," blogged equine journalist Donna Campbell Smith.[51] Indeed it is, but what statement was his owner trying to make?

Equine historian Edward Bowen recalls Patrice Wolfson explaining that Affirmed's name came from a situation in which the couple expected to have an opinion affirmed on appeal.[52] While an intriguing theory, *Merritt-Chapman & Scott Corp. v. Wolfson*, decided on May 31, 1974, is the only known case involving Louis Wolfson that may have been on appeal at the time of Affirmed's birth. Research and correspondence with Jack B. Jacobs, now a justice of the Delaware Supreme Court and one of Wolfson's attorneys in the case, reveals no evidence that the decision of the Delaware Superior Court was ever appealed.[53] Another of Wolfson's lawyers, Bruce Stargatt, believes the case may simply have been affirmed without opinion, although he also was unable to find any evidence of its having been appealed.[54]

It has been suggested that the name Affirmed is emblematic of the vindication Wolfson spent the second half of his life seeking to gain. "A guess might be made that Patrice Jacobs sees in Affirmed a chance for vindication of both men in her life — for the attainment of the one goal denied her father and a way of bringing honor to her husband, who has been attacked so often in the past."[55] "I think she wanted vindication for him, as he wanted for himself."[56] Michael Goldman, a Delaware attorney who represented MCS in *Merritt-Chapman & Scott Corp. v. Wolfson*, puts a slightly different spin on this theory. He believes Wolfson was angry at the Supreme Court for refusing to hear his appeal of the Continental Enterprises case. The naming of Affirmed was Wolfson's way of demonstrating contempt for the judicial process that had treated him so unfairly. "Affirmed? I'll give you 'Affirmed'!"[57] At his sentencing in the MCS case, Wolfson addressed the court in bitter terms claiming he was a victim of bias and discrimination, and led to conclude "that there is one set of rules for me and one set of rules for the others."[58] According to his son Stephen, "If you ever said the word *judge*, he'd bring out a stack of papers to show you how he was railroaded."[59]

There is no evidence that Wolfson was a student of psychology. So, it may be sheer coincidence that the name he selected for his champion Thoroughbred is the term used to describe the mechanism for coping with a threat to one's self-integrity by seeking an alternative source of self-worth in another competency. First proposed by psychologist Claude M. Steele, self-affirmation theory holds there is a basic human need to defend one's self-integrity, *i.e.*, the sense that one is a "good" person. When a person's valued self-image is threatened, as when one feels humiliated and ashamed rather than proud and pleased, a person may adopt a defensive strategy aimed at restoring one's sense of self-worth by affirming a valued sense of the self in a domain unrelated to the threat.

With his meteoric business career in ruins, Wolfson seemed to channel the power and determination of Affirmed to give his own life new direction and purpose. There is no doubt that Wolfson appeared to bask in Affirmed's success. In the words of equine historian Timothy Capps, "the horse was clearly a restorative to him."[60] According to son Stephen, "Affirmed and his offspring took Dad back to a world where he felt good about life again."[61] "He, Patrice, and the whole family rose again. Affirmed was the catalyst to the return of my father."[62]

It seems fitting that Louis Wolfson's most loyal and trusted confidante should have the last word on the subject. Monteen C. Tomberlin was associated with Wolfson since 1935, when she went to work for Florida Pipe and Supply Company at the age of 16. Mrs.

Tomberlin has said that Patrice Wolfson "gave Affirmed his name based on many important decisions, personal, business and otherwise that have been affirmed over the years."[63]

VII. Conclusion

Louis Wolfson died at home in Bal Harbour, Florida on December 30, 2007, his 35th wedding anniversary, at the age of 95. Official causes of death were Alzheimer's disease and colon cancer, although he had been substantially incapacitated for several years after suffering several small strokes. He was survived by his wife, Patrice, daughter Marcia, sons Stephen, Gary and Martin, three brothers, nine grandchildren and five great-grandchildren. His is a complex tale of respectability and social status gained, lost and re-gained through extraordinary effort and innate skill. The American ideal of the self-made man, Wolfson did it twice by inventing himself in the role of corporate raider in the 1950's, and then repurposing himself through horse-racing in the 1970's.

Although he would achieve great wealth and celebrity, Wolfson would always be a first-generation Floridian and the son of poor Russian Jewish immigrants. He seemed to embrace the role of quintessential outsider, perhaps realizing he had no choice in the matter. Racing historian Capps believes Wolfson reveled in being identified as the "enfant terrible" of corporate America.[64] Always a maverick in business, Wolfson was considered a menace by leaders of the nation's major corporations and their political allies. Captain Thomas A. Scott, who preceded Wolfson as board chairman of MCS, was a surprising exception. "I can't speak highly enough of Lou Wolfson. He bought the stock. Anybody could have bought it . . . Wolfson is an extremely able businessman who expects performance and gets it."[65] Wolfson was also reported to have had admirers within the SEC itself. According to Paul Windels,

> Even to some of the staff people of the SEC, the lawyers down in Washington, Wolfson was something of a hero. He was kind of an outsider who was busting up the cabal that was running the country economically . . . He had a following, and that's where a bit of the sadness was, and the hurt.[66]

Wolfson considered himself the victim of a vendetta waged by those who felt threatened by his activities. Even after he achieved extraordinary success in horse racing, membership in the exclusive Jockey Club, "that Caucasian circle of Anglo-Saxons who for generations controlled the racing industry," was denied to him, as it had been denied to his illustrious father-in-law before him.[67]

Wolfson built a career by identifying companies ripe for take-over because the value of their net assets exceeded share prices that were discounted by the market to reflect inefficient management. Remembered as the inventor of the modern conglomerate and the original corporate raider, the use of the hostile tender offer as a disciplinary force on managerial behavior is Wolfson's legacy. As economist Peter Klein explains, "Before Wolfson's innovation, executing a 'hostile' (*i.e.*, against the wishes of incumbent management) takeover required winning a long and potentially costly proxy contest. Now, potential bidders could appeal directly to shareholders, asking them to 'tender' their shares at the offered price, bypassing the incumbent management team altogether."[68]

Wolfson is said to have worked assiduously and flawlessly to create his own legend while still living. According to Wolfson, management discounted the importance of the American investor. Wolfson believed managers failed to appreciate the significance of the transition that had taken place in the U.S. economy, whose industries had long been owned by a handful of plutocrats with names like Mellon, Morgan, Vanderbilt and Rockefeller. "Without his [the average joe stockholder's] willingness to provide the funds to build factories and buy machinery, management would have nothing to manage."[69]

In a trope to be perfected in the 1980's by Carl Icahn, T. Boone Pickens, Michael Milken and Sir James Goldsmith, Wolfson articulated his role as a crusader for stockholders against entrenched incumbent management. Sir James Goldsmith, for example, has described his role as corporate raider as being in the nature of a "cleansing" agent. Like another shipbuilder, George Steinbrenner, who decades later would arise as a self-styled surrogate for baseball fans, Wolfson saw himself as a strong voice for the interests of shareholders, including interests that stockholders may not have understood themselves. It is ironic, therefore, that Wolfson would twice stand accused of selling unregistered securities and defrauding stockholders in his own companies, and it would be his downfall. It is unclear whether Wolfson himself understood his own impact on corporate governance. "I met Wolfson in his later years," Henry Manne reported.

> As an academic interested in the theory of the market for corporate control, I pressed him for his understanding of the real thrust of his innovation and of the merciless animosity that it generated. He seemed to harbor no grudge — or even to understand what I was talking about. Happily, the market does not require theoretical understanding, just action.[70]

If not a true visionary, Wolfson was certainly a forerunner decades ahead of his time. In Wolfson's own words following the Montgomery Ward proxy fight, "[S]hareholders will recognize that they are not voiceless and directors and executives will become aware of the power of the investor to hold management to account for their stewardship."[71] Conglomeration would become commonplace in the 1970's. By the 1980's the role of corporate raider would achieve the respectability it lacked in Wolfson's time. If it was Wolfson's tragedy to have been born too soon, it was his good fortune to enjoy a successful second act.

Long regarded as an enigma himself, his life story was distilled into the enigmatic name Wolfson gave his champion racehorse. "[A]lthough countless attempts have been made to produce the 'real' Wolfson, none has succeeded . . . . The enigma — what makes Wolfson run and what is he after — is also intact and unresolved."[72]

If and when a movie is made about the lives of Louis Wolfson and Affirmed, "Seabiscuit" will surely provide a tempting model. The story of Affirmed, much like Seabiscuit's before him, illustrates the redemptive power of the sport of horse racing on the lives of the connections to a champion Thoroughbred. However, Orson Welles' "Citizen Kane," featuring a reporter's obsessive search for the meaning behind the title character's famous last word, "Rosebud," may be the better cinematic model. Toward the end of "Citizen Kane," the reporter-narrator Jerry Thompson remarks, "I don't think any word can explain a man's life."[73] Like "Rosebud," Affirmed may well represent something Wolfson felt he could not obtain or something he lost. "Had he been capable of accepting his place as a successful horse owner and breeder who achieved things very few such people do, without tilting at windmills in an effort to resurrect his own view of himself, he might well have left this life a more content person."[74] In the naming of Affirmed, Louis Wolfson succeeded in capturing the essence of a long and difficult journey.

II

Henry Ford's Wingman: A Perspective on the Centennial of *Dodge v. Ford*

I. Introduction

Almost as enigmatic as Henry Ford himself, *Dodge v. Ford Motor Company* has defied understanding for 100 years. Although it has become fashionable to question its continuing relevance, the case retains its claim to our attention at its centennial. The case "should be celebrated in political economy as the trial of Socrates in philosophy or that of Galileo in astronomy,"[1] because it heralded some of the most important developments in corporate law in the past century.

It announced the business judgment rule, declaring that "judges are not business experts." The rule establishes a rebuttable presumption that, absent proof of fraud, illegality or conflict of interest, the substantive merits of business decisions made by directors are protected from second-guessing by courts, so long as the directors reached their decisions through a deliberative process.

It presaged recognition of a fiduciary duty owed by majority shareholders not to engage in a pattern of conduct designed to squeeze out minority shareholders. A "squeeze out" occurs when a majority shareholder oppresses a minority shareholder through the exercise of control over the payment of dividends (or salary or other terms of employment) as the initial step in an intimidation process designed to influence the minority shareholder to accept an offer to sell the latter's shares to the majority shareholder at a bargain price.

Finally, it presaged the recent emergence of the so-called B corporation. A benefit or "B" corporation is a relatively new form of limited liability entity, available in states that have enacted enabling legislation, in which the managers are free to consider the impact of their environmental and other decisions on societal interests, without regard to the effect on maximization of shareholder profit. The ice cream maker Ben & Jerry's, a wholly owned autonomous subsidiary of Unilever, claims to have been among the first to take advantage of this choice of entity. *Dodge v. Ford* has been cited for the proposition that Ben & Jerry's directors were obligated to accept Unilever's rich offer to purchase the company in 2000 by their primary duty to maximize shareholder value, notwithstanding the founders' efforts to maintain the company's social mission and independence.[2]

Ahead of his time in many ways, Henry Ford was confident the American people would elect as their President a successful businessman, without pretense to political correctness, or a mechanism to filter the expression of his most outrageous thoughts, or any previous experience in government or the military. Ford would discover that his outspoken pacifism, combined with rabid antisemitism, rendered him unelectable to public office. In an interview at the time of the case, Ford said, "The Jew is a mere huckster, a trader, who doesn't want to produce, but to make something out of what somebody else produces." Ford published a series of articles and pamphlets that made this and other negative observations about Jews.[3] Ford also believed that the Catholic Church was out to get him. Adding to the improbability of his suitability for public office, Ford avoided speaking engagements, never wrote anything of substance, and was likely incapable of digesting complex written memoranda.

Every founder needs a wingman. For Henry Ford, that role belonged to James Couzens, whose contributions to the early success of the Ford Motor Company are considered equal to those of Ford himself. The first decade of the company has been described as the "Couzens Years." Each brought critical skills to the business that the other lacked. A contemporary observer noted that, "[f]or practical purposes, Couzens was boss," and that "[t]he genius of the two men so perfectly complemented each other that it is doubtful if there ever was a more perfect alliance in the annals of industrial history."[4] Ford Bryan, a historian and descendant of the Ford family, wrote that "Ford by himself could not have managed a small grocery store, and Couzens could not have assembled a child's kiddie car. Yet together they built an organization that astounded the world."[5] Historian Richard Snow quipped that "Couzens . . . understood everything about the car business except how a car worked."[6] In an interview with a journalist, Couzens described his role as follows: "They used to tell it around the automobile shows and so forth that Couzens is the brains of the organization. Couzens is the front door. If you want anything you will have to see Couzens."[7]

From its inception in 1903 and for a decade thereafter, the spheres of influence in the Ford Motor Company were clear. Henry Ford devoted his attention to product design and production. He ceded control of business operations, including finance and marketing, to Couzens. "A lot of industry observers, then and now," noted journalist Richard Bak, "felt the Ford Motor Company would not have survived, much less prospered without James Couzens."[8] John W. Anderson, an attorney and one of a dozen original shareholders, said "it was due to [Couzens'] efforts that the company became a success."[9] Charles Sorensen, a principal of the Ford Motor Company during its first four decades, reminisced that, "Without the bulldog driving energy of Couzens . . . the Ford company would have fallen apart almost before it had been put together."[10] During this period, and as a direct result of their partnership, the company "prospered beyond all expectations and . . . met with unparalleled success."[11]

Like Ford, Couzens also believed he could have been President. "I can never become King of England," he observed, "but if I had been born in the United States, I could be president."[12] Because his mother gave birth to him in Canada, however, Couzens would have to be content to become one of the wealthiest industrialists of his generation, mayor of Detroit, and a U.S. Senator.

Couzens is less well-remembered than he deserves. Although he was a profligate philanthropist who gave away most of his fortune, Couzens refused to perpetuate his memory by permitting buildings or institutions to be named for him. Couzens' low profile is also the result of a strategic business decision that Henry Ford be the public face of the company that bore his name. In his role as chief craftsman of the Ford image, Couzens personally directed the company's campaign to enhance Ford's reputation as pioneer and inventor in the pre-1914 period. What he lacked in political correctness and public speaking prowess, Ford made up for as a master of public relations. "His actions and statements," wrote University of Chicago Law Professor Tod Henderson, "were carefully crafted into a message about the virtues of the automobiles he was selling. Buying a Ford meant not only buying a particular car, but also buying an idea and an image."[13]

This chapter seeks to open a window into *Dodge v. Ford* by focusing on the pivotal role played by Couzens at the Ford Motor Company during its fraught formative years. Couzens' personal and official papers from 1903 to 1940, spanning his career as industrialist and politician, were conveyed to the Library of Congress by the administrators of the estate of his son, Frank. Consisting of 350 containers of correspondence, articles and speeches, they represent a treasure trove of information, which illuminates the internal decision-making process of the Ford Motor Company during its formative years.

Primary source material is valuable in understanding the circumstances surrounding historical cases and in telling the stories behind the litigation. According to Derrick Bell, "People are moved by stories more than by legal theories."[14] Although once a subject of controversy, the value of narrative in legal scholarship and education is no longer a matter of dispute. "Every lawsuit is a potential drama: a story of conflict, often with victims and villains, leading to justice done or denied."[15] A high-stakes tale of motors and money, ambition and intrigue, it would be difficult to find a better example of the analogy than *Dodge v. Ford.*

Following the Introduction, Part II explores the backstory of *Dodge v. Ford.* Part III describes the proceedings at the trial and appellate court levels, from which the principals appear to have been strangely disassociated. Context is critical to a full understanding of most legal disputes, and *Dodge v. Ford* is no exception. Part IV argues that, perhaps more than the facts and legal doctrine involved, *Dodge v. Ford* is a product of the surrounding circumstances at the historical moment when the case arose.

II. The Couzens Years

By the close of the 19th century, Henry Ford had become well-known in the Detroit area for experimenting successfully with cars designed for racing. Among his car racing exploits was a world record for speed which has been variably estimated between 90 to more than 100 miles per hour. He thought it might be possible to parlay his fame into developing a scalable motorized vehicle for public consumption. His earliest backer in this venture was Alexander Y. Malcolmson, a Detroit coal dealer, whose initial investment was equal to Ford's.

Malcolmson had expanded his business through heavy reliance on credit. Strapped for cash, Malcolmson needed to conceal from creditors his financial involvement in a risky start-up venture with the unproven Henry Ford. Before the Ford Motor Company, Henry Ford had failed in two previous automobile-making ventures, primarily because of his inability to perfect a machine that satisfied his own standards. Accordingly, Malcolmson made his investment through an account in the name of his principal assistant, James Couzens.

Born in Chatham, Ontario in 1872, Couzens had moved to Detroit in 1890 where he found work as an inspector and later as manager for the Michigan Central Railroad's freight office. While serving in that capacity, Couzens met and impressed Malcolmson, a shipper of coal. Malcolmson hired Couzens as office manager and financial advisor. In what may have been his greatest contribution to the new company's remarkable success, Malcolmson delegated to Couzens responsibility for personally monitoring Malcolmson's investment with Ford.

To save on plant and machinery expenses, Couzens suggested that, rather than manufacture cars, the enterprise should assemble finished vehicles almost entirely from parts supplied by others. Ford and Malcolmson arranged for John F. and Horace E. Dodge to become the principal supplier of parts for the Model A, the first automobile designed by Ford for sale to the public. Except for the body, wheels and tires, the Dodges made the entire Model A. It was priced at $750–$850 (about $20,000 in today's dollars), and each sale generated $150 in profit.

The Dodge brothers had previously supplied engines to Ford's competitor, Ransom Olds. From 1903 until 1914, when they started their own company, the Dodge brothers provided components exclusively for Ford. Their relationship did not go smoothly. The supply contract with the Dodges was renegotiated annually, and the Dodge brothers regarded the yearly haggling over prices with Ford and Couzens as a source of aggravation. For his part, Ford complained about the poor quality of components produced by the Dodges, and parts shortages resulting from their inability to keep pace with Ford's requirements.

The Ford Motor Company was incorporated on June 16, 1903 by a dozen original shareholders with $19,500 cash on hand. Upon the incorporation, the Dodges agreed to accept 50 shares each, constituting a 10 percent ownership interest, in exchange for writing off overdue payments of $7,000 and extending Ford $3,000 in credit. The other shareholders were Ford, Malcolmson, Couzens, law partners Horace Rackham and John W. Anderson (Malcolmson's attorneys who prepared the incorporation documents and the contract with the Dodges to manufacture Ford components), Vernon Fry (a member of Malcolmson's church), Charles Bennett (a friend of Malcolmson), John S. Gray (Malcolmson's uncle), Charles Woodall (Malcolmson's bookkeeper), and Albert Strelow (supplier of the first assembly plant).

Ford and Malcolmson each received 255 shares representing 25.5%. Malcolmson contributed working capital. Ford's shares were issued in consideration for his contribution of his patents, designs and ideas. Couzens' initial ownership interest of 25 shares constituted 2.5 percent. Couzens invested his entire life's savings of $400, and borrowed most of the balance of the $2,500 purchase price from Malcolmson. He borrowed $100 from his sister, Rosetta Hauss, an amount equal to a third of her life's savings. Couzens wanted his sister to be the thirteenth shareholder, but Ford objected to the idea of a female shareholder. Instead, Couzens held one of his shares as nominee for his sister. As the only two employees of the company who owned shares, Ford and Couzens were considered partners by themselves and others, and regarded their fellow stockholders as parasites.

Ford and Couzens often worked 16-hour days, seven days a week. Couzens was responsible for keeping track of expenses for parts, salaries and rent. By July 11, 1903 the bank balance had been reduced to $223.65.

Luckily, a check for $850 in payment of the sale of the first Model A to Dr. Ernst Pfennig, a Chicago dentist, arrived on July 15. It was long believed that Dr. Pfennig was a medical doctor. His historic purchase was cited to support the narrative that physicians were among the first to perceive the professional benefit of owning a horseless carriage. In preparation for the 75th anniversary of the Ford Motor Company in 1978, researchers located Dr. Pfennig's granddaughter who corrected the record. Sales for the period from July 16 to September 30, 1903 amounted to $132,482, on which the company realized a net profit of $36,958. Couzen's tally after the first nine and one-half months of operation showed the sale of 658 units for a net profit of $98,851.

Like Malcolmson, Ford was impressed with Couzens' business acumen.

> [Couzens] was as much of a genius in business as Ford was in everything else. It was because of him that Ford stopped experimenting with improvements on the Model A and got it into production, which started the meteoric rise in the company's fortunes. It was Couzens' tightfisted and brilliant guidance of those fortunes that turned the company into an unprecedented business success in under a dozen years.[16]

Possessed with "the soul of an accountant,"[17] Couzens would eventually come to oversee all of Ford's business affairs, including sales, advertising, public relations, and negotiations with dealers and suppliers. As vice president and treasurer, Couzens made sure revenue was collected and bills were paid. The spectacular success of the company in its formative years has been attributed to the fact that neither Ford nor Couzens interfered in the other's sphere of influence. "To Ford, looking back from the vantage point of many years later, 'the business went along almost as by magic,' and for this, Couzens was almost solely responsible."[18]

Personality, however, was not Couzens' strong suit. "Able, exacting, truculent, he had a don't-tread-on-me attitude reinforced by outspokenness and a terrible temper."[19] Couzens has been described as brusque of manner, and often overbearing, vain, and self-interested.

"Couzens . . . was so humorless it was later said of him that the ice on the Great Lakes broke when he cracked his annual smile."[20]

Both Ford and Couzens were self-made, meticulous perfectionists and equally strong willed. But theirs was an unlikely partnership given that Ford previously had never demonstrated the ability to work closely with other strong men. Ford, who obsessed about every minor detail, was continually seeking to improve the design of his automobiles and the processes of production. Ford's failure to get his product to market was one of the reasons for his two previous business failures. Although he appreciated Couzens' ability, Ford believed the heart of an enterprise was its product, and the business office was a necessary evil to be tolerated.

Unlike Ford, Couzens could be pragmatic when circumstances required. Tasked with responsibility for the timely payment of bills, Couzens was mindful of the desperate need for cash in the company's early days. Rather than wait for Ford to produce a perfect model, Couzens insisted on shipping products first, and later sending Ford mechanics by train to make repairs for customers with overheating engines, disintegrating brakes and the like. Couzens reportedly accompanied Ford to the train station and personally nailed shut the doors to a boxcar, to make sure that Ford did not interfere with an early shipment of vehicles that he considered unready for sale. Although the business was cash-poor in its infancy, Couzens forbade discounting, believing that maintaining the car at one price to every buyer was a fixed principle of business honesty.

While Ford concentrated his efforts on the design of a series of models, Couzens established a network of 7,000 dealers that was critical to the early success of the company. Couzens insisted that Ford dealerships were spotlessly clean. It was Couzens' idea to keep the service department enclosed and separate from the showroom, so prospective buyers would not be distracted by complaints from owners of defective cars in need of repair. He instructed Ford dealers to arrange for disabled vehicles to be taken into the shop after dark so as not to draw attention to the unreliability of the Model A.

Ford acquiesced to Malcolmson's pressure to build cars for the upscale market. The Model B was priced at $2,000, and the 6-cylinder Model K at $2,800. Meanwhile, the car Ford wanted to build was a lightweight, sturdily-built vehicle, at a price point affordable by 95% of the population, capable of lasting five years (double the industry standard) and of being repaired by nonskilled tradesmen. Vanadium steel alloy turned out to be the key to accomplishing Ford's vision. Ford rejected the conventional wisdom that consumers associated weight with quality, a mistake that would be repeated by U.S. automakers in competing with Japanese manufacturers in the 1970's. Lighter in weight and three times stronger than ordinary steel, vanadium was also superior in its ability to resist shock and vibration, and thus better able to withstand the strain imposed by poor American roads. To successfully manufacture vanadium steel, Ford financed construction of a mill in Canton, Ohio capable of operating a furnace that was 300 degrees hotter than the typical furnace used to manufacture steel at the time.

Couzens sided with Ford in his conflict with Malcolmson over the direction of the business. In what may have been his most important contribution during the company's first decade, Couzens was reportedly responsible for engineering the ouster of the man who had given both Ford and Couzens their start. Malcolmson sold his quarter interest to Ford in 1907 for $175,000, realizing a nearly 700% gain on his $25,500 investment. Other shareholders followed Malcolmson's lead and sold their shares to Ford, reducing the number of stockholders to seven. Ford wound up owning 58.5% of the shares. As part of the reorganization, Couzens purchased shares held by original stockholder Albert Strelow, making Couzens second only to Ford as the largest shareholder with 11 percent. Strelow, unfortunately, invested the $25,000 he received from the sale of his shares to Couzens in a Canadian gold mine that went broke.

Ford's "universal" vehicle, the Model T, ranks as the ninth best-selling car in history with 16.5 million units sold from 1908 to 1927. It was also the first car manufactured on an assembly line. The assembly line had previously been used in the meat packing industry and large bakeries, and automobile manufacturers had used it for sub-components, but not for an entire vehicle. An endlessly moving chain attached to a power conveyor, the first automobile assembly line began operating in October 1913. Instead of completing an entire vehicle at his own bench, each worker repeatedly performed only a single operation at his station as the chassis was dragged across the floor to the next worker, who did the same. The line was adjusted to a convenient height to keep workers from developing back pain. Cars were spaced and the line paced to speed up slow workers and slow down the swift. Within the first year, the coordinated group effort reduced the time of assembly of a Model T from more than twelve hours under the stationary assembly system to one and one-half hours.

Ford recreated a truncated version of the moving automobile assembly line at the 1915 Panama-Pacific Exposition in San Francisco where it was one of the most popular exhibits. "[A] Model T would actually come together from several piles of inert parts. . . . Then, fueled, oiled, watered, and crank-started, it left the transfixed spectators' mouths agape as it motored nicely out into the courtyard to make a circuit around the statue of Neptune's daughter. It was no wonder that every Model T was sold on the spot. . . ."[21] On opening day, fair officials asked Ford representatives to shut down the model assembly line temporarily until they could arrange for additional crowd control.

Arguably the most important social engineering innovation in the field of labor economics, the five-dollar minimum wage for an eight-hour day was adopted on January 5, 1914 at a meeting attended by Ford, Couzens and a handful of others. As part of the policy, Ford created a "sociological department" to enforce a paternalistic program by which company investigators made home inspections to assure that workers adhered to standards of cleanliness and hygiene. Consumption of alcoholic beverages, and failure to save for the future or otherwise comport with character traits valued by Ford would result in disqualification for the new wage. The plan was coupled with a policy of hiring handicapped workers. Couzens explained the rationale for why female workers were excluded from the plan.

> The average woman employee cannot be regarded as a fixture in a business as a man can be. A woman will leave at almost any time, for almost any reason, and when she stays long enough to be dependable worker, she is apt to get married and have someone else support her. It is the man we aim to benefit.[22]

John Dodge was among many who believed the Five-Dollar Day was Couzens' idea. According to Dodge's biographer, Harry Barnard, and David Lewis, a leading expert on the history of the Ford Motor Company, it was Couzens who conceived the plan and brought it to Ford's attention.[23] Consistent with the strategy of keeping Ford's name in the public eye, Couzens abdicated the limelight and credited Ford with originating the idea. However, by 1915, Couzens was openly claiming credit.

Couzens persisted in advocating for the Five-Dollar Day until he had overcome Ford's repeated objections. Mindful of Ford's aversion to altruism and philanthropy, Couzens focused on economic justifications, pitching the new policy as a remedy for persistent problems of absenteeism and turnover. Ford was not having trouble recruiting workers at the prevailing wage rate of $2.34 per day. Rather, the problem was an annual turnover of 370%, a 10% per day rate of absenteeism (anathema to the assembly line method of production), and the threat of unionization. Muckraking journalist Ida Tarbell, who visited the Ford plant in 1913 to research a book, reported that Ford was hiring 60,000 employees per year to maintain a workforce of 12,000.

Announcement of the Five-Dollar Day created pandemonium among business leaders, some of whom predicted bankruptcy. The *Wall Street Journal* reported that Ford was injecting "Biblical and spiritual principles into a field where they do not belong." While Ford became involved in charitable enterprises later in life, Journalist E. G. Pipp (a contemporary of Ford) described Ford as being "as selfish a man as God permitted to breathe."[24] Couzens wrote about Ford, "He has never given anything . . . to charity, and in fact declares against it."[25] "Ford claimed not to believe in charity, because, he argued, it took away a man's ambition and self-respect."[26] In his autobiography, Ford described the new wage in purely economic terms: "The payment of five dollars a day for an eight-hour day was one of the finest cost-cutting moves we ever made. . . ."[27] Turnover declined from 370% to 50% almost immediately after introduction of the plan, and to 15% within one year.

The morning after the announcement, 10,000 men lined up in 10-degree weather outside the Ford plant looking for work. Police deployed fire hoses to disperse the tumultuous mob of job applicants. In response, Couzens announced a policy of giving preference in hiring to local residents in an attempt to stem the tide of job seekers who arrived in Detroit by freight train.

Relations between Ford and Couzens began to deteriorate in 1914. The previous year, while still serving as a company executive, Couzens was appointed chairman of the Detroit Street Railway Commission. As public service consumed an increasing amount of Couzens' time and attention, Ford complained about Couzens' absence from the factory. Couzens had also taken time off to travel to California where his son had died in an accident when his new Model T plunged off a steep, narrow mountain road and sank in a lake below.

By 1915, Couzens' disagreement with Ford's aggressive pacifism led to a showdown. That year Ford chartered a "Peace Ship" and, as head of a delegation he organized, sailed across the Atlantic in a quixotic publicity campaign to end the conflict in Europe. While the typical reaction to the Peace Ship episode was ridicule, former President Theodore Roosevelt offered a harsh denunciation. "Mr. Henry Ford takes some of his fellow pacifists on a peace-junket to Europe, in the effort to bring about a peace more degrading to humanity than the worst war — a peace which would consecrate successful wrong, and trample righteousness in the dust."[28] The kind of peace that Ford sought is evident in the pamphlets and public statements he published blaming bankers and Jews for fomenting preparedness for World War I.

Couzens was incensed when Ford published his views about neutrality and non-involvement in the house organ, *Ford Times*, which Couzens believed was supposed to be under his control. A proponent of military intervention, Couzens argued that pacifist editorials published in Ford's name would alienate customers and cost the company sales. Ford believed his stance resonated with the public. Their differences resulted in Couzens' resignation as an officer on October 12, 1915, although he remained a stockholder and director until 1919.

Relations between Ford and the Dodge brothers also deteriorated. While the Ford Motor Company had evolved from a mere assembling plant into a manufacturing plant that made many of the parts which in the beginning it had purchased from others, the Company still depended on the Dodges for many automobile components, and Ford depended on Couzens to maintain a cordial relationship with the Dodge brothers. In the summer of 1912, Couzens successfully brokered a delay of the Dodge brothers' split with Ford. In a letter to Couzens dated July 26, 1912, John Dodge agreed to reconsider his and his brother's decision to cease providing parts to Ford and to resign as directors. A letter to Ford from Couzens dated July 29, 1912 informed Ford of Couzens' efforts to maintain the relationship with the Dodge brothers "in the same happy and harmonious condition as it exists today."

In July 1913, despite Couzens' efforts, the Dodges served notice that they would cease providing parts for Ford. By letter to Couzens dated August 18, 1913, the brothers resigned as directors to manufacture their own car, larger and more expensive than the Model T. They offered to sell their shares to Ford, but he refused to purchase them. As a result, the Dodges maintained their 10 percent interest as shareholders.

Profits from manufacturing parts for Ford, combined with their dividends, enabled the Dodge brothers to go into competition with Ford. Beginning in 1908, Ford Motor Company paid regular annual dividends of $1.2 million per year. Between 1911 and 1915, Ford also paid special dividends totaling $41 million. The Dodges were relying upon future dividends to finance expansion of their own business.

In January 1916, after announcing a record profit of $60 million, Ford disclosed his intent to pay only regular dividends of $1.2 million a year. With the company having a cash surplus of $52 million in 1916, stockholders could have expected to receive special dividends of at least $25 million. Instead, all but a small fraction of profits would be reinvested to build a massive manufacturing facility and iron smelting plant on the River Rouge to increase production, and to further lower the price of the Model T.

Increasing production and lowering prices may have made good, long-term business sense. But, at least in the short term, these strategies subordinated shareholder wealth maximization. Ford had never been able to satisfy customer demand for the Model T regardless of price. When first introduced in 1908, the car sold for more than $900. Annual adjustments thereafter reduced the cost to $440 by 1916. Ford's stated goal was to lower the price to $220. While the scope of his envisioned expansion may not have been clear, Ford's plans clashed with the Dodge brothers' assumption that the flow of dividends would not diminish. Ford denied the Dodge brothers' allegation that his expansion plans included the purchase of iron ore mines in Michigan's Upper Peninsula or in Minnesota, and the acquisition or construction of ships to transport ore to the new River Rouge smelter. Couzens, whose more cautious approach to expansion had been a restraining influence on Ford, was no longer involved in the business. In August 1916 Ford announced a price cut to $360, and a suppression of dividends.

III. Wheels of Justice

On the evening of November 1, 1916, Henry and Clara Fords' only son, Edsel, married Eleanor Lothian Clay, niece of Detroit department store magnate J. L. Hudson, at his mansion. The Dodge brothers attended the wedding as guests of the bride's family. It would be announced in the newspapers the following day that the Dodges had filed suit in Wayne County Circuit Court on November 2nd against Ford for subordinating the goal of shareholder wealth maximization to other interests.

The Dodge brothers claimed Ford had increased wages unnecessarily for the benefit of employees, and sold cars more cheaply than necessary to benefit customers, at the expense of profits and to the detriment of shareholders. Their complaint sought to require Ford to distribute 75% of the company's cash surplus, or about $39 million, as dividends. On the day suit was filed, at the Dodges' request, the court issued an order temporarily restraining use of company funds for construction of the River Rouge assembly plant. On December 22, the state supreme court lifted the injunction on the condition of the company posting a $10 million bond. Ford had no trouble posting the bond. A letter from E. O. Rice, a bank executive, to Couzens dated December 23 expressed The Bank of Detroit's willingness to provide the bond at no cost if the company maintained a corresponding balance in an interest-bearing account.

Ford wasted no time before litigating the case in the media. He called E. G. Pipp, editor-in-chief of the *Detroit News*, which reported on November 4 that Ford said,

> . . . . I do not believe we should make such an awful profit on our cars. A reasonable profit is right, but not too much. So it has been my policy to force the price of the car down as fast as production would permit, and give the benefits to users and laborers, with resulting surprisingly enormous benefits to ourselves.[29]

Trial began on May 21, 1917 before Circuit Judge George S. Hosmer. Ford's cross-examination by Elliott G. Stevenson, counsel for the Dodges, occupies more than a third of the record. In his questioning, Stevenson seized upon Ford's statement published in the *Detroit News*. Ford doubled down, saying not only that the goal of the business was to consider a wide range of constituencies, but also that the shareholders' interests should not be considered primary to others. Ford's testimony has been described as "among the worst testimony given by any corporate defendant in any trial at any time."[30]

> STEVENSON: Now I will ask you again, do you still think that those profits were "awful profits," and not right?
>
> FORD: Well, I guess I do, yes.
>
> STEVENSON: And for that reason you were not satisfied to continue to make such awful profits?
>
> FORD: We don't seem to be able to keep the profits down.
>
> STEVENSON: [A]re you trying to keep them down? What is the Ford Motor Company organized for except profits, will you tell me Mr. Ford?
>
> FORD: Organized to do as much good as we can, everywhere, for everybody concerned . . . [a]nd incidentally make money.
>
> STEVENSON: Incidentally make money?
>
> FORD: Yes, sir.

With Ford seemingly on the defensive, Stevenson committed a classic trial lawyer's mistake, asking one question too many after receiving a favorable answer from a hostile witness:

> STEVENSON: But your controlling feature . . . is to employ a great army of men at high wages, to reduce the selling price of your car, so that a lot of people can buy it at a cheap price, and give everybody a car that wants one?
>
> FORD: If you give all that, the money will fall into your hands; you can't get out of it.

Stevenson violated the rule known as "Younger's Ninth Commandment on Cross Examination," attributed to famed trial advocate Irving Younger. The most common example is likely apocryphal: "Q: So, if you didn't see my client bite off the victim's nose, how do you know he did it? A: Because I saw him spit it out."[31]

Nevertheless, Stevenson was able to get Ford to make a serious admission which arguably cost Ford the case. In response to questioning, Ford testified that he had made up his mind not to pay any more dividends except regular dividends "for the present." Had Ford been willing to commit to a time certain for ending the suspension, it would have made for a much stronger case.

> STEVENSON: For how long? Had you fixed in your mind any time in the future when you were going to pay.
>
> . . .
>
> FORD: No.
>
> STEVENSON: That was indefinite in the future?
>
> FORD: That was indefinite, yes, sir.

On October 31, 1917, in a 23-page opinion, Judge Hosmer ordered Ford to pay $19,275,385 in dividends, 50% of the company's cash surplus, and permanently enjoined further use of company resources to finance construction of the River Rouge plant.

Ford appealed to the Michigan Supreme Court the following day. On February 7, 1919 the court issued its decision in *Dodge v. Ford.* Describing Ford as the "dominant force" in the company, Chief Justice Russell C. Ostrander cited the following pretrial publicity as reflecting

Ford's attitude that shareholders "should be content to take what he chooses to give." *Dodge v. Ford*, 170 N.W. 668, 683 (Mich. 1919).

> My ambition, declared Mr. Ford, is to employ still more men; to spread the benefits of this industrial system to the greatest possible number, to help them build up their lives and their homes. To do this, we are putting the greatest share of our profits back into the business. *Id.* at 683.

According to the court, Ford's testimony

> creates the impression . . . that he thinks the Ford Motor Company has made too much money, has had too large profits and . . . a sharing of them with the public, by reducing the price of the output of the company, ought to be undertaken. We have no doubt that certain sentiments, philanthropic and altruistic, creditable to Mr. Ford, had large influence in determining the policy to be pursued by the Ford Motor Company. . . . *Id.* at 683–84.

Justice Ostrander's opinion is most frequently cited for the following proposition, one of the most iconic passages in the history of corporate law:

> A business corporation is organized and carried on primarily for the profit of the stockholders. The powers of the directors are employed for that end. The discretion of the directors is to be exercised in the choice of means to that end, and does not extend to a change in the end itself, to the reduction of profits or to the non-distribution of profits among stockholders in order to devote them to other purposes. *Id.* at 684.

Justice Ostrander expressly acknowledged that directors have implied power to authorize ". . . an incidental humanitarian expenditure of corporate funds for the benefit of employees. . . ." *Id.* Thus, the opinion limits the extent to which directors can subordinate shareholder profit to other concerns, rather than imposing a duty to exclusively engage in profit maximization.

The language for which *Dodge v. Ford* is most often cited is dicta. The state supreme court reversed the trial court's decision to enjoin the proposed expansion of the company's manufacturing capacity. Although the decision never uses the phrase "business judgment rule," the analysis foreshadows this doctrine. Saying that "judges are not business experts," Justice Ostrander implicitly acknowledged that judicial interference would have a chilling effect on business decision-making. His opinion provides the rationale for why the considered decisions of corporate managers that are plausibly related to a rational business purpose should be shielded from judicial second-guessing.

> It is recognized that plans must often be for a long future, for expected competition, for a continuing as well as an immediately profitable venture. The experience of the Ford Motor Company is evidence of capable management of its affairs. . . . We are not satisfied that the alleged motives of the directors, in so far as they are reflected in the conduct of the business, menace the interests of shareholders. *Id.*

The court affirmed the trial court decision to require the issuance of a portion of the dividend requested by the Dodge brothers. Again, while the decision never uses the phrase "minority oppression," the analysis is prophetic. First, the court noted Ford's position as controlling stockholder. "Mr. Henry Ford is the dominant force in the business of the Ford Motor Company. No plan of operations could be adopted unless he consented, and no board of directors can be elected whom he does not favor." *Id.* at 683. Next, the court posited the fiduciary duty of good faith owed by a controlling stockholder not to oppress the minority stockholders in the context of a closely held corporation. "There should be no confusion . . . of the duties which Mr. Ford conceives that he and the stockholders owe to the general public and the duties which in law he and his codirectors owe to protesting, minority stockholders." *Id.* at 684.

We may never know with certainty why Ford insisted on litigating the case to a finish. Anxious to begin production of their own vehicles, the prospect of a lengthy trial and certain appeal would likely have motivated the Dodges to accept a settlement that would have permitted construction of the River Rouge plant, and accommodated Ford's stated goal of further reducing the price of the Model T.

Financing construction of the River Rouge assembly plant cannot account for Ford's insistence on litigating the case. Ford Motor Company was debt-free at the time of the litigation, and the company spent more than $60 million on construction throughout the litigation. Even after payment of the special divided the Dodges demanded, the company had sufficient cash surplus to complete construction.

It is conventional wisdom among historians and legal scholars that Ford was motivated by resentment over the Dodge brothers' using dividend income to compete. Denying the Dodges access to cash would make it more expensive for them to finance expansion of a rival company. But Ford surely realized that the Dodges' intended vehicle would not be in direct competition with Ford's. And, even if it were, Ford understood that an attempt to monopolize the market would raise antitrust problems.

There is a similar consensus that Ford's otherwise inexplicable litigation strategy was motivated by political ambition. Ford likely would have prevailed in the litigation had he been willing to testify that lowering the price of cars was intended to boost profits by increasing sales volume. Instead, he took the unnecessarily candid and indefensible position in pretrial comments and testimony that stockholders had made "enough" money, and that consumers and workers deserved to benefit at stockholders' expense, an altruistic position, the sincerity of which is belied by his reputation.

The case presented Ford with a timely opportunity to strengthen his appeal as a populist. A calculated public relations campaign cast Ford as an everyman by way of contrast with robber barons of the period, such as Carnegie, Mellon and Rockefeller. According to a story planted in a California newspaper, "Personally there is not much outward difference between Henry Ford, maker and dispenser of millions, and many of his workmen. Money has not made the slightest difference in his habits, his manner of life, or his friendships."[32]

Ford also viewed litigation as part of a personal and corporate branding strategy to enhance his public image as folk hero, and to stimulate demand for his product through media attention. In another instance of branding by litigation, a legal battle with George Selden, inventor of the gasoline-powered engine, lasted seven years until a trial court decision that Ford had infringed upon Selden's patent was reversed on appeal in 1911. Ford's involvement in high-profile litigation made good copy and created strong feelings of loyalty among the general public, and it was about fighting rather than winning. For example, Ford sued the *Chicago Tribune* for defamation after it published an editorial under the headline, "Ford is an Anarchist," falsely claiming that Ford employees would forfeit their jobs if they reported for duty after President Wilson mobilized the national guard during a conflict with Mexico in June 1916. After a four-month trial, a jury returned a verdict for the plaintiff, and awarded Ford damages of 6 cents.

Couzens and Ford agreed about the value of litigation as a means of enhancing the Ford legend by influencing public opinion and attitudes about Ford. "Ford's well-publicized views were enthusiastically received by millions of people. They served immeasurably to identify the industrialist with the best interests of the common man."[33] Otherwise, Couzens was scornful about publicity generally. In a letter to I. G. English dated January 16, 1917, Couzens described it as "propaganda." In a letter to John Dodge dated February 17, 1917, Couzens wrote:

> [M]ost all kinds of publicity that can be given a car cannot, in any respect, equal the results from the performance of the car itself. Most publicity is superfluous, and I think most companies spend entirely too much money for publicity, in fact, much more than is necessary. . . . [T]he product itself is the best kind of advertising.

Historians and legal scholars also agree that Ford's suspension of dividends was the first step in a squeeze-out plan. Before trial began, Ford announced that he and Edsel would start a new company to build a cheaper vehicle than the Model T. As intended, this thinly disguised effort at intimidation created panic among the minority stockholders. Announcement of Ford's intention to compete eliminated any possibility of trying to sell a minority interest in Ford Motor Company on the open market. Ford then announced a tender offer, on the condition that he acquire 100% of the shares. By July 1919 Ford had arranged to buy the minority stockholders' shares for $106 million. Ford paid $12,500 per share, except to Couzens who held out until he was offered $13,000 per share in consideration for his services as an officer. Couzens received $29.3 million. His sister, a school teacher, received $262,000 in return for her $100 investment. Including dividends, Couzens' $2,500 investment yielded about $40 million. Still, Ford's buyout likely was far below market value. Ford reportedly danced a jig when he learned of the final agreement, and shortly after the 1919 sale, he received a $1 billion offer for the company, representing four times the per share value paid to Couzens.

Ford's motivation to suspend dividends has been variously attributed to resentment over the Dodges using the dividend to compete, political ambition, the prospect of enhancing the Ford legend through litigation, and the desire to squeeze-out minority shareholders. But Ford had another powerful motivation for suspending dividends, which will be explored in Part IV.

IV. The Sixteenth Amendment and the Great War

Tax avoidance was likely the critical motivation for Ford's decision to suspend dividends, and would later motivate Ford to create one of the world's largest foundations. To understand why requires a brief digression into the history of the modern graduated income tax. An assumed part of contemporary American life, the progressive income tax — taxing higher incomes at higher marginal tax rates — traces its origin to the 16th Amendment and the mass mobilization for World War I. The 16th Amendment provides that "The Congress shall have power to lay and collect taxes on incomes, from whatever source derived, without apportionment among the several States, and without regard to any census or enumeration."

Averse to taxation generally, the Founders viewed taxing individuals directly as a last resort, to be implemented only during wartime or other emergencies. Thomas Paine famously warned against "the greedy hand of government thrusting itself into every corner and crevice of industry. . . . It watches prosperity as its prey and permits none to escape without a tribute."[34] Before the Civil War, and for a brief period thereafter, the federal government's principal source of income was tariffs and excise taxes collected on imported goods. Increasing the price of consumer goods by as much as 50 percent, tariffs operate as an indirect form of taxation in the nature of a silent sales tax. Because the poor spend a larger percentage of their income on basic goods than the affluent, the burden of consumption-based taxes falls more heavily on the less wealthy segments of society, making the tariff system highly regressive.

The Civil War prompted enactment by Congress of the first progressive national income tax in 1861. Annual incomes above $600 were taxed at a rate starting at 3%, with increasing percentages on income above $10,000. The Civil War era income tax was repealed in 1872. In 1894, Congress enacted a 4% tax on annual income above $4,000, but it was struck down as unconstitutional by the Supreme Court in 1895 in the so-called *Income Tax Cases*.

Following the Supreme Court's invalidation of the 1894 income tax, a coalition of Democrats and progressive Republicans sought to firmly establish the federal government's authority to levy a direct tax on individual and corporate incomes. On July 12, 1909, Congress passed a joint resolution proposing a constitutional amendment enabling enactment of a federal income tax, and sent it to the states for consideration. "There was a floor debate on whether to put a 10 percent cap in the constitutional amendment. The answer was no — largely because people thought the idea that the tax might ever rise that high too absurd to address."[35]

Proponents of ratification portrayed the old tariff system as a perpetual subsidy of tycoons by the working class. The amendment was successfully marketed to the public as a way to make families like the Vanderbilts, Mellons, Carnegies and Rockefellers pay an equitable share of the cost of funding the federal government. The required three-fourths of the states ratified the 16th Amendment within four years.

On April 8, 1913, President Woodrow Wilson appeared before a joint session of Congress to introduce a bill calling for a progressive income tax. The House passed the income tax bill on May 8, 1913. The Senate followed suit four months later. President Wilson signed the bill into law on October 3, 1913.

Intended to be experimental in nature, a combination of low rates and high exemption amounts was designed to minimize the number of people affected by what President Wilson and Congress expected would be an unpopular law, and to permit the governmental infrastructure necessary to administer the law to develop. The 1913 Act imposed a 1% base tax on net income and a surtax, ranging from 1-6%, on income above certain thresholds. However, a generous exemption (equal to $90,000 in current value) meant that only about 2% of households paid any tax at all. It was well understood at the time that the 1913 Act was intended to be only a preliminary step in what would gradually evolve into a more comprehensive, and remunerative, tax regime.

Eruption of war in Europe, and eventual U.S. intervention, thwarted the plan for incremental development of federal income taxation. Known as the "Great War" and the "War to End All Wars," World War I was triggered by the assassination of Austrian archduke Franz Ferdinand and his wife in Sarajevo on June 28, 1914. President Wilson pledged strict and impartial neutrality. However, public opinion grew increasingly negative toward Germany following the sinking of the Cunard passenger liner *Lusitania* off the Ireland coast without warning on May 7, 1915, resulting in the deaths of 1,198 civilian passengers, including 128 Americans.

Although he narrowly won re-election to a second term as President in November 1916 under the slogan, "He Kept Us Out of War," subsequent events forced Wilson's hand. In January 1917, German U-boats began sinking American merchant ships in the North Atlantic without warning. The German High Command calculated that by sinking 600,000 tons of Allied and neutral merchant marine shipping per month, Great Britain would run out of ships and be forced to the peace table before the United States could effectively intervene in the war. The chief of the German Admiralty staff assured the Kaiser, "I give your majesty my word as an officer that not one American will land on the Continent." [36] The Kaiser was hopeful this decision would be the final decisive stroke of the war. By provoking U.S. entry into the conflict, the decision indeed changed the course of the war, although not in the way the Kaiser intended. Public opinion in America tilted toward intervention. Faced with a direct challenge to the U.S., a reluctant Wilson appeared before a joint session of Congress on April 2, 1917 to ask for a declaration of war against Germany. "The world must be made safe for democracy," Wilson urged.[37]

Long believing it was kept safe by oceans, and with no tradition of maintaining a large peacetime army, the U.S. was underprepared for large-scale intervention in Europe. Winston Churchill noted that Great Britain similarly relied upon her island position in forbearing from conscription to maintain military readiness during peacetime. American industry had no experience making artillery, military vehicles, tanks or airplanes. "Henry Ford, for example, had promised thousands of tanks coming out of his new factory at River Rouge. The war ended long before any were made." [38] American soldiers fought with British-made weapons; pilots flew French-built aircraft. Even as war raged for two years, Wilson remained reluctant to increase the size of the military. Wilson's guiding principle was "that preparation tends to invoke war, and therefore that war can be avoided by abstention from preparation."[39]

The country was fortunate to be able to draw upon the 1913 income tax statute at this moment of crisis. In a fundamental policy decision that would influence the tax system for generations, Congress opted for a progressive approach to financing the cost of mass mobilization for war. World War I would eventually cost the United States about $16 billion. The size of the federal budget increased from $742 million in 1916 to almost $14 billion in 1918. In 1916 Congress raised the base tax to 2%, and surtax rates to a maximum of 13%. In 1917 Congress increased the maximum surtax rate to 63%, and again in 1918 to 65%. Between 1913 and 1918, the base rate on individuals increased from the original 1% to 12%. In five years, the maximum combined individual income tax rate rose from 7% to an unprecedented 77%. At the time, American economist Edwin R.A. Seligman wrote: "[n]ever before, in the annals of civilization, has an attempt been made to take as much as two-thirds of a man's income by taxation."[40] During the same five years, the Bureau of Internal Revenue expanded from 4,000 to 15,800 employees. The change in income tax rates during this period is starkly summarized in Table 1 below. Table 2 illustrates the dramatic changes in marginal income tax rates during the Ford Motor Company's formative years.

Table 1

	Change in Income Tax Rates Between 1913 and 1918	
	1913	*1918*
Base Tax on Individuals	1% on net income	6% on net income up to $4000 12% on additional net income
Surtax on Individuals	1% to 6%, beginning at net income over $20,000	1% to 65%, beginning at net income over $5000

Table 2

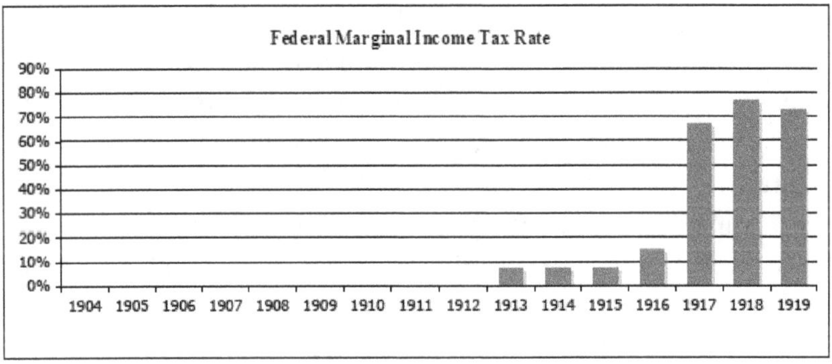

Known for his "instinctive feel for nuances of public mood,"[41] Ford would have sensed the shift in opinion toward preparedness. His personal diplomatic effort, the Peace Ship episode, ended in failure in December 1915. After, Ford's opposition to the war seemed to harden, and his stubbornness to intensify, as a result of the ridicule his project encountered. The growing inevitability of U.S. intervention in the Great War surely would require the government to raise revenue on a different order of magnitude than was generated by the 1913 Act. Ford and Couzens together would receive 70% of any dividends, on which they would owe an increasing share in taxes. Did the prospect of dramatically higher tax rates weigh on Ford's mind when he announced the decision to suspend dividends in January 1916?

Although entirely legal, tax avoidance is typically not the subject of a paper trail, particularly for taxpayers with political aspirations like Ford and Couzens, and especially during wartime exigency. The evidence that Henry Ford was motivated by tax avoidance, therefore, is necessarily circumstantial.

It explains the strange disassociation of the principals from the litigation. While their counsel clashed "almost savagely," Ford and the Dodges were courteous in their references to each other on the witness stand, and the suit did not rupture the social relationships among their families. There is reason to believe that the Dodge brothers may have been stalking horses for powerful steel firms seeking to protect their monopoly position by thwarting Ford's plans to develop his own smelting capacity, or other powerful interests alienated by Ford's campaign against U.S. involvement in World War I. From 1915 until the time of the Michigan Supreme Court decision in 1919, the Dodges' production increased from 18,000 to 120,000 units. Their sales rose from $11 million to $120 million, and their profits from $300,000 to $24 million. "The reason the dividend they demanded did not really matter to the Dodges is they could (and did) easily raise funds from other sources. . . ."[42]

Might Ford have been grateful to the Dodge brothers for helping to preserve Ford's political viability by providing him with a convenient cover story for the suspension of dividends during wartime? Ford received a letter from the Dodges in September 1916 threatening to sue if Ford did not resume the payment of dividends. "Ford rebuffed the Dodges' demand without response or acknowledgment. This is unusual and seems designed to invite conflict."[43]

Tax avoidance explains why Couzens, and other stockholders similarly situated, did not side with the Dodges in demanding payment of dividends in the immediate prewar period, when Congress could be expected to roll back wartime tax rates at the end of hostilities. Indeed, a series of tax cuts in the 1920s reduced the top marginal income tax rate from a war-era high of 77% to 24% by 1932.

It explains Couzens' uncharacteristic reaction to the Dodges' complaint. Although personally named as a defendant in his capacity as a director, Couzens never filed an answer or other responsive pleading. Couzens ignored a telegram he received on December 15, 1916 from Ford's lawyer Alfred Lucking warning that, by failing to answer the complaint, Couzens would be deemed to have acknowledged the truth of the Dodge brothers' allegations. Lucking followed up by sending Couzens a copy of an affidavit by Ford's chief construction engineer William B. Mayo describing the loss that would result to the company from a delay in the construction schedule, including damages for breach of contracts with members of the building trades.

Failing to answer a complaint bespeaks untidiness and leaves loose ends. Couzens was punctilious, if not obsessive, about responding promptly to every piece of correspondence, even the most mundane letter seeking a job reference, or a political or philanthropic contribution. But how could Couzens respond to the Dodges' allegations and preserve his intellectual honesty? Couzens was described by a writer in the *New Republic* as the "perfect example of the honest man in politics . . . the most intellectually honest man . . . in Washington."[44] Couzens, who actually believed in altruism and progressive policies towards workers, may have decided it was better to remain mute than to dissemble about the rationale for discontinuing dividends on the public record.

Couzens' ambivalence on the subject of dividends is evident in his response to an inquiry about a possible sale of his shares. On September 22, 1916, Couzens received a letter from New York City attorney and business broker Theodore H. Price posing what the writer described as a "hypothetical question:"

> If John D. Rockefeller could be induced to buy a minority interest in the Ford Company for the Rockefeller Foundation, do you think Mr. Ford could be induced to give any assurance with respect to the declaration of dividends, provided he were satisfied that the income derived from the stock so purchased would be devoted to the philanthropic purposes for which the Rockefeller Foundation was established?

In September 1916, Couzens responded cryptically to Price:

> I do not believe there is any inducement that would get [Ford] to declare himself as to dividends. I do not blame him for this, particularly, because conditions and earnings enter materially into that question and I think it would be unwise for anyone to commit themselves, for any period

> of time, in any such proposition. If I were competent to answer at all, I would answer 'no.'

Couzens, a social friend of the Dodge brothers, and by then openly antagonistic to Ford, remained strictly neutral. Couzens helped the Dodge brothers gain admission to elite society, despite their well-deserved reputation as hard partiers. "Grosse Pointe society would have nothing to do with them because of all the trouble that they had in the bars of Detroit."[45] Couzens facilitated John Dodge's election to membership in the prestigious Detroit Club, for which the latter expressed gratitude. In a letter dated July 5, 1917, John Dodge wrote "[I] sincerely hope that when in the Club I will behave myself well enough so that you will never have any regrets." On the eve of the filing of the complaint in *Dodge v. Ford*, Couzens was arranging Horace Dodge's membership. In a cover letter forwarding a blank application to Horace Dodge on November 1, 1916, Couzens wrote, "If you will sign this and return it to me I will be very glad to propose your name and get a second to it. I know the Club will be glad to have you with them, and I will be very glad to be instrumental in getting you." Horace Dodge promptly returned the completed application to Couzens in a letter dated November 3, 1916.

When compelled to comment on the case, Couzens was noncommittal. In a letter dated December 27, 1916 responding to newspaper editor I. G. English who had made Couzens aware of an editorial critical of Henry Ford, Couzens wrote, "I am neutral on the question of the suit between Messrs. Dodge Brothers and Mr. Ford. . . . It has been my desire from the beginning to have the whole controversy settled out of court, but both sides seemed to be determined to go through with it to a finish." Couzens' ambivalence is understandable. He was the second largest beneficiary of Ford's decision to suspend dividends. However, unlike Ford, Couzens believed in preparedness and intervention. The relatively low amount of taxes paid by Couzens in the period following his resignation from Ford Motor Company, notwithstanding the high rates in effect for much of this period, would be a source of vulnerability for Couzens in his political career.

The outcome of the case found Couzens at the center of a flurry of stockholder correspondence and activity, none of which involved who won or who lost, or the implication of the decision for corporate governance or shareholder primacy. The focus was exclusively on how to minimize the tax consequences of what the stockholders described as the "Big Dividend," the name they gave to the dividend declared as a result of the decision in *Dodge v. Ford*.

In a letter to Henry S. Morgan, Couzens' general secretary, dated February 14, 1919, stockholder John W. Anderson suggested that the dividend be payable out of cash surplus accumulated prior to enactment of the 1913 Act, so as to be exempt from taxation entirely.

> The first chance you get to have a talk with Mr. Couzens, in view of the outcome of the Dodge Bros.–Ford litigation in ordering distribution to stockholders of nearly $20,000,000.00 from accumulated surplus, I wish you would please urge upon him, as one of the Directors who will be called upon to pass the resolution declaring such dividend . . . the great importance of having the phraseology of the same worded that there can be left no doubt as to WHEN the surplus from which such dividend was declared payable, was accumulated. . . . If, for example, there was in the Treas. of the corporation, on March 1st, 1913, $20,000,000.00 . . . then a resolution expressly setting forth the fact that such dividend be paid out of surplus accumulated prior to March first, 1913, would make the dividend tax exempt in the hands of the recipient.

By letter dated February 20, 1919, Morgan informed Anderson that, at Couzens' request, Morgan had called on Lucking. "Mr. Lucking assured me that the resolution to be passed would be properly worded so as to positively cover the year in which the various amounts accrued, and I, therefore, believe we should have no worry regarding this." In another letter to Morgan dated March 3, 1919, Anderson reiterated that, while tax rates for 1913, 1914 and 1915 are the same, there was an increase in 1916, and "there was a very considerable increase in the 1917 rate."

Ultimately the board of directors adopted a resolution specifying that the dividend ordered by the court be paid out of accumulated cash surplus on hand on August 1, 1916, so as to be taxable at the maximum rate of 15% then in effect.

V. Conclusion

There were no losers in *Dodge v. Ford.* Construction of the River Rouge assembly plant was not interrupted because the Michigan Supreme Court had previously lifted the trial court's injunction. In a Solomonic decision, the court ordered Ford to pay a $19 million special dividend, half the amount the Dodge brothers sought. Ford succeeded in deferring for three years the payment of taxes on the $12 million in dividends he received as his share. He received no dividends taxable at wartime rates he would have considered confiscatory, and intended to raise revenue for a cause he morally opposed.

Ford was able to use the platform of litigation to espouse his populist business philosophy and strengthen his appeal to the "hearts of ordinary American citizens."[46] Ford was spared the vituperation in which the public held the robber barons of his era, such as John D. Rockefeller, J. P. Morgan, the Vanderbilts and the Mellons.

Ford was unable to parlay his fame and popularity into public office. After being defeated in the Republican primary, he ran on the Democratic ticket for senator from Michigan in 1918, losing to Truman H. Newberry, Secretary of the Navy under Theodore Roosevelt, by 7,500 votes. A recount demanded by Ford brought him within 5,000 votes of victory. Edsel Ford's draft deferment was raised as an issue in the campaign by Ford's opponent. According to John Kenneth Galbraith, "In his campaign, Ford made no speeches, most likely because he could not speak."[47]

Until the early 1920's, Ford was often mentioned as a presidential prospect. The *New York Times* reported Couzens' reaction to Ford's possible candidacy. "Why Ford for President? . . . How can a man over sixty years old, who has done nothing but make motors, who has no training, no experience, aspire to such an office? It is most ridiculous."[48] For his part, Ford made no secret of his presidential ambitions. He published an article in *Collier's* in 1923 entitled, "If I Were President." Various explanations have been offered for why Ford ultimately decided not to run for president. Perhaps he realized his controversial opinions likely made him unelectable. Ford may have been dissuaded following a conversation with President Calvin Coolidge in which Ford reportedly received assurances of business concessions as a *quid pro quo.* According to Henry Lewis, a leading authority on Henry Ford, "[T]he Ford boomlet fizzled after Clara declared she would have none of it. Henry, who valued domestic peace at any price, bowed to her dictate."[49]

As their case made its way through the dispute resolution process, the Ford and Dodge families maintained a cordial social relationship. Ford was described as visibly shaken when he received news of John Dodge's untimely and sudden death at 55 from Spanish influenza, contracted while attending the New York auto show in January 1920. Famously inseparable from his brother in life, Horace Dodge died the following year at 52.

Couzens was elected mayor of Detroit in 1918, on the same day Ford lost his senatorial election to Newberry. As mayor, Couzens installed a system of public mass transit to ease Detroit's traffic problem resulting in large part from the success of his former employer. He is credited with instituting measures to accommodate the growing number of cars with streetcars and pedestrian traffic, including marking lanes, stop signs at intersections, signage for one-way streets, and traffic signals. "What James Couzens accomplished in Detroit began to spread across the country. . . . By the mid-1920s Detroit would be recognized as one of the most innovative cities in the country for traffic management and safety."[50]

Ironically, in 1922, Couzens — then a member of Congress — was appointed to fill the vacancy created when Newberry resigned from the U.S. Senate amid allegations of finance law violations committed during his campaign against Ford. Couzens was reportedly the wealthiest member of Congress at the time of his appointment to the Senate. Although Couzens claimed to have paid more than $8 million in federal income taxes during the decade prior to his appointment, more than $7 million was tax on the profit from his sale of Ford stock in 1919. Accordingly, Couzens paid only about $1 million in taxes between 1913 and 1922, "not an especially large sum given the amount of his wealth (and presumed level of income) and the applicable income tax rates during a portion of that period." During debate on controversial tax legislation in

1924, Couzens was pointedly asked on the Senate floor whether he had "paid any income tax whatsoever" in the prior four years and, if so, how much?" Couzens replied that the question was "impudent and irrelevant."[51]

Couzens served in the Senate for 14 years. A Republican by affiliation, Couzens' long-standing independence alienated party leaders. In a July 2, 1917 response to a fund-raising solicitation from the finance chairman of the National Republican Congressional Committee R. W. Austin, Couzens expressed his unwillingness "to contribute to any Republican who might be a candidate. While I am anxious that the United States Senate and House of Representatives be controlled by the Republican Party, I am more interested in who the party is, than in that he is a Republican."

Couzens' progressive attitudes have been attributed to "pangs of guilt over his wealth."[52] Couzens' long-standing support for a progressive agenda spelled disaster for his political career when he gave an enthusiastic reelection endorsement to Franklin D. Roosevelt in 1936. Couzens faced opposition in the Republican primary that year, and was defeated. He died in October 1936. Ford served as a pallbearer at the funeral.

In seeking to resolve the enigma that is Henry Ford, it seems appropriate to give his wingman the last word. "James Couzens simply chalked up the mystery to the man's genius, which is something he thought could never be analyzed."[53] According to one historian, "Henry Ford can be understood only in the context of his times."[54] The same can be said of *Dodge v. Ford.* As its relevance in corporate law wanes, it may not be time to stop teaching the case, but to repurpose it in the curriculum — perhaps as a case in tax history.

III

Up From *Javins*: A 50-Year Retrospective on the Implied Warranty of Habitability

I. Introduction

Come hell or high water. Although its origin has been lost to time, this phrase describes with remarkable precision the common law governing the tenant's obligation to pay rent in full on the first of the month, regardless of the circumstances.

For centuries, under a variety of hardship circumstances, courts consistently declined to excuse tenants from paying rent. In 1647, an English court held that a tenant's obligation to pay rent was not excused by an invasion of the realm by Prince Rupert and a hostile band of men. *Paradine v. Jane*, 82 Eng. Rep. 897 (King's Bench 1647). One rationale offered by way of explanation is that the landlord bargains for a fixed return, regardless of tenant's success. The court in *Paradine* reasoned that "as the lessee is to have the advantage of casual profits, so he must run the hazard of casual losses, and not lay the whole burden of them upon his lessor . . . ." In fairness, according to the *Paradine* court, tenant should therefore bear the risk of adverse conditions beyond the control of either party. A more intellectually honest explanation is that the interests of creditors are protected by this rule: The certainty of timely rent receipts enables landlords to make their mortgage payments.

A long-standing principle of Anglo-American land law, the tenant's seemingly immutable obligation to pay rent in full persisted for centuries until recognition of an implied warranty of habitability 50 years ago in the groundbreaking case of *Javins v. First National Realty Corporation,* 428 F.2d 1071 (D.C. Cir. 1970), *cert. denied,* 400 U.S. 925 (1970). *Javins* is widely regarded as the first case to recognize an implied warranty of habitability, perhaps because the D.C. Circuit's reputation as arguably the most important inferior appellate court helped spur acceptance of the concept by other courts. The New Jersey Supreme Court had recognized an implied warranty in a commercial landlord-tenant case a year earlier. *Reste Realty Corporation v. Cooper*, 251 A.2d 268 (N.J. 1969). The Hawaii Supreme Court held that an implied warranty of habitability was implied in residential leases the year before *Javins*. *Lemle v. Breeden*, 462 P.2d 470 (Haw. 1969).

Both of the 1969 decisions arose in the context of constructive evictions, a judicially created remedy that allowed tenants who vacated unsafe or defective premises to assert defenses to rent based on the condition of the property. *Javins*, on the other hand, was the first case to unequivocally hold that tenants could raise an implied warranty of habitability as a defense to eviction. Almost all Property casebooks either include *Javins* as a principal case, or cite the decision in notes and comments.

It is impossible to over-emphasize the scope of the law reform triggered by *Javins*. It has been described as "arguably the most influential landlord-tenant case of the twentieth century."[1] Two years after *Javins,* the National Conference of Commissioners on Uniform State Laws drafted the Uniform Residential Landlord and Tenant Act. Section 2.104(a) codifies landlords' duty to make all repairs necessary to put and keep the premises in a fit and habitable condition, some version of which has since been adopted by statute in almost half the states. The implied warranty of habitability is now recognized by statute or judicial decision in 49 states, Arkansas being the only exception. Perhaps unsurprisingly, according to an annual study by the National Low Income Housing Coalition, Arkansas has the lowest market rent for a two-bedroom apartment in the country at $720 per month.[2]

Javins radically altered the relationship of landlords and tenants. It is credited with setting the tone for later decisions substituting contract law principles for the feudal rules of Property law that governed the landlord-tenant relationship for the previous eight centuries. Subsequent court decisions constrained the rights of landlords, increased the obligations of landlords, and expanded the legal rights and remedies available to residential tenants. The implied warranty of habitability, prohibitions against self-help and retaliatory eviction, requirement of mitigation of damages, limits on landlords' ability to refuse to lease to certain tenants or to approve transfers of leasehold interests, are examples of the transformation in landlord-tenant law that took place within the last 50 years following in the wake of *Javins*.

Long understood as involving the conveyance of an estate in land, leasing had been governed exclusively by principles of Property law. From this common law tradition emerged the doctrine of *caveat* lessee, in which tenant accepted possession of the premises "as is" and the lessor owed no further duty thereafter. Under common law Property principles, landlords were only obligated to provide tenants with the legal right to possession, and quiet enjoyment of the premises. Unless the parties expressly agreed, landlords were not required to deliver or maintain premises fit for the contracted use. Furthermore, Property law long held that each party's obligations were independent of the other; therefore, tenant's obligation to pay rent was not dependent on landlord providing habitable premises. In 1870, an American court held:

> It is now well settled, both here and in England, that in a lease of a building for a dwelling-house or store no covenant is implied that it should be fit for occupation. And the English authorities, ancient and modern, are conclusive, that even where the landlord is bound by custom or express covenant to repair, and by his failure to do so the premises become uninhabitable, or unfit for the purpose for which they were leased, the tenant has no right to quit the premises, or to refuse to pay rent according to his covenant, but his only remedy is by action for damages. *Royce v. Guggenheim*, 106 Mass. 201, 202-03 (1870).

These rules made sense in the rural agrarian society in which they originated, but created harsh results in cases where a tenant was more interested in the improvements than the land on which they were situated. By the early 19th century, as a judicially-created response to this problem, the remedy of constructive eviction had become available to tenants willing to vacate unsafe or defective premises in order to assert defenses to rent based on the condition of the property. The Massachusetts Supreme Court described the constructive eviction doctrine as creating:

> . . . the legal fiction that the tenant had been 'evicted' to show that the tenant's possessory interest in the property itself was destroyed by the landlord's failure to provide adequate maintenance services. It was the loss of the tenant's possessory interest which excused him from paying rent. The constructive eviction defense gave the tenant the option of abandoning the demised premises in order to extinguish his rental obligation if the court shared the tenant's view as to what acts or omissions on the landlord's part constituted a breach of his duty to assure quiet possession. *Boston Housing Authority v. Hemingway*, 293 N.E.2d 831, at 837–38 (1973).

In theory, the remedy of constructive eviction allowed tenants to secure habitable housing, but tenants seeking to invoke the legal fiction often faced practical hurdles. In addition to taking the risk that a judge might not agree about the seriousness of the deficiency in the condition of the premises, a tenant would need the first-month's rent and security deposit in liquid funds necessary to secure new housing. Finally, constructive eviction was cold comfort for tenants in times of housing shortages.

Because of its practical limitations, constructive eviction did nothing to improve the living conditions of the urban poor. Landlords simply replaced vacating tenants with new occupants with a higher threshold for slum living conditions. What it would take to get landlords' attention was a more effective remedy by which a tenant could withhold rent and remain in possession.

As rural populations shifted to urban centers, courts came to accept that a lease was a contract of mutual rights and obligations between the parties. The Supreme Court of Hawaii recognized that "In an urban society where the vast majority of tenants do not reap the rent directly from the land but bargain primarily for living purposes . . . common law conceptions of a lease . . . are no longer viable." *Lemle v. Breeden*, 462 P.2d 470, 473 (Haw. 1969). The recognition of a lease as a contract resulted in the application of rules of law founded on intent and expectations, and has freed parties from archaic doctrines.

By the late 1960's, *caveat* lessee eroded as courts recognized the modern residential tenant's interest in acquiring habitable premises, and not merely the conveyance of a leasehold estate. It became obvious that urban residential tenants had different expectations than their agricultural predecessors. Tenants in feudal England were more capable of inspecting and repairing the premises than tenants of today. Furthermore, the improvements were incidental to the transaction, the essence of which was obtaining access to land for agricultural purposes. Modern tenants, by contrast, seek a package of services, not a bare possessory interest in land.

In a series of decisions, Judge J. Skelly Wright of the U.S. Court of Appeals for the District of Columbia Circuit, played a leadership role in the development of modern landlord-tenant law. In addition to his opinion in *Javins*, Judge Wright wrote an opinion that prohibited landlords from evicting tenants in retaliation for reporting housing code violations. *Edwards v. Habib*, 397 F.2d 687 (D.C. Cir. 1968). In another case, Judge Wright held that a landlord may not take premises off the market in retaliation for tenant reporting housing code violations. *Robinson v. Diamond Housing Corp.*, 463 F.2d 853 (D.C. Cir. 1970).

Judge Wright analogized residential tenants to consumers buying a product; if the tenant was obligated to pay the same amount of rent throughout the entire lease term, then the premises should stay in the same condition throughout. From this analogy arose a duty on landlord's part to deliver and maintain leased premises, and essential common areas, in a fit, safe and habitable condition. The implied warranty of habitability was soon joined by a growing list of duties imposed on landlords. For example, at common law, a landlord was not liable for personal or physical injuries caused by defects in the leased premises; today, most courts reject this theory of landlord tort immunity and impose a duty of reasonable care on the landlord. In addition, landlords have been found liable for rapes, burglaries and assaults committed by criminal intruders and, more recently, fellow tenants, when tenant can show that landlord did not take due care to protect against such occurrences.

The official account contained in an appellate opinion may have only the most tenuous relationship to the events that actually lead the parties to court. Context is critical to a full understanding of most legal disputes, and *Javins* is no exception. Perhaps more than the facts and legal doctrine involved, *Javins* is a product of the circumstances and the historical moment when the case arose. It is not coincidental that *Javins* was decided at about the apogee of legal services funding. As part of the War on Poverty, a component of the Great Society envisioned by President Lyndon B. Johnson, battalions of lawyers were deployed nationwide to provide legal representation to low-income Americans facing issues including housing.

One of these lawyers was Edmund E. ("Gene") Fleming. A staff attorney for the Neighborhood Legal Services Program, which was located on the first floor of Clifton Terrace, Fleming would represent the Clifton Terrace tenants throughout the trial and appellate stages of the *Javins* litigation. The complex would become ground zero in the effort by legal services attorneys to forge a relationship between tenant's duty to pay rent, and landlord's obligation to provide premises that were clean, safe and fit for habitation, in the context of tenant remaining in possession. Achieving reform in the nation's housing laws through litigation was an intentional strategy on the part of legal services attorneys. According to Willie Cook, Jr., managing attorney at Neighborhood Legal Services Program and a colleague of Fleming, "It was planned in staff meetings, memos, conferences. . . . There was a conscious strategy to re-write property law, to alter the playing field."[3]

Clifton Terrace was home to Journalist Molly McCardle from the age of 15. Her chapbook, entitled "Amenities: Four Stories of Clifton Terrace,"[4] is the closest thing available to a first-person account of life at Clifton Terrace at the time of the *Javins* case. McCardle provides a description of Gene Fleming as seen through the eyes of her tenant protagonist, Doris:

> Gene is a thick, square man with ruddy skin . . . and a full head of fine yellow hair. He looks more like a quarterback than a lawyer, but he owns a pair of thick black framed glasses that he wears in court and it sure makes Doris feel better to look at him. . . . When Gene Fleming, a nice young man from George Washington law school and the only white man she's seen round here in years, started getting together folks from the building to file suit, Doris

> signed up. Even if they kick her out eventually, good riddance. Clifton Terrace would be no great loss on her mind.[5]

McCardle's vivid narrative descriptions of the substandard living conditions of Clifton Terrace are critical for understanding the *Javins* story. Although once a subject of controversy, the value of narrative in legal scholarship and education is no longer a matter of dispute. People learn from narratives in ways they cannot learn from objective analyses and traditional scholarly presentations.

> Stories and counter-stories, to be effective, must be or must appear to be noncoercive. They invite the reader to suspend judgment, listen for their point or message, and then decide what measure of truth they contain. . . . [T]hey offer a respite from the linear, coercive discourse that characterizes much legal writing.[6]

"Every lawsuit is a potential drama: a story of conflict, often with victims and villains, leading to justice done or denied."[7] As a tale of the power of courts to reverse centuries-old doctrine and to make a difference in peoples' lives, *Javins* is a very good story. Following the Introduction, Part II explores the backstory of events that led to the litigation. Part III analyzes the proceedings at the trial and appellate court levels.

Javins is also a cautionary tale about the limits of judicial intervention to achieve social reform. The tenants' rights revolution triggered by *Javins* has not produced meaningful improvement in the living conditions of the urban poor. Notwithstanding the transformation in the law over the past half-century, landlords have managed to preserve the dominant position in the landlord-tenant relationship. Fearful of the pervasive threat of eviction, tenants fail to exercise their legal rights and remedies. Further, the erosion of public support for legal services in recent decades limits the availability of attorneys willing to enforce the rights of residential tenants. The disconnect between landlord-tenant law as taught in the Property course, and as practiced in the courtrooms and corridors of the housing courts, is the subject of Part IV.

II. Murder Capital

A drama is more than a set of actions. It is a set of actions that occurred in a specific moment in time and place in space. The place in which events unfold can profoundly influence the outcome. In the *Javins* drama, the Clifton Terrace Apartments in Washington, D.C. function as a principal character.

Built as Wardman Court by architect Harry Wardman between 1916 and 1918, Clifton Terrace was part of an explosive growth of residential construction to accommodate the burgeoning federal government during the World War I era. Harry Wardman was one of the most prolific real estate developers in the history of the District of Columbia. Born in England in 1872, Wardman came to this country by accident. At the age of 17, he stowed away on a ship bound from London to Australia. When discovered, he was put off the ship at the first port, which turned out to be New York City. Wardman is credited with building 400 apartment buildings containing 80,000 housing units, a dozen office buildings, two embassies, and eight hotels, including the iconic Wardman Park Hotel, considered the largest and grandest hotel in the capital up to that time. Wardman lost his entire fortune, estimated at $30 million, during the Depression. By the time of his death in 1938, it was estimated that 10 percent of Washingtonians lived in a residence designed by Harry Wardman.

Clifton Terrace is located in the neighborhood named for Francis Cardozo, African American educator and politician. Born a free man in Charleston, South Carolina in 1836, Cardozo was elected Secretary of State in South Carolina, the first African American elected to statewide office. He moved to Washington, D.C. and became principal of an African-American high school now named after him. He was a cousin of Supreme Court Justice Benjamin Cardozo. Encompassing 1308, 1312 and 1350 Clifton Street, N.W. between 13th and 14th Streets, N.W., Clifton Terrace was the largest luxury apartment complex in Washington, consisting of 284 units, complete with uniformed doormen. Built in the Colonial Revival style, it was placed on the National Register of Historic Places in 2001. The complex was inspired by the ideals of the garden apartment movement, which encouraged the integration of green space into multifamily urban design. Clifton Terrace featured superior air circulation, maximization of light, and apartments with balconies offering pleasing views of the landscaped courtyard.

Molly McCardle describes the hill atop which the complex sits, enjoying a panoramic view of the capital:

> It is the most dramatic thrust of an inevitable rise from the Potomac, where the land heaves itself upward and away from the politicians and lobbyists and lawyers, men who want nothing to do with Clifton Terrace and its history. The corner of 13th and Clifton is its peak, where residential DC definitively tears itself from the marble knot of Washington.[8]

In McCardle's words, the three identical buildings that comprise Clifton Terrace were "beautiful":

> Harry Wardman poured more than a million dollars into the three sand colored brick buildings that stretched up five stories high on Washington's possibly third highest hill. The buildings, each shaped like the letter E, had their three prongs facing Clifton Street and their connecting spine facing the slope of the hill down towards the river. They were arranged in a row, with the far left and right building sitting right up on the road. The middle building was pushed back so that it began just when the other two ended, sitting comfortably on the crest of the hill with a long narrow courtyard stretching out in front of it, which bridged the two neighboring buildings in a long swath of green. The doormen had matching uniforms and there was a swimming pool. Each of the three lobbies had marble floors and crystal chandeliers. The newspapers would add exclamation points after these facts if their style guide allowed it. Marble floors! Crystal chandeliers! Really! Here![9]

Sidney J. Brown had been editor-in-chief of the New York University Law Review, and a prosecutor in the Nuremberg war crime trials. But when he died in 2000 at age 86, the lead sentence of his obituary identified Brown as the slumlord who owned the Clifton Terrace

Apartments, notorious as the murder capital of northwest Washington, D.C. Brown was convicted of multiple housing code violations, including failure to provide heat, ordered to pay a $5,000 fine, and sentenced to 60 days in prison. Although the jail sentence was reversed on appeal, Brown's legacy has not improved with the passage of time. A recent retrospective described him as "a notoriously rapacious slumlord — the kind of owner who drove down values all over the area."[10]

Beginning in the 1960s and continuing into the 1990s, Clifton Terrace was considered one of the city's deadliest neighborhoods, home to an active open-air drug market, and the scene of turf wars between hit squads representing organized drug gangs from out of town and local dealers. One gang adopted the nickname "Clifton Terrace University." On their Facebook page, "alumni" of CTU, as they call themselves, reminisce about old times and marvel how Clifton Terrace has since been transformed.[11]

When Sidney Brown purchased Clifton Terrace for $1,475,000 in 1963, the buildings remained home to middle to upper-middle class families. Through the eyes of her tenant protagonist named Doris, McCardle paints a vivid word picture of the decline in living conditions under Brown:

> [E]ver since that rat of a man bought the place in '63 there is no doubt that he has turned it into a slum. It makes Doris sick to think about. There was a swimming pool once, but he filled it up with dirt. After a time, her brass chandelier in the sitting room started to weep a thin stream of water and she began to eat her suppers in front of the open stove on cold nights. When the men came to board up her balcony on account of safety regulations, all she could do was sit on her bed and cry.[12]

By the mid-1960's, the capital was a majority-black city. Clifton Terrace became a symbol of the frustration of inner-city blacks living in substandard housing owned by whites. In 1967, the Washington Post described Clifton Terrace as a place where

> the lobbies are dim and damp . . . ceiling light fixtures are missing, paint on the walls peels, plaster crumbles . . . the

> stench of urine and garbage is diluted by the brisk draft in the hallway — a draft that whips through the broken window panes and open doors of the lobby . . . electrical panels have no covers leaving the wiring exposed . . . the elevator in this five story building doesn't work.[13]

By 1970 the Government Accountability Office (GAO) would report to Congress that the appraised value of Clifton Terrace had declined to $1 million, "a substantial drop in the fair market value of the property . . . attributable to deterioration of the buildings from an apparent lack of maintenance which had resulted in over 1,000 violations of the D.C. building code."[14] The GAO report of living conditions at Clifton Terrace is an example of bureaucratic understatement. More graphic accounts are provided by other sources:

> With shootings in the laundry rooms, crack dealers in its hallways, and prostitutes in the stairwells, resident security and safety was nothing more than an afterthought.[15]

> Broken glass covered the sidewalks, grounds and hallways. Lobby windows were boarded up. Eighteen apartments had collapsed ceilings and buckled floors from water damage. The faulty furnace was going through 13 tons of coal every day and broke at least once a month in the winter. On Thanksgiving Day in 1967, 60% of the apartments had no heat.[16]

> In 1965, [tenant] Pat Garris walked into the law clinic office to say she'd had enough of the conditions in the building. She encountered attorney Gene Fleming and took him upstairs for a look around. He took one look at the mess and agreed to support her and her neighbors in a rent strike.[17]

Brown responded by a public shaming of the striking tenants.

> Mr. Brown sent men marching into each of Clifton Terrace's three buildings and posted up a sign on the rental office doors. It was a list of everyone in the whole complex who had not paid their rent, those on strike as

> well as those flat-out broke. It listed their names, their apartment number and the amount of rent they owed right down to the last penny in neat columns.[18]

Brown's intimidation tactics were successful. Of the 29 Clifton Terrace tenants who began the rent strike, only four would remain on strike throughout the trial and appellate proceedings, which are the subject of Part III, below.

III. Trial and Error

On April 8, 1966, Sidney Brown filed suit seeking possession of apartments occupied by six striking Clifton Terrace tenants who were still in arrears in the payment of rent. As a yet unproven litigation strategy, Gene Fleming intended to rely on the existence of more than 1,000 violations of the D.C. housing regulations at Clifton Terrace as a defense to eviction.

A jury trial was scheduled to commence on June 17, 1966 in the courtroom of Judge Austin Fickling of the District of Columbia Court of General Sessions. Fleming's litigation strategy, apparent from the scene in the courtroom on the day set for trial, was to introduce graphic evidence of living conditions at Clifton Terrace, consisting of bags containing mouse feces, dead mice and roaches, and images of tenants' apartments. Herman Miller, counsel for First National Realty Corporation, moved to bar the admission of evidence of housing code violations, claiming it would exacerbate the jury. Fleming opposed Miller's motion. Fleming argued he should be able to introduce evidence of more than 1,500 housing code violations, as well as testimony by Robert Gold, Chief of Research for the National Capital Planning Commission, to prove that low-income families, especially African Americans, had trouble finding housing that met codes.

Judge Fickling ruled the evidence inadmissible, based on the long-standing refusal of courts to allow tenants to raise the physical condition of the premises as a defense in eviction cases. Brown's complaint sought only possession and not a monetary judgment for unpaid rent. Accordingly, under D.C. landlord-tenant court rules, no equitable defense by way of recoupment or set-off was available, nor could tenants counterclaim for money damages. Each tenant having stipulated that rent was in arrears, and with no other relevant facts remaining to be determined, Judge Fickling entered judgments of possession as a matter of law, and dismissed the jury by the end of the day.

McCardle described the scene in the courtroom following Judge Fickling's decision. "Gene patted the backs of the men and hugged the women. 'This isn't over,' he said. 'We were prepared for this outcome. I've already got our appeal together and we're going to keep going with this. You *won't* be evicted.'"[19]

Notices of appeal were filed in the District of Columbia Court of Appeals on behalf of four of the original six tenants — Rudolph Saunders, Ethel Javins, Gladys Grant and Stanley Gross. Fleming wanted Saunders to serve as the central figure because he was "staunch, 30ish, slender, quiet and determined."[20] Both parties' briefs having been filed by November 16, 1966, the case was ready to be heard by Thanksgiving. However, oral argument did not occur until March 11, 1968. Meanwhile, the District of Columbia Court of Appeals rendered its decision in *Brown v. Southall Realty Co.*, 237 A.2d 834 (D.C. 1968), invalidating a residential lease that had been executed with the landlord aware of housing code violations at the time of lease commencement.

Fleming expected to rely heavily on *Brown*. He began his oral argument pleading the similarities between the two cases. Fleming next advanced the argument that, merely by their promulgation, the housing regulations were intended to significantly alter the common law tenant-landlord relationship by creating a contractual duty on the landlord's part to comply. Miller responded by attacking *Brown*, claiming the decision allowed tenants to create violations and then refuse to pay rent. Miller also argued that the existence of criminal penalties for code violations meant only the city should be entitled to enforce the regulations.

On September 23, 1968, Chief Judge Andrew Hood rendered the court's decision. Judge Hood distinguished *Brown* as pertaining only to leases executed with the landlord aware of housing code violations existing *prior* to lease commencement. "[W]e did not hold and we now refuse to hold, that violations occurring after the tenancy is created void the lease," Judge Hood wrote. *Saunders v. First Nat'l Realty Corp.*, 245 A.2d 836, 838 (D.C. 1968).

Turning to Fleming's principal argument, Judge Hood cited the long-established common law rule: "[I]n the absence of express covenant in the lease, a landlord does not impliedly covenant or warrant that the leased premises are in habitable condition and the landlord is not obligated to make ordinary repairs to the leased premises in the exclusive control of the tenant." *Id.* Although violations of the housing code expose landlords to legal liability, nothing express or implied in the housing regulations created a contractual duty owed by landlords to comply with the regulations. Judge Hood concluded a landlord's violation of housing regulations is not a defense to an action for possession for nonpayment of rent.

Tenants filed a petition for review by the U.S. Court of Appeals for the District of Columbia Circuit. At the time of *Javins*, the federal government controlled every aspect of life in the District of Columbia, which explains why the U.S. Court of Appeals for the D.C. Circuit had discretionary jurisdiction to hear appeals of cases decided by the D.C. Court of Appeals. The District of Columbia was finally granted home rule, subject to federal oversight, in 1973.

On January 16, 1969, three of the four tenants' petitions for appeal were granted. Gladys Grant's motion was denied for lack of jurisdiction. Because Grant had paid her rent arrearages after Clifton Terrace changed hands, the landlord-tenant court lacked jurisdiction to entertain an eviction action against her.

In his brief, Fleming sought to incorporate principles of contract law into the landlord-tenant relationship. Citing the challenges black residents of inner-city Washington encounter in seeking housing, Fleming urged that compliance with housing regulations be implied as an obligation of landlord in residential leases. Fleming cited *Whetzel v. Jess Fisher Management Co.*, as precedent for courts imposing a duty on landlords to correct housing code violations, with nonpayment of rent as a remedy for noncompliance.

Miller's brief reiterated the same argument made successfully in the D.C. courts that housing regulations do not create contractual rights for tenants because enforcement rests solely with government. He criticized the decision in *Brown*, claiming it usurped enforcement of housing regulations from the appropriate authority. In a novel argument, Miller accused legal services attorneys and law students of interference in the administration of justice by informing tenants not to pay rent and to demand a jury trial, perniciously clogging dockets in housing courts. Landlords inevitably would be coerced into settlement to avoid long delays, during which rent would be uncollectable.

The case was assigned to a three-judge panel consisting of J. Skelly Wright, Carl McGowan and Roger Robb. Skelly Wright has been described as "the most courageous and influential lower court judge of his generation,"[21] and the foremost judicial activist of modern times. As a United States District Court Judge prior to his nomination by President Kennedy to the D.C. Circuit Court of Appeals in 1962, Wright became known as the "integration judge" for his role in the controversial desegregation of New Orleans' public schools in 1960, invalidating a state statute that gave the governor authority to take over the city's schools and continue segregation.

> By the end of 1960, Skelly Wright had become the most hated man in New Orleans. Pairs of federal marshals alternated in eight-hour shifts at his home to ensure his physical safety, and they escorted him to and from work. With few exceptions, old friends would step across the street to avoid speaking to him.[22]

As Fleming approached the podium, Judge Wright told him that he could take as much time as he needed for oral argument. Minutes of oral argument time in the U.S. Circuit Courts of Appeal are a precious commodity tightly rationed by the clerk of the court after reviewing the briefs submitted by appellate counsel, fifteen minutes per side being typical. Fleming argued for an hour and forty-five minutes on behalf of the appellant. As counsel for the appellee, Miller's argument lasted ten minutes.

Oral argument had gone well for Fleming, but reversal on appeal would require the court to discard, as a matter of common law interpretation rather than legislative action, three classical rules, acceptance of any one of which would result in affirmance: (i) the landlord's lack of any duties with respect to the physical condition of the premises not expressly provided in the lease; (ii) the independence of tenant's duty to pay rent from the landlord's obligations (if any) with respect to the premises; and (iii) the adequacy and exclusivity of the long-standing remedy of constructive eviction that required tenants to vacate before asserting a defense to nonpayment of rent based on condition of the premises.

On May 7, 1970, Judge Wright issued the court's decision. His opinion acknowledged a duty to "reappraise old doctrines in the light of the facts and values of contemporary life — particularly old common law doctrines which the courts themselves created and developed." *Javins*, 428 F.2d. at 1074. Based on factual and contextual changes in the landlord-tenant relationship, Judge Wright concluded that a warranty of habitability should be implied in all leases for space in urban dwellings, imposing an obligation on landlord to ensure that the premises, and essential common areas, are in habitable condition on the lease commencement date, and remain habitable throughout the term.

Judge Wright began by addressing the dichotomy of whether residential leases should be governed by centuries-old principles of property law or modern contract law. The traditional view of leases as being nothing more than the conveyance of a non-freehold estate in land may have been appropriate in a rural environment, where the land itself was the subject matter of the lease. With the passage of time, and the evolution from an agrarian to urban society, this understanding no longer reflected the expectation of the parties, especially tenants. According to Judge Wright, the purpose of the modern apartment lease is to provide "shelter," defined as not merely the walls and ceilings, but also "adequate heat, light and ventilation, serviceable plumbing facilities, secure windows and doors, proper sanitation, and proper maintenance." *Id.* To accomplish this purpose it would be necessary to introduce principles of contract law in the construction and interpretation of leases.

Judge Wright believed that residential leases resembled the typical contract involving consumer products. *Id.* at 1075. Wright elaborated on the implied warranties of fitness and merchantability, and how each has not been limited to cases involving sales. *Id.* As with any such contract, the court should seek to protect the legitimate expectations of the consumer, and hold the provider accountable for the quality of services through implied warranties. The inflexible doctrine that lessor was under no obligation to make repairs, unless it had expressly covenanted to do so, was outmoded. According to Judge Wright, "the old no-repair rule cannot coexist with the obligations imposed on the landlord by a typical modern housing code, and must be abandoned in favor of an implied warranty of habitability." *Id.* at 1076-77.

At common law, when land was leased to a tenant, the lease was essentially a sale of the premises for a term, and the lessee became the owner and occupier subject to the doctrine of *caveat emptor*. The lessee had the opportunity to inspect the premises prior to execution of the lease, but must accept the premises "as is" if execution followed. Under this doctrine, once an estate was leased, there were no further acts to be performed by the landlord, unless expressly covenanted in the lease. The old rule of *caveat emptor* was based upon factual assumptions that no longer apply. Unlike the "jack-of-all-trades" farmer, the contemporary urban tenant is likely to possess a single, specialized skill, that is likely unrelated to maintenance. In an increasingly mobile society, the time and effort required for tenants to repair dwellings of growing complexity cannot be justified. In times of housing shortages, tenants have no alternative but to accept premises "as is," with the expectation that landlord will make necessary repairs.

Judge Wright found support in prior court decisions holding vendors and developers of real property accountable on consumer protection principles for the quality of their products. He invoked the inequality in bargaining power between landlords and tenants, a rationale he had used two years earlier to establish the retaliatory eviction defense in *Edwards v. Habib*, 397 F.2d 687, 701 (D.C. Cir. 1968). In *Edwards*, Wright held that a tenant could defend eviction action on grounds that landlord terminated month-to-month tenancy in retaliation for tenant reporting housing code violations to governmental authorities. Interestingly, Miller had represented the landlord in *Edwards*. Judge Wright catalogued the factors that contribute to the inequality of bargaining power, including racial and class discrimination, standardized form leases presented to tenants on a "take it or leave it" basis, and the severe shortage of adequate housing.

Judge Wright addressed the question of whether this was a matter better left for legislative development. He responded that the very existence of housing regulations in the District of Columbia reflects the legislative intention that a warranty of habitability be implied in leases of all housing that it covers. He found precedential support in *Whetzel,* which held that housing regulations created legal rights and duties enforceable in tort against private parties. A 1922 opinion by Judge Cardozo in *Altz v. Lieberson*, concluded the housing code imposed a duty of repair upon the landlord, and provided a remedy to a tenant injured by landlord's breach of duty. In dismissing the argument that government officials should have exclusive housing code enforcement power, Judge Cardozo wrote:

> We may be sure that the framers of this statute, when regulating tenement life, had uppermost in thought the care of those who are unable to care for themselves. The Legislature must have known that unless repairs in the rooms of the poor were made by the landlord, they would not be made by any one. The duty imposed became commensurate with the need. The right to seek redress is not limited to the city or its officers. The right extends to all whom there was a purpose to protect. *Lieberson*, 134 N.E. 703, at 704.

Judge Wright acknowledged the holding in *Brown* stated the "basic validity of every housing contract depends upon substantial compliance with the housing code at the beginning of the lease term." *Javins*, 428 F.2d at 1081. But he interpreted Section 2501 of the housing regulations, to evidence the D.C. council's intention that this section cover defects arising after a lease has been signed. Section 2501 of the Housing Regulations provides:

> Every premises accommodating one or more habitations shall be maintained and kept in repair so as to provide decent living accommodations for the occupants. This part of this Code contemplates more than mere basic repairs and maintenance to keep out the elements; its

purpose is to include repairs and maintenance designed to make a premises or neighborhood healthy and safe.

The implied warranty is not absolute. The trier of fact must first determine whether the alleged violation existed during the period for which past rent was due, and what portion of the tenant's rent obligation may be withheld due to landlord's breach. Not all housing code violations give tenant the right to withhold rent. One or two *de minimis* violations that do not affect habitability, or violations arising from tenant's own wrongful conduct, do not justify withholding rent. If the fact-finder determines only a portion of withheld rent is appropriate, tenant must pay the remaining amount due to avoid judgment for possession. The full amount of rent once again becomes due after landlord makes the necessary repairs.

In the final footnote of his opinion, Judge Wright addressed Miller's argument about the pernicious impact of legal services attorneys in eviction cases, and the negative consequences for the administration of justice. Judge Wright agreed that an "excellent protective procedure" would be to have tenants deposit the full amount of their rent into the court's registry during a pending action to assure the availability of funds to pay landlord if a tenant is found to have wrongfully withheld rent.

IV. Up from *Javins*

In a seminal 1965 article, Yale Kamisar identified the disconnect between the Constitutional protections afforded criminal defendants in courts of law (mansions) compared with the treatment they receive in police station interrogation rooms (gatehouses). The Supreme Court cited Professor Kamisar's article and adopted its reasoning in *Miranda v. Arizona*, holding that the Fifth Amendment requires police to advise suspects under arrest of their right to remain silent and to counsel before custodial interrogation.

"Evicted: Poverty and Profit in the American City," an ethnographic study of low-income rental housing in Milwaukee by Matthew Desmond, won the Pulitzer Prize for nonfiction in 2017. Desmond, a professor of sociology at Princeton University, also received the 2017 American Bar Association Silver Gavel Award for fostering public understanding of law and the legal system, and a fellowship, commonly known as "Genius Award," from the MacArthur Foundation, which has a long-standing interest in the condition of rental housing in the U.S. Before the publication of "Evicted," rental housing had become the "neglected child of American life."[23] The U.S. is an "ownership society" in which the detached single-family house has long represented the American dream, strongly encouraged through lavish tax subsidies. It is estimated the tax benefits of homeownership amount to $147 billion dollars per year. "Evicted" placed rental housing quality at the top of America's housing policy agenda, a position previously occupied by affordability.

Like Professor Kamisar, Desmond identified a similar disconnect between the theoretical legal rights available to tenants facing eviction in housing court, and the obstacles tenants encounter along the way. Desmond found that tenants who fell behind were unable to summon a building inspector for fear of eviction, or withhold rent until repairs are made. A recent empirical study of 40,000 residential eviction actions filed in Essex County, New Jersey in one year similarly found only 80 cases of tenants asserting landlord's breach of the implied warranty of habitability as a defense to nonpayment of rent, notwithstanding significant reported instances of grossly substandard rental housing known to exist within the county. Asserting a defense based on the condition of the premises can be daunting.

> Some courts require written answers, which *pro se* litigants may not know how to generate. Even those courts that allow tenants to respond orally in open courtroom on a particular day require a presence of mind and sense of timing that *pro se* litigants are likely to lack: the tenant may have only a few seconds to decide what to say, and the judge's cue (such as "is this the amount you owe?") may steer tenants into responding to the landlord's accounting rather than raising an affirmative defense that may seem unresponsive.[24]

Crowded housing court dockets spawn an assembly-line process to resolve a high volume of cases as efficiently as possible. The resulting system is a closed, static environment with patterns of behavior that have evolved over decades. The courthouse culture features repeat players who interact daily — judges, court clerks, landlords, landlords' lawyers and unrepresented tenants. "The process is a morass, the language is different, and the stakes are high. It is an intimidating experience to navigate, even for a lawyer."[25] A tenant facing eviction encounters a Byzantine web of rules and practices.

> Your landlord's lawyer finds you and suggests that you go with him to an office to talk about your case. You sit down across from him in the office, intimidated but resolute as he hands you documents and says that your landlord will drop the case against you if you agree to move out within 30 days. . . . The lawyer says if you don't take the deal today, then you'll need to go through the court process and prove to a jury that you didn't do anything wrong. Your palms sweat and your head swims. You think to yourself that you don't know how to prove something to jury. You don't have a lawyer, and you can't afford one. What do you do?[26]

The fast-moving housing court chaos forces parties to settle cases in crowded hallways, or makeshift offices crammed with old furniture and broken file cabinets.

> Settlement discussions occur in the hallways, within earshot of everyone, because there is no other space for them. Since there is little seating, these conversations usually happen standing up. It's hard to think clearly when you can't even sit down. A report on the court years ago said it resembled a hospital waiting room, and that seems about right. The hallways, though, feel like a bustling bazaar. Negotiations deal not with textiles or pottery, but with homes. Litigants trade money for time, until there is no more money and therefore no more time. And therefore no more home. . . . Tenants wind up signing all sorts of dubious [stipulations]. Because they're scared. Or bewildered. Or ashamed. Or have children to pick up from school. Or can't skip another day of work. Or think they're speaking to an impartial court official when it's actually the landlord's lawyer.[27]

The overwhelming number of tenants either lose their cases in housing court or, more likely, agree to disadvantageous settlements. Either way, they are evicted or they give up and vacate. Most tenants facing eviction never reach housing court. They are removed by other, cheaper and quicker, ways than eviction. In "Evicted," Desmond writes that courts

> . . . have come to depend on this because each day brings a pile of eviction cases, and the goal of every person working in housing court is just to get through the pile because the next day another pile will be waiting. The principle of due process has been replaced by mere process: pushing cases through. Tenant lawyers would change that. . . . Every housing court would need to be adequately funded so that it could function like a court, instead of an eviction assembly line: *stamp, stamp, stamp.* Desmond at 304.

Landlords leverage the threat of eviction to incentivize tenants to forfeit their right to be heard. Desmond described a poor black couple living in a house with exposed wires and water flowing inside when it rained. As the court date approached, landlord's lawyer offered tenants a stipulation agreeing to move, which tenants accepted so no eviction would appear on their record.

> If they signed a stipulation and agreed to leave, according to the housing court judge, 'the eviction part [of the case] would dismiss. So on your record, which anyone can see, it wouldn't say you were evicted. . . . If you think you really have paid the rent or have some other reason that is a legal defense here, then you can tell me all about that. That's your one choice. Your other choice would be to go ahead with some agreement that you'll leave and save [the landlord] and ultimately yourself some headache.' Desmond at 305 n. 38.

Desmond found that half of forced moves were informal evictions that take place in the shadow of the law: off-the-books displacements not processed through the court, as when a landlord pays a tenant to leave, "or hires a couple of heavies to throw you out." Desmond at 330. Formal eviction was less common — 24% of forced moves. Twenty-three percent of forced moves were due to landlord foreclosure, and 5% to condemnation. Tenants also prefer informal evictions because an official record does not accompany them, whereas an eviction filing shows up on background checks. The advent of the Internet encourages tenants to skip court and quietly move out of a home riddled with dangerous problems when their landlord threatens to evict. "[F]or every eviction executed through the judicial system, there are two others executed beyond the purview of the court, without any form of due process. Some landlords pay tenants a couple hundred dollars to leave by the end of the week. Some take off the front door." Desmond at 4.

The absence of counsel for tenants facing eviction is well-documented. Between 90 and 95 percent of landlords have legal representation, compared with only five to ten percent of tenants. When tenants have lawyers, their chances of keeping their homes increase dramatically. A 2016 report by the New York City Civil Justice Coordinator's office found that representation reduced evictions by 24%.[28] Desmond concluded that extending the right to counsel in housing court "would be a major step on the path to a more fair and equitable society." Desmond at 305. "Good lawyers will raise defenses tenants often don't, because they are either unaware of them or . . . are too nervous and intimidated." Desmond at 303.

Low-income tenants facing eviction have limited access to legal services. D.C. Law Students in Court is among the oldest and most successful programs that protect clients experiencing housing instability. Operated by a consortium of D.C.-area law schools, students are available to stay evictions and assist clients in seeking rental assistance from local social service agencies.

Beginning in 2017, New York City became the first jurisdiction to guarantee legal representation to low-income tenants facing eviction. All tenants sued for possession in housing court are entitled to individual consultation with lawyers, and low-income tenants who face eviction proceedings are entitled to legal representation. The law requires the city to build up the capacity of its nonprofit legal services organizations so that, by July 31, 2022, the organizations will be able to provide free legal representation for every low-income individual (defined as households with a family of four earning below $49,200 per year) sued for eviction in housing court. The city also requires that the availability of access to legal assistance be publicized on public transportation. There is no reason why rental housing accommodations with more than a handful of units should not be required to make tenants aware of this service, in the same manner as casinos and race tracks are required to publicize the availability of assistance for problem gamblers.

Legal aid to the poor decreased steadily since the Reagan era, and was decimated by the Great Recession. The reality is that there is unlikely to be enough pro bono or affordable attorneys to satisfy demand. Legal services organizations suffer chronic underfunding and regularly combat political threats of extinction. It will be necessary to explore creative ways to level the landlord-tenant playing field by minimizing the cost of access to justice. One such initiative is the result of a partnership consisting of attorneys with the Wilson Sonsini law firm and law students at the University of Arizona and Brigham Young University. "Hello Landlord" is an on-line program that generates correspondence designed to help tenants inform landlords of conditions that affect habitability.

Counseling residential tenants is an example of a type of "law practice" that could be performed by trained persons with less than a three-year J.D. degree and law license. Tenants facing eviction would benefit from assistance offered by trained and licensed legal service providers. Armed with basic legal advice, tenants can be empowered to navigate the system and exercise their legal rights without a lawyer.

Washington State was the first in the country to introduce an affordable legal services option for low- and moderate-income individuals with unmet legal needs. It represented the first time in the American legal profession that non-lawyers could openly, legally and ethically engage in activities constituting the practice of law. Created by order of the state supreme court in 2012, it required limited license legal technicians to meet educational requirements, pass three licensing exams, and complete 3,000 hours of supervised work experience, the equivalent of almost 18 months of full-time work. The Washington State Supreme Court stated, "[w]e have a duty to ensure that the public can access affordable legal and law related services, and that they are not left to fall prey to the perils of the unregulated market place."[29]

This model is a promising legal services option for those unable to afford a lawyer. The program is similar to nurse practitioners who have reduced the cost and increased the availability of health care. Like nurse practitioners, limited license legal technicians would not have significant student loan debt. According to the most recent data from the National Center for Education Statistics, law students graduate with an average student loan debt of $145,550, including undergraduate loans, for which the average monthly loan payment is $1,656.

V. Conclusion

Clifton Terrace Apartments have been given a new lease on life. Even the name is different. The current ownership group restored the original name, "Wardman Court Apartments." On the day the Author visited in March 2019, there were no vacancies in the two buildings still operated as rental housing, and the waiting list was closed.

Fifty years later, it is hard to picture the "maze of drugs, gangs, and prostitution"[30] that was Clifton Terrace at the time of *Javins*. "[A]bout the only thing the development, now called Wardman Court, has in common with the old Clifton Terrace is that it still consists of three buildings."[31] Residents enjoy a variety of services including ESL and computer training, and classes in vegan cooking and Tae Kwon Do. The entire Cardozo neighborhood is a different place with a different population. The gentrification of the thriving Cardozo neighborhood is largely attributable to the proximity of the U Street/Cardozo and Columbia Heights Metro Stations. The Green Line, which was designed on paper but not yet built, was rerouted to spur revitalization of the neighborhood in the aftermath of the riots following the assassination of Rev. Martin Luther King, Jr.

HUD gained control of the project from the previous owner through foreclosure in 1996. The current ownership group acquired the complex from HUD for $1 in 1999, and spent $16 million on restoration. Its marketing literature describes the return of "turn-of-the-century elegance based on studies of other buildings in the area created by the same architect," buried behind decades of drywall renovations. The current ownership is a partnership between the Community Preservation and Development Corporation, a non-profit organization dedicated to revitalizing housing complexes, and the Michaels Development Company, which claims to have developed more than 22,000 housing units in 19 states. To qualify for HUD financing, the partnership agreed to maintain the apartments as housing for low- and moderate-income families for at least 20 years, reduce density from 289 to 232 units, and provide child care and job training services. The combined family income of residents cannot exceed $56,280. Rent starts at $1,245 for a one-bedroom apartment, and increases to $1,713 for a three-bedroom unit.

Tenants and visitors enter the buildings after passing through the newly landscaped courtyard, formerly an open-air drug market. The well-appointed lobby features tall ceilings, chair-rail and ceiling molding, and chrome and glass chandeliers. On display in the lobby is a collection of vintage photographs and historical documents, including the original 1914 building permit and a 1915 newspaper story featuring an artist's rendering of Wardman Court before commencement of construction. Absent from the display is any reference to the tumultuous but transformative role of Clifton Terrace in the history of landlord-tenant law.

The tenants' rights revolution of the past half-century represents one of the most extraordinary reforms in modern Property law. Reversing centuries-old doctrine, *Javins* radically altered the allocation of legal rights and responsibilities in the landlord-tenant relationship by shifting obligations and liability to landlords. *Javins* illustrates Judge Skelly Wright's willingness to create law when he thought the circumstances warranted, and his intentional use of judicial power as an engine to achieve social change.

Article III judges typically prefer to remain anonymous or, at least, largely unknown. It is uncommon for appellate judges to refute critiques, preferring to let their opinions speak for themselves as the voice of the court. Ethical considerations dictate the exercise of caution by judges in their public comments even when a case is no longer pending. For example, judges in New Jersey are cautioned not to "clarify, defend, or justify any of the judge's decisions or opinions, or reasoning therein."[32]

An uncommon judge, Skelly Wright was certainly more candid, and probably more intellectually honest, than most in admitting that his opinions were result-oriented, visceral reactions to the context in which they arose, strong enough to overcome precedent which stood in the way. Judge Wright certainly breaks the mold of judicial propriety cast by Richard Posner, former Chief Judge of the United States Court of Appeals for the Seventh Circuit, who wrote:

> Unfortunately judges tend not to be candid about how they decide cases. They like to say they just apply the law — given to them, not created by them — to the facts. They do this to deflect criticism and hostility on the part of losing parties and others who will be displeased with the result, and to reassure the other branches of government that they are not competing with them — that they are not legislating and thus encroaching on legislators' prerogatives, or usurping executive-branch powers.[33]

In an extraordinary exchange of correspondence with a law professor in 1982, Judge Wright reflected on his landlord-tenant decisions. He acknowledged the influence of the nationwide racial turmoil of the sixties, the injustice of racially selective service during the Vietnam War, and his belief that legal doctrine had helped create and perpetuate systematic class bias. The context for the *Edwards* and *Javins* decisions included the 1963 March on Washington, urban rioting in summer 1967 and following the assassination of Dr. Martin Luther King Jr. in summer 1968, and passage of the Civil Rights Acts of 1964 and 1968. Judge Wright acknowledged he

> . . .did what he could to ameliorate, if not eliminate, the injustice involved in the way many of the poor were required to live in the nation's capital. . . . I offer no apology for failing to follow more closely the legal precedents which had cooperated in creating the conditions that I found unjust.[34]

Skelly Wright was under no illusion that the systemic problems of the urban poor would be remedied by individual judicial decisions, no matter how significant. Judicial intervention would not "solve the housing crisis in the District of Columbia. That crisis is the product of a constellation of social and economic forces over which no court — and perhaps no legislature — can exercise full control. . . . [T]he judicial process is not a *deus ex machina* which can magically solve problems where the legislature and the executive have failed." *Robinson v. Diamond Housing Corp.*, 463 F.2d 853, 871 (D.C. Cir. 1972).

Clifton Terrace's troubled history persisted following *Javins*. In 1978 HUD acquired the property after foreclosing on a loan to an ownership group led by Mayor Marion Barry's ex-wife, Mary Treadwell. Treadwell was convicted in 1984 of conspiracy charges for skimming off $600,000 in rental payments and other federal funds intended for the complex's upkeep, allegedly affording Treadwell an apartment in the Watergate and a Jaguar.

At its 50th anniversary, *Javins* illustrates a disconnect between the legal doctrine of the Property class and the assembly-line justice of landlord-tenant court. Of considerable influence and staying power among academics, the implied warranty of habitability has been rendered virtually irrelevant in practice. Unaware of their legal rights and how to raise them, unrepresented tenants in housing court confront a daunting array of procedural obstacles. The legacy of *Javins* depends upon the ability to deliver basic and affordable legal services to tenants facing eviction.

IV

Forever Young: *Texas Gulf Sulphur* Rules at Fifty

I. Introduction

It does not happen often. But sometimes, while writing an opinion, a judge has an inkling, or perhaps an intention, that it is destined for law school casebooks — not merely as a note case but as a principal decision, and not just for a couple of editions but for a half-century or more. Circuit Judge Alex Kozinski of the U.S. Court of Appeals for the Ninth Circuit is more candid than most on this subject. In a law review article entitled, *Who Gives a Hoot About Legal Scholarship*, he described how he once wrote an opinion on contract law for the purpose of getting it published in a law school casebook. Likewise, Judge Kozinski acknowledged in an interview that his dissent in a constitutional law case involving Vanna White was written with a view to its possible inclusion in a casebook.[1] Circuit Judge Richard Posner, on the other hand, has denied that he thinks about writing an opinion for casebooks, "in part because I don't know any more what casebook editors are looking for."[2]

Whether or not Circuit Judge Sterry Robinson Waterman had the idea or purpose of publication in mind in 1968, his majority opinion for the United States Court of Appeals for the Second Circuit in the landmark case of *SEC v. Texas Gulf Sulphur* certainly had that effect. Suggesting that he may have had such an idea, Judge Waterman told a *Wall Street Journal* reporter that *Texas Gulf Sulphur* was "going to have a hell of an impact on the financial world. Everyone in the United States has been waiting for this."[3] In this chapter, *Texas Gulf Sulphur* refers to *Texas Gulf Sulphur II*, 401 F.2d 833 (2d Cir. 1968) (en banc), *cert. denied sub nom.* Coates v. SEC, 394 U.S. 976 (1969).

While not the first insider trading case, *Texas Gulf Sulphur* promulgated the evergreen rule that a purchaser of securities is required to disclose material information unknown to the seller, or otherwise abstain from trading. It was the critical first step toward creating the modern system of insider trading enforcement despite the absence of a specific legal definition of the offense. *Texas Gulf Sulphur* has been described as a "landmark" decision by the Securities and Exchange Commission Historical Society, and legal commentators have echoed this characterization. It appears not only in Securities Regulation casebooks, but also in casebooks for courses in Corporations and Business Associations.[4]

"Every lawsuit is a potential drama: a story of conflict, often with victims and villains, leading to justice done or denied."[5] A tale of bonanza, greed and deceit, including a cameo appearance by the Queen of England, it would be hard to find a better example of the analogy than *Texas Gulf Sulphur.*

Following extensive geophysical exploration in the early 1960s, Texas Gulf Sulphur Company (Texas Gulf), an American mining corporation, acquired property in Northern Ontario known as the Kidd Creek Mine. At 3,000 meters, it is the world's deepest mine below sea level, making it the closest accessible point to the center of the earth. Kidd Creek generates 2.25 million metric tons of ore per year and contains deposits of zinc and copper ore with a value of $2 billion. Zinc is valued, primarily, as an anti-corrosion (*i.e.,* galvanizing) agent for coating iron and steel in the automotive and construction industries, in the production of batteries and, together with copper, in the composition of brass. Today's penny is ninety-eight percent zinc. Zinc replaced copper as the principal component of the penny in 1982 when the value of copper in the coin rose above one cent.

In order to keep the discovery a secret, Texas Gulf geologists took evasive action in conducting their exploration activities in a manner designed to throw competitors off the scent, and not tip off the landowners regarding the extent of mineral deposits located on their property until after the company was able to acquire fee simple title or mining rights.

During the course of exploration and subsequent land acquisition negotiations, and after becoming confident of the extent and likely value of the orebody, Texas Gulf geologists and managers took advantage of the opportunity to acquire shares of the company's stock, and options to purchase additional shares, before knowledge of the discovery was made public. Several recommended the stock to friends and family members, who in turn recommended it to others.

In 1965 the Securities and Exchange Commission (SEC) charged the company with securities fraud and twelve of its managers and employees, including the company president, with insider trading. For the first time in its history the SEC sought to hold insiders responsible not only for disgorgement of their own profits but also the profits of their tippees. It is unlikely that the commission would have brought such unprecedented charges on its own initiative, and President Lyndon B. Johnson was reported to have encouraged the SEC, perhaps in retaliation for Texas Gulf's failure to heed White House admonitions against raising prices. While the District Court dismissed the charges against the company and all but two of the individual defendants, the Second Circuit reversed the findings of the lower court and reinstated the charges against the company and nine individual defendants.

After the landowners discovered the true value of the deposits and the inadequacy of the consideration they received, lawsuits were filed against Texas Gulf directly challenging its ownership of the Kidd Creek Mine by claiming the company wrongfully withheld relevant information. In November 1968, three months after the decision in *Texas Gulf Sulphur*, the Ontario High Court of Justice found that Texas Gulf was only doing "what any prudent mining company would have done to acquire property in which it knew a very promising anomaly lay." *Leitch Golf Mines, Ltd. v. Texas Gulf Sulphur Co.*, 1 O.R. 469, 493 (1969).

Context is critical to a full understanding of most legal disputes. Following the Introduction, Part II of this chapter explores the events leading to litigation in the U.S. and Canada as a result of Texas Gulf's exploration activities. It has become conventional in scholarly discussion of *Texas Gulf Sulphur* to use a stylized version of the facts of the dispute "without slavish adherence to the actual facts." In commemorating the 50th anniversary of the decision, Part II defies that convention by exploring the backstory *in extenso*.

Texas Gulf Sulphur continues to accurately represent controlling legal principles, even after the ebb and flow of decades of litigation first contracted and later expanded the scope of insider trading regulation. Part III analyzes both the decision at the trial court level and the appellate court's categorical reversal. An unanswered question raised by *Texas Gulf Sulphur* asks why it is considered "prudent" to withhold material information from unsuspecting landowners in real estate transactions, but unlawful to conceal the same information in the purchase of securities. In Part IV we consider this apparent anomaly.

II. The City with a Heart of Gold

In any drama, the place in which events unfold can profoundly influence the outcome. In *Texas Gulf Sulphur*, the town of Timmins itself functions as a principal character.

Located in Northern Ontario about 450 miles northwest of Toronto,[6] Timmins markets itself as "The City With a Heart of Gold." Paradoxically described as "the most barren and God-forsaken country" and "the most beautiful place on Earth," Northern Ontario contains ninety percent of the Province's land but only six percent of its population. In 1903, railroad workers found massive deposits of high-grade silver, triggering the Cobalt silver rush and attracting the Timmins brothers to the area. Noah Timmins, one of two brothers who made their fortunes in silver mining, founded the town bearing his name. The area was a wilderness before news of the discovery of gold near Porcupine Lake in 1906 attracted a community of 30,000 people. The Porcupine gold rush, which lasted from 1906 to 1912, surpassed the better-known North American gold rushes in the Klondike and the Yukon in terms of production. Timmins owes its origin to the discovery of gold, and its continued existence to subsequent discoveries of base-metal ore in mineable quantities.

Timmins remained a boom town for the next several decades supported by three major gold mines — Dome, Hollinger and McIntyre — and dozens of smaller operators. More than fifty gold mines once operated in the Timmins area. By 2011 the Porcupine region produced more than

70 million ounces of gold, worth $100 billion at current market value. Although some Canadians travelled north seeking work, mine owners preferred to hire immigrants thought to be more willing to endure the harsh weather and working conditions, and less susceptible to unionization, if for no other reason than the language barrier. Gold mining revenue sustained Timmins during the Great Depression, when out-of-work musicians from the rest of North America were attracted to the Porcupine region to entertain the large population of young single miners with disposable income and time to spend. Jack Kent Cooke, who would later amass a fortune in the fledgling cable television industry and own the Washington Redskins, Los Angeles Lakers and Los Angeles Kings, started his career in Timmins as advertising manager for the local radio station which featured live broadcasts of performances by dance bands in the 1930s. "Timmins was a boom town and certainly had its share of characters . . . . The chief of police . . . made headlines by booking his sister on prostitution charges; he also closed down his mother's boot-legging operation."[7]

Between 1956 and 1968, most of the gold mining operations in the Porcupine region were abandoned as the region's gold reserves were depleted. "Many families found themselves without a source of income and there were genuine fears Timmins would become a ghost town."[8] Then, Texas Gulf's successful exploration activities were made public in spring 1964. The news triggered the most frantic land rush and financial market hysteria in Canadian history. "For Timmins, a dying gold-mine town . . . the Texas Gulf bonanza was a dramatic rescue from oblivion."[9]

Gulf Sulphur Company was founded in 1909 by two St. Louisans, A.C. Einstein and John W. Harrison, who went to Texas in search of sulphur. The First World War having expanded demand for sulphur, Eastern bankers J. P. Morgan, Bernard Baruch and W. B. Thompson purchased Gulf Sulphur Company in 1918 and renamed it Texas Gulf Sulphur. The company weathered the Great Depression without laying off employees by shortening its work week to four days. Once the world's leading producer of sulphur, Texas Gulf's management realized that the company's future depended upon diversification as the market price of sulphur plunged in the 1950s. Sulphur prices declined from $28 per ton in

1956 to below $20 in 1962. Texas Gulf's earnings correspondingly fell from $3.23 a share in 1955 to 93 cents in 1963. The dividend which had been $2 per year in the mid-1950s was reduced to 40 cents in 1962. The company's stock price declined from $45 in the mid-1950s to $11 in 1963. Other setbacks suffered by Texas Gulf in the early 1960s included loss of the *S.S. Marine Sulphur Queen,* which disappeared in the Florida Straits en route from Texas to Virginia carrying a crew of 39 and 900,000 tons of sulphur, and an explosion in a potash mine in Utah in which 25 miners died.

In response to these setbacks, the company turned its attention to locating mineral deposits, including an area in northeastern Canada known as the Canadian Shield, whose mineral-rich rocks are among the oldest on earth. The Shield is a vast, barren area formed thousands of years ago by a receding glacier that left behind a lake covering tens of thousands of square miles. Streams carried billions of tons of sediment into the lake which settled to the bottom building up beds of clay which attracted deposits of gold, silver and base metals including zinc and nickel. Although southern portions of the Shield support forests, it is largely unsuitable for all but a narrow range of agricultural crops, the poorly drained clay soil being too thin and low in fertility. Northern Ontario winter temperatures dip to minus 40 degrees Celsius, and frost persists into June.

The lengthy and complex process of discovering and developing a mineable orebody has not changed significantly in the past half-century. It involves technology, human incentive, patience and luck, in roughly equal parts. Metaphorically as well as statistically, locating a mineable orebody is analogous to finding a random needle in a haystack, with the needle serving as a pocket of minerals and the earth's crust as the haystack.

The ever-narrowing selection process begins with aerial geophysical surveys of what is believed to be promising terrain, followed by ground investigation of the sites indicated by aerial survey. Although other companies had been surveying with fixed-wing airplanes, Texas Gulf designed a system that could be affixed to light helicopters capable of flying at tree-level for greater accuracy. A camera attached to the helicopter was synchronized with electromagnetic equipment to record the precise location which produced responses that were a deviation from the norm, known as "anomalous" readings. The point on the ground which produces an anomalous reading is described as an "anomaly." Aerial surveys by Texas Gulf of the Canadian Shield detected thousands of anomalies, only one of which proved to be a mineable body of ore. The high probability of false positive responses generated by worthless graphite, metal fences and other ground conditions makes aerial reconnaissance tedious and costly. At locations deemed favorable by aerial reconnaissance, a portable diamond-head drill is used to extract a cylindrical core sample of subsurface rock. An independent chemical assay of the core sample is the ultimate determining factor in locating an orebody that is economically feasible to mine and market.

If ore deposits of commercially exploitable quality and quantity are proven to exist, the next step is to acquire the right to mine the area of interest. This sequence necessarily exposes entities engaged in natural resources extraction to liability for damages for trespass, a risk that is accepted by the industry as a cost of doing business. In Part IV of this chapter we will see that willful violation of the rights of unsuspecting landowners may also provide a basis for granting equitable relief.

While speaking to a law school class at Vanderbilt University Law School in 1980, Harold Kline, an administrative vice president of Texas Gulf at the time of the discovery who became general counsel in January 1964, remarked that:

> After you've done [aerial surveying] then you trespass on the ground below without permission to find deposits because you can't be sure from the overflight exactly what property they are on. Now, it's customary to do that trespass and, if anybody sued you, they would recover damage for whatever damage you did while doing that.[10]

Kline's description conflicts with Texas Gulf's account of the timeline of events. Texas Gulf maintained that it acquired an option to purchase the first of four lots overlying the orebody, including the right to explore the property, from Royal Trust Company, executor of the Estate of Murray Hendrie, in June 1963, and conducted ground geophysical surveys to locate a drill site, in which event the successful hole drilled on

November 9 may not have involved a trespass to land. Kline is not alone in casting doubt on Texas Gulf's version. A law review article by Berkeley Law Professor Melvin A. Eisenberg, entitled *Disclosure in Contract Law*, stated that "Texas Gulf might have unlawfully entered on the Estate's land." Although he did not purchase any shares of Texas Gulf before public announcement of the discovery on April 16, 1964, Kline was named as a defendant by the SEC for having accepted stock options from a committee of non-management directors on February 20, 1964. He denied having material nonpublic information at the time he accepted the options, but the credibility of his testimony was called into question. Kline and other corporate officers traveled to Salt Lake City where the drill core sample had been sent for assay immediately after the discovery. In his testimony regarding the trip, he described attending a football game in Utah Stadium between Arkansas and Utah on November 16, which he said Utah won. A sports-savvy SEC attorney, doubtful that Arkansas would schedule a road game against a strong non-conference opponent so late in the season, investigated and determined that Utah had not played Arkansas, and had lost the game it did play, opening the door for the SEC to question the accuracy of Kline's recollection of the trip.

Texas Gulf began prospecting for minerals in Northern Ontario in 1957. By 1959 airborne surveys of more than 15,000 miles of the Canadian Shield generated electromagnetic responses indicating the presence of ore-bearing rock north of Timmins, in an area known as Kidd Creek. Although prospectors had long since combed every square foot of the Timmins area searching for gold, the Kidd Creek orebody had been protected from visual observation by the terrain, a quagmire composed of layers of grassy bog known as "muskeg" (a Native American term for dead vegetation in various stages of decomposition). Reflights of the area in 1960 confirmed the likelihood of commercially significant mineral deposits.

During an initial test boring conducted on November 9, 1963, the glimmer of metals was visible to crew members as the 1-1/4 inch cylindrical core containing ore sample was pulled from the ground. Among them was Kenneth Darke, a 29-year old Texas Gulf geologist who had zealously advocated exploration of the region, and convinced his more skeptical and conservative superiors of the region's promise by offering to explore the Porcupine using his own funds and personal vacation time. Clearly excited by the results, Darke jeeped twelve miles to a motel in Timmins where he called his immediate superior, Texas Gulf chief geologist Dr. Walter Holyk, at his home at midnight. Holyk, in turn, immediately got President Claude O. Stephens out of bed. Holyk arrived in Timmins on November 12 to personally view the core sample before it was shipped to Salt Lake City, Utah for assay.

Sensitive to the delicacy of a large company acquiring title or mineral rights to land in an area where it was known to be engaged in mining exploration, Holyk ordered that drilling be suspended and the discovery site camouflaged. Tractor tracks were covered by branches. Trees were planted over the original drill hole. "A second test hole was drilled, as ostentatiously as possible, some distance away, at a place where a barren core was expected — and found."[11] To confuse pilots working for competing mining companies who might fly overhead, the drill team set up an identical camp at the opposite end of the township.

At this point, land assembly necessarily took priority over further geological investigation. Texas Gulf not only required mineral rights to the orebody itself. The company also needed sufficient land for mining operations and access to roads in the event the site proved to be mineable.

Since 1959, Texas Gulf had been engaged in protracted negotiations with the owners of four 160-acre lots in the area designated on company maps as the Kidd 55 segment. Previously their land had only limited commercial value as a timber site. Texas Gulf deliberately conducted its land acquisition negotiations at a leisurely pace designed to conceal from the prospective vendors how highly the company valued their properties. Harold Kline later explained his company's negotiating strategy with respect to geological information:

> You don't tell them about it because . . . if they knew there was an anomaly on the property they would ask more money for the property . . . . You don't tell them anything. As a matter of fact, it's important that you don't. It's a corporate responsibility to keep silent in that regard.[12]

The property was owned by the Murray Hendrie Estate, the Elliot Estate, the Roberts Estate and T.S. Woolings and Company, Ltd., a subsidiary of

Curtis Publishing Company, publisher of the *Saturday Evening Post.* Murray Hendrie had been granted title by the Canadian government in consideration for services rendered as a veteran of the Boer War. He married Agnes Gilmour, a widow with a young son, William. The couple had no other children. Following protracted litigation, stepson William Gilmour was adjudged sole heir of Murray Hendrie's estate, surviving a challenge to his will by one hundred relatives. Texas Gulf acquired title to the Hendrie Estate property in settlement of a lawsuit filed by Royal Trust Company, executor of the estate. After entering into an agreement with Woolings to pay $11,588.50 for its land, Texas Gulf obtained beneficial ownership by purchasing 100% of Woolings' stock. The purchase price Texas Gulf paid to the Roberts and Elliott Estates was unreported. The Elliott Estate's land turned out not to contain any portion of the orebody.

Meanwhile, with time on their hands and material nonpublic information in their possession, Darke, Holyk, and other Texas Gulf insiders, including company president Claude O. Stephens, and family members and friends, took advantage of the opportunity to acquire shares of Texas Gulf stock, and options to purchase additional shares, before any announcement of the discovery would or could be made.

From the time of the first test boring in fall 1963, Texas Gulf made numerous denials of its discovery until it was able to complete its property acquisition objectives by the end of March 1964. Nevertheless, rumors began to circulate in February 1964, triggering intense speculation in Canadian mining stocks. Trading volume and price fluctuations were so spectacular as to attract the attention of Queen Elizabeth II, who appointed a Royal Commission to investigate the possibility of irregularities. Following several months of hearings, the commission issued a 122-page report in 1965 that resulted in reforms to the Ontario Securities Commission. Representatives of the SEC attended the hearings, which detailed the chronology of events leading to the discovery.

On April 9, 1964 the *Northern Miner*, a weekly publication, reported Texas Gulf's exploration north of Timmins. Similar reports appeared in the *Toronto Daily Star* and the *Globe and Mail*. In response to these published stories, Texas Gulf issued a press release on April 12, 1964 (the "First Press Release") stating in part,

> During the past few days, the exploration activities of Texas Gulf Sulphur in the area of Timmins, Ontario have been widely reported . . . . These reports exaggerate the scale of operations . . . . Recent drilling on one property near Timmins has led to preliminary indications that more drilling would be required for proper evaluation of this prospect . . . . The drilling done to date has not been conclusive . . . . *Texas Gulf Sulphur* at 855.

On April 16, 1964 the *Northern Miner* reported the extent of the orebody, accompanied by a sketch showing its location. Texas Gulf confirmed discovery of the Kidd Creek Mine at a press conference the same day (the "Second Press Release"). The company's stock increased from about $18 per share at the time the orebody was discovered to more than $31 at the time the discovery was made public, and to $58 a month later. Texas Gulf was the most actively traded stock on the New York Stock Exchange in 1964.

Texas Gulf ultimately acquired fee simple title to all the property in which the orebody lay. Texas Gulf transferred the land and mining rights to Ecstall Mining Ltd., a wholly-owned subsidiary in 1967. Since 2013 the mine has been owned by Glencore PLC, a multinational mining corporation based in Switzerland, as a result of its takeover of Xstrata Copper which acquired the mine by *mesne* conveyances in 2006. Potash Corporation of Saskatchewan acquired all of the outstanding shares of Texas Gulf in 1995.

Kidd Creek Mine transformed Texas Gulf from a domestic sulphur company into a diversified international mining giant. The company's sales increased from $59 million in 1962 to $271 million in 1971, largely as a result of ore mined from Kidd Creek.

Similarly, Kidd Creek Mine transformed Timmins' economic base, and ushered in a new era of prosperity. "[Timmins] became more secure . . . . [P]eople were spending money, they were expanding businesses, they were opening new businesses. The boom in the mining sector quickly spread to the retail sector and even to the property sector … which sent the value of properties upward."[13] By 1972, the population reached about 41,000. Three daily Air Canada flights linked Timmins to Toronto. The promise of long-term economic activity resulting from the

Kidd Creek Mine was evidenced by new suburban housing and office building construction, and a new 300-bed psychiatric hospital. Once expected to live and die on gold and timber, the Porcupine region now had a multi-generational economic engine. The Kidd Creek Mine took Timmins "out of the uncertain here-today-gone-tomorrow atmosphere of gold mining and gave it a future rooted in the more lasting world of industrial metals."[14] While the life expectancy of a gold mine is measured in years, a base metal mine can remain productive for decades. Of the more than fifty operators that once mined for gold in the Porcupine region, only the Dome Mine remains in business. A scheduled closing date in 2016 was extended due to the continued high price of gold.

Texas Gulf became not only Timmins' largest taxpayer and employer, but also one of its more enlightened. Texas Gulf placed all Kidd Creek Mine employees on salary, making them the highest paid in Timmins. Placing miners on salary may have been motivated in part by a desire to avoid paying productivity bonuses. The company offered loans to enable miners to afford to buy houses. As a result, unlike the gold mines in the Porcupine region, Kidd Creek Mine was never unionized. To monitor the environmental impact of its activities, Texas Gulf maintained a herd of 60 bison (non-indigenous to Northern Ontario but known to be particularly sensitive to air pollution) on 300 acres downwind of the mine. The annual culling of the herd and sale of bison meat was a community event. The mine's award-winning safety record is a source of community pride. A "zero acceptance program" encourages self-evaluation of safety preparedness. Staff members are encouraged to begin each shift with a discussion of what happened during the previous shift. Kidd Creek Mine has received the John T. Ryan National Safety Trophy, the Canadian mining industry's most prestigious safety award (comparable in Canadian mining circles to hockey's Stanley Cup) eleven times.

By the time Kidd Creek Mine opened for business in November 1966, Texas Gulf Sulphur was already defending itself not only against the SEC, but also in two separate lawsuits filed in the Canadian courts directly challenging its ownership of the mine on the basis of its concealment of information about the discovery. Texas Gulf settled one at a high cost. The company's conduct was vindicated in the other.

A suit filed in 1966 by Royal Trust Company, executor for the Murray Hendrie Estate, accused Texas Gulf of fraudulent misrepresentation and concealment of knowledge that the estate's property was worth far more than the consideration paid. The suit was settled in 1970 by Texas Gulf paying $27 million to acquire fee simple title, including a 10% interest in net profits generated from minerals underlying its property to which the estate was entitled under the terms of its agreement to convey mining rights to Texas Gulf.

In February 1963, Leitch Gold Mines, Ltd., a Canadian mining company, entered into a contract with Texas Gulf to share exploration data with a view toward acquiring mineral rights to promising properties for exploitation by a joint venture to be formed between the two companies. In a suit filed in 1964, Leitch claimed that Texas Gulf wrongfully withheld geophysical data and reports to which Leitch was contractually entitled. The suit asked that title to the Kidd Creek property be placed in a constructive trust or alternatively for damages. Leitch Gold Mines was not one of the four landowners, and the specific issue before the court was a narrow question involving contract interpretation. However, the opinion includes an extensive account of Texas Gulf's negotiations with the vendors, and the decision is often cited as authority that a land purchaser owes no duty to disclose information to the seller before contract formation, although the language in the opinion on this subject is *dicta*.[15]

A non-jury trial of the *Leitch* case commenced in fall 1966 and lasted 164 days, a record in the Province of Ontario. Chief Justice George A. Gale of the Ontario High Court of Justice ruled in favor of Texas Gulf and awarded costs to the company.

Justice Gale determined that Texas Gulf

> . . . had decided to attempt to acquire the properties in which the Kidd 55 anomaly was located . . . with great caution and diplomacy . . . for if a hint was conveyed to any of the owners . . . that a discovery had been made, Texas Gulf would have had great difficulty thereafter in getting the properties. *Leitch*, 1 O.R. at 503.

When Dr. Holyk's credibility as a witness was challenged by reason of his evasiveness and deception in dealing with the landowners, Justice Gale came to his defense. "I do not condemn Dr. Holyk for what he did in that respect, for he was in a very delicate and perhaps dangerous position as to all of them." *Id.* Justice Gale concluded, "Under the circumstances, I believe that Texas Gulf did what any prudent mining company would have done to acquire property in which it knew a very promising anomaly lay." *Id.* The parties subsequently reached a settlement by which Texas Gulf relinquished its right to receive the payment of costs in exchange for plaintiff's agreement not to appeal the judgment. The *Wall Street Journal* reported that estimates of the costs ranged as high as $650,000.

We will return in Part IV of this Article to examine the extent to which Justice Gale's reasoning reflects the current state of Anglo-American law regarding a purchaser's duty to disclose information to the seller under the circumstances. The land law case was pending in Canada at the time the Second Circuit announced its decision in *Texas Gulf Sulphur*, which is the subject of Part III.

III. After the Gold Rush

William Cary, a former law professor, became chair of the SEC at the outset of the Kennedy administration with a primary goal of combating stock trading through unfair advantage by corporate or stock exchange officials. Cary had written the *Cady, Roberts* decision in which the SEC had been successful in pursuing this objective administratively by internal disciplinary action. As chair, Cary wanted the imprimatur of a decision by a federal court.

It was in this context that, in 1966, the SEC charged Texas Gulf and twelve individual defendants, including the company's president, general counsel, and two directors, with violations of Section 10(b) of the Securities Exchange Act of 1934 ("the '34 Act") and Rule 10b-5 promulgated thereunder. A Texas Gulf accountant (*i.e.,* a fourteenth defendant) was also charged. He failed to answer, and his case was treated as a separate, default proceeding. The company was charged with violating the anti-fraud provisions of the federal securities laws by issuing a misleading press release deliberately intended to deceive the investing public. The charges against the individual defendants related to stock and options trading between November 12, 1963 (coinciding with the successful Kidd 55 drilling) and April 16, 1964 (the date of the Second Press Release).

The District Court bench trial featured extensive and detailed expert geological testimony over the course of seventeen trial days. For reasons that would become apparent, District Court Judge Dudley Baldwin Bonsal began his opinion with a granular description of the process of mineral exploration. He characterized Texas Gulf's decision to suspend drilling following the November 1963 discovery and maintain strict confidentiality during land acquisition negotiations as "usual practice in the mining industry," a description that would be echoed by Justice Gale two years later. He provided a chronology of securities trading by insiders, wives, and friends from November 1963 to April 1964. His fact-finding ended with the issuance of the Second Press Release, which acknowledged a significant ore discovery on April 16 1964, four days after the longer First Press Release had discounted the importance of the Kidd 55 drilling. *See Texas Gulf Sulphur I*, 258 F. Supp. 262, 269 (S.D.N.Y. 1966).

Perhaps designed to demonstrate his faithfulness to text, Judge Bonsal began his legal analysis with the preamble to the '34 Act, and navigated through the subsections addressing agency authority, the public interest in the fairness of securities market prices, and the danger presented by stock manipulation.

The opinion next addressed Rule 10b-5, and two subsections of the '34 Act conferring the SEC's rule-making jurisdiction. As it existed in 1966, Rule 10b-5 prohibited the following:

1. to employ any device, scheme, or artifice to defraud,
2. to make any untrue of a material statement necessary in order to make the statements made, in light of the circumstances under which they were made, not misleading, or
3. to engage in any act, practice, or course of business which operates or would operate as a fraud, or deceit upon any person, in connection with the purchase or sale of any security. 17 C.F.R. § 240.10b-5.

This portion of Judge Bonsal's decision contained significant doctrinal victories for the Commission. He acknowledged the non-trivial argument that, while Rule 10b-5 says nothing about insider trading, Section 16(b) of the '34 Act was enacted for the express purpose of preventing trading by officers, directors and significant shareholders on the basis of inside information. Section 16(b) of the '34 Act provides for a cause of action by shareholders against officers, directors, and 10% shareholders of exchange-registered public companies for any profits gained through purchase and sale of company stock within a six-month time frame. 15 U.S.C. § 78p. Judge Bonsal held that Section 16(b) was non-exclusive and did not limit the Commission's discretion to regulate insider trading as a violation of Rule 10b-5. He rejected defendants' claim that the Commission needed to satisfy traditional elements of common law fraud. Finally, the court held that, for purposes of insider trading, the term "insider" included not only managers but all employees.

Judge Bonsal's ultimate decision was heavily influenced by his interpretation of the concept of materiality, a core element of Rule 10b-5. It is "obvious" that insiders always know more about a company's affairs than outside stockholders. Outside shareholders want insiders to own a stake in their companies, which necessarily includes the ability to trade. "[I]t is important under our free enterprise system," wrote Judge Bonsal, "that insiders, including directors, officers, and employees, be encouraged to own securities of their company." *Texas Gulf Sulphur I* at 280. Accordingly, Judge Bonsal thought that the concept of materiality should be governed by a conservative standard, "particularly since any actions under Section 10(b) are brought on the basis of hindsight." A broader test would "prevent some management trading that represents an abuse, but only at the cost of possibly exposing management to meritless litigation."

Hours of expert testimony by geologists and engineers had persuaded Judge Bonsal that those familiar with the mining industry would consider results from a single drill hole unreliable because they prove nothing about the shape of the orebody. It would be speculative to make assumptions about the value of mineral deposits, and investment decisions, in reliance on such results. Judge Bonsal concluded that any trading before April 9, 1964 was based on information at best regarded as "remote." He found as a matter of fact that material information did not surface until a point very late in the chronology, and as a matter of law that most defendants had engaged in speculative trading. Finally, Judge Bonsal found the Second Press Release to have accurately disclosed news once it became material, undermining the SEC's claim that the First Press Release was misleading. These determinations exonerated the company and ten of the twelve individual defendants.

Doubtlessly anticipating an appeal, and perhaps as a signal to the Second Circuit, Judge Bonsal acknowledged the restraints on a trial judge's discretion in the absence of binding precedent:

> It may be that the 'fairness' overtones of Cady, Roberts indicate a trend toward the elimination of all insider purchasing. But even were the court prepared to accept the proposition that all insider trading is unfair, a proposition of doubtful validity at best, it would be deterred by the admonition of Judge Learned Hand that it is not 'desirable for a lower court to embrace the exhilarating opportunity of anticipating a doctrine which may be in the womb of time, but whose birth is distant' (cites omitted). *Texas Gulf Sulphur I* at 284.

The SEC filed an appeal, and the case was argued before a three-judge panel on March 20, 1967. On May 2, 1968, after a year of deliberation, the case was submitted without further oral argument to the nine active judges on the Second Circuit to be considered *en banc* on the basis of the record, the briefs and the opinions written by the judges who heard the oral argument. The extraordinary procedure in *Texas Gulf Sulphur* avoided the inefficiency of an inevitable rehearing *en banc* after a panel has rendered a decision. Rule 35(a) of the Federal Rules of Appellate Procedure, which became effective on July 1, 1968, codified the common law practice of granting initial *en banc* consideration to cases of exceptional importance. *Texas Gulf Sulphur* was the first in a series of cases interpreting Rule 10b-5 granted initial *en banc* consideration by the Second Circuit. Judge Hayes concurred in part and dissented in part. Judge Moore wrote a vigorous dissenting opinion. Judge Waterman's majority opinion, issued on August 13, 1968, spoke for himself and six colleagues. The Second Circuit reversed the dismissals by the District Court, and reinstated charges against the company and nine individual defendants. Thomas Lamont, an outside director, who had been exonerated by the district court, died while the appeal was pending and charges against him were dropped. After appeal, no other defendant was exonerated; several had their cases deemed moot because stock options had been rescinded or canceled.

Responding to Judge Bonsal's exercise of judicial restraint, Judge Waterman wrote that "inequities based upon unequal access to knowledge should not be shrugged off as inevitable in our way of life, or, in view of the congressional concern in the area, remain uncorrected." *Texas Gulf Sulphur* at 852.

The Second Circuit addressed and rejected an argument that had not been considered below that profits derived from insider trading constitute a "normal emolument of corporate office" that should not be denied to captains of industry. The court gave short shrift to the concern that "elimination of insider trading benefits will deplete the ranks of capable corporate managers."

Addressing the key issue of materiality, the Second Circuit disagreed with the District Court's conclusion that the test should be "conservative." Under SEC Rule 405 (which contains the traditional definition of "material"), the term broadly encompasses information which "would have been important to a reasonable investor," whose decisions may be based on fundamental, technical or sentimental (sometimes known as "contrarian") analysis, and including information that might be regarded as speculative. The definition within Rule 405 — a guidebook for SEC filings — reads as follows:

> *Material.* The term *material*, when used to qualify a requirement for the furnishing of information as to any subject, limits the information required to those matters to which there is a substantial likelihood that a reasonable investor would attach importance in determining whether to purchase the security registered. 17 C.F.R. § 230.405.

Traders self-demonstrate the materiality of information by the uncharacteristic nature of their investment conduct (*e.g.*, purchasing securities on margin or investing an inordinately large portion of their net worth in one security). One investor convicted of insider trading had become the world's largest holder of options to purchase shares of the subject company, mortgaging his house in the process.[16] As first-time purchasers of short-term call options (an exotic form of investment at the time), several defendants in *Texas Gulf Sulphur* demonstrated the importance they attached to preliminary information obtained well before final test results became available in April 1964. Unlike corporate stock that has intrinsic value, call options eventually become worthless unless the underlying stock appreciates in value before the expiration date of the option. Texas Gulf insiders were in a position to know not only that the value of the company's stock was going to rise dramatically, but also when it would rise.

The Second Circuit decision foreshadowed the test of materiality that would later be announced by the Supreme Court in which courts should balance "the indicated probability that the event will occur and the anticipated magnitude of the event." For example, the Court would hold that preliminary merger negotiations were material because board meeting minutes indicated that the merger was probable and the merger was an event of great magnitude. *Basic, Inc. v. Levinson*, 485 U.S. 224 (1988). Relatedly, the Court would hold that a pharmaceutical company's failure to disclose adverse event reports may be material although the reports did not reveal a statistically significant number of adverse events. *Matrixx Initiatives, Inc. v. Siracusano*, 563 U.S. 27 (2011).

The Second Circuit addressed the issue of when insiders may lawfully trade on the basis of material information. The court rejected the District Court's concern that a judge-made rule requiring insiders to wait until the financial markets had "absorbed" information would lead to hopeless uncertainty. Judge Bonsal had specifically opined:

> It may be, as the Commission contends, that a more effective rule should be established to preclude insiders from acting on information after it has been announced but before it has been absorbed by the public . . . . Should the representatives of the news media and the wire houses be subjected to such a rule since they are in possession of material information which the average stockholder has not had an opportunity to absorb? . . . This could only lead to uncertainty. A decision in one case would not control another case with different facts. No insider would know whether he had waited long enough after an

> announcement had been made. *Texas Gulf Sulphur I* at 289.

The Second Circuit criticized the testimony of a defendant who expressed his desire to "beat the news." Investors were cautioned to exercise forbearance until the effective dissemination of a material news announcement to investors generally through the Dow Jones tape, wire services, or other media.

The court refused to recognize a good faith defense to charges of Rule 10b-5 violations. Three defendants claimed that they honestly believed information regarding the ore strike had been made public by the time they entered their purchase orders. Following case law that had established that specific intent was unnecessary, the Second Circuit held that even "negligent insider conduct" was unlawful.

By rejecting Texas Gulf's argument that the First Press Release was outside the coverage of Rule 10b-5, the court relaxed the "in connection with" requirement that appears at the end of the Rule. For support of this interpretation, Judge Waterman cited '34 Act legislative history as reflecting Congressional intent that "[t]here cannot be honest markets without honest publicity."

Texas Gulf Sulphur introduced the terms "tipper" and "tippee" to describe the source and recipient of insider information, respectively, which *Cady, Roberts* had rather awkwardly described collectively as "persons who [were] in a special relationship with a company and privy to its affairs." Although the doctrinal basis for their liability would evolve, the terms "tipper" and "tippee" continue to be used to describe these defendants. Upon remand, individual defendants who recommended purchase of Texas Gulf shares by others were ordered to disgorge profits earned by their tippees. Emboldened by its victory in *Texas Gulf Sulphur*, the SEC moved swiftly to assert its enforcement power, obtaining a consent judgment against Merrill Lynch, Pierce, Fenner & Smith formally recognizing "tippee" liability.

Texas Gulf Sulphur promulgated the duty to abstain from trading in securities, or recommending trading by others, until material nonpublic information has been disclosed and digested by the market. A half-century later, this duty remains the central organizing principle of insider trading regulation. According to Judge Waterman, the duty is owed by anyone in possession of inside information, with a view to "the implementation of the Congressional purpose that all investors should have equal access to the rewards of participation."

Opponents of insider trading regulation criticized the notion of equality of access as reflecting a quixotic vision of the securities markets that suggests to unsophisticated investors that government regulation will level the playing field for their benefit. The prevalence of insider trading and the inability of government to detect and prevent it was acknowledged by passage of the Insider Trading and Securities Fraud Enforcement Act of 1988 giving the SEC authority to seek substantial penalties against companies whose employees engage in insider trading. The act conscripts publicly-traded companies to police insider trading by creating a strong economic incentive for companies to adopt and implement compliance programs. Companies that fail to take appropriate steps to prevent insider trading face penalties of $1 million, or three times the profit realized by employees who engage in insider trading and their tippees, whichever is greater. The act was passed by unanimous vote of both houses of Congress in response to public perception that insider trading had reached epidemic proportions.[17]

Five insider trading cases have been decided by the U.S. Supreme Court since *Texas Gulf Sulphur*. In *Chiarella v. United States*, in a setback for the SEC, the Court substituted its own rationale for the duty to disclose or abstain, and narrowed the categories of traders and tippers who owed the duty. 445 U.S. 222, 239 (1980). In *Chiarella*, an employee of a financial printer purchased stock in a company after obtaining knowledge of an impending tender offer. The Court held that the disclose or abstain duty does not arise from the mere possession of material nonpublic information but from the existence of a fiduciary relationship. The insider trading prohibition is a function of the fiduciary duty of loyalty owed by a company's directors, officers and employees to its shareholders. It is unlawful for insiders with secret information to purchase securities from, or sell securities to, their own shareholders. The Court held there could be no violation of Rule 10b-5 in the absence of a fiduciary relationship between the defendant and those trading on the other side of the transaction. *Chiarella* effectively limited insider trading to traditional insiders (*i.e.*, company managers and employees).

In *United States v. O'Hagan*, the Court adopted the Commission's argument, known as the misappropriation theory, that trading on the basis of information wrongfully obtained from an employer or other source constitutes a violation of Rule 10b-5. 521 U.S. 642 (1997). The Court held that an attorney in a law firm representing a corporate raider violated Rule 10b-5 by acquiring options to purchase target company's stock based on knowledge of an impending tender offer. By appropriating for personal profit secret information required to be held in the strictest confidence, a trader betrays the trust and confidence of the trader's employer, patient or client. The Court had previously considered the misappropriation theory in a case involving R. Foster Winans, a *Wall Street Journal* columnist, who passed along information to tippees identifying stocks that he knew would be mentioned in the paper. *Carpenter v. United States*, 484 U.S. 19 (1987). Although the Supreme Court upheld his conviction, its equally divided opinion was without precedential value. Judicial acceptance of the misappropriation theory in *O'Hagan* may explain why the SEC has been reluctant to push for a statutory definition of insider trading, which might be more constrictive than what has been achieved through common law development.

Judicial acceptance of the misappropriation theory constituted a significant expansion of the scope of insider trading regulation. For example, the government charged a psychiatrist with breaching the physician-patient duty of confidentiality when he purchased BankAmerica stock after learning from a patient that her husband would become its chief executive officer. *United States v. Willis*, 737 F. Supp. 269 (S.D.N.Y. 1990). His insider trading conviction has been cited as the "paradigmatic example" of the misappropriation theory run amok. *United States v. O'Hagan*, 92 F. 3d 612, 622 n.14 (8th Cir. 1996). Because it is virtually certain to generate more losses than gains, a strategy of trading on tips from psychotherapy patients poses little risk to the integrity of the securities markets. The case became the poster child for opponents of the misappropriation theory who feared that, in the hands of over-zealous enforcement authorities, it may reach conduct outside the scope of Rule

10b-5.[18] Like any government agency, the SEC loses cases it probably should have won, and wins cases that arguably should never have been filed. For an example of the former, *see SEC v. Switzer*, 590 F. Supp. 756 (W.D. Okla. 1984) (trading on the basis of market information obtained by chance as a result of an overheard conversation is not a violation of Rule 10b-5). In *Salman v. United States*, 137 S. Ct. 420 (2016), the Court held that a tipper breached his fiduciary duty because he benefited personally from disclosing confidential information to a relative.

In Part IV of this chapter we will see that these same two categories of purchasers (those in a fiduciary relationship and those who misappropriate information from its owner) are also required to disclose their superior knowledge about the value of real property to unsuspecting landowners.

IV. Silence is Golden?

In his classic treatise, *Contract as Promise,* Charles Fried described this thinly disguised version of the Texas Gulf Sulphur story as being ". . . just on the moving edge of the law's developing frontal system . . .":

> An oil company has made extensive geological surveys seeking to identify possible oil and gas reserves. These surveys are extremely expensive. Having identified one promising site, the oil company . . . buys a large tract of land from its prosperous farmer owner, revealing nothing about its survey . . . . The price paid is the going price for farmland of that quality in that region.

Professor Fried's characterization notwithstanding, at first blush the law appears well-settled on the subject. In an arm's length transaction, when information has not been requested, prospective purchasers are under no duty to disclose facts within their knowledge materially affecting the value of the property that the seller could have discovered by its own due diligence. Thus, proprietary information obtained through geological investigation need not be disclosed in the course of bargaining as a matter of law, although private morality and conscience may inform a buyer's decision to volunteer such information. Early English courts came to similar conclusions:

> Suppose, for instance, that A, knowing there to be a mine in the estate of B, of which he knew B was ignorant, should enter into a contract to purchase the estate of B for the price of the estate, without considering the mine, could the court set it aside? . . . The court will not correct a contract merely because a man of nice honor would not have entered into it . . . . *Fox v. Mackreth*, 2 Bro. Ch. 400, 420; s.c., 2 Cox, 320 (1788).

Commenting positively on this case, Chancellor Kent observed that

> . . . human laws are not so perfect as the dictates of conscience, and the sphere of morality is more enlarged than the limits of civil jurisdiction. There are many duties that belong to the class of imperfect obligations which are binding on conscience, but which human laws do not and cannot undertake directly to enforce.[19]

Stated more colorfully and memorably, "A person who knows that there is a mine on the land of another may nevertheless buy it . . . . A purchaser is not by our laws bound to make the man he buys from as wise as himself." *Harris v. Tyson*, 24 Pa. St. 347, S.C., 64, Am. Dec. 661 (1855).

Other American court have come to similar conclusions. The Tenth Circuit reasoned that:

> The superior scientific knowledge and skill which enables a prospective lessee of mineral lands to acquire information about their mineral qualities by geophysical methods is no different in principle than any other type of superior knowledge whereby a prospective purchaser in enable to judge the soundness of a horse, the genuineness of a picture or the quality of a diamond. *Peterson v. Koch Indus., Inc.*, 684 F.2d 667, 671 (10th Cir. 1982).

See also Garbutt v. Southern Clays, Inc., 894 F. Supp. 456, 461 (M.D. Ga. 1995) (a buyer-seller relationship does not require that the buyer disclose information regarding the value of the seller's property); *Nusbaum v. Weeks*, 214 Cal. App. 3d 1589 (Cal. App. Ct. 1989) (public official owed no duty to disclose to seller information about his intention to influence policy change that would affect the value of the property); *Zaschak v. Traverse Corp.*, 333 N.W. 2d 191 (Mich. Ct. App. 1983) (purchaser with graduate degree in geology, and aware of oil and gas in the area, had no duty to disclose his knowledge to seller); *Harrell v. Powell*, 106 S.E. 2d 160 (N.C. 1958) (dicta) (no duty to disclose purchaser's knowledge of gold mine on land).

Fortified by long-standing precedent, the drafters of the *Restatement (Second) of Contracts* definitively assert that "[a] buyer of property . . . is not ordinarily expected to disclose circumstances that make the property more valuable than the seller supposes." If an unsuspecting landowner "is indolent, inexperienced or ignorant, or if his judgment is bad or he lacks access to adequate information his adversary is not generally expected to compensate for these deficiencies."

However, by including the words "ordinarily" and "generally," the drafters acknowledge the existence of exceptions to the right to remain silent. Perhaps signaling their dissatisfaction with the general rule, courts have demonstrated a willingness to interpret these exceptions expansively in natural resources transactions. For example, one court interpreted the phrase "if any" in a mineral deed prepared by the buyer as creating a misleading impression that the buyer did not know whether or not there had been any oil and gas production, giving rise to a duty to disclose its knowledge of the existence of mineralization. *Croslin v. Enerlex, Inc.*, 308 P.3d 1041 (Okla. 2013).

Just as some courts have demonstrated dissatisfaction with the general rule, Professor Fried has expressed ambivalence about the outcome of his own hypothetical. Similarly, a past president of the Colorado Bar Association has called upon lawyers in natural resources transactions to adhere to a higher standard of professionalism, arguing that reliance on rules that have developed to justify deceptive conduct in negotiations undermines the integrity of the profession, their clients and the process.[20]

There are so many well-recognized categorical exceptions to the silence-is-golden rule that they almost swallow the rule whole. In this Part

IV we examine the exceptions most relevant to the Texas Gulf Sulphur story.

The existence of a fiduciary relationship between the parties changes everything. As a consequence of being in a fiduciary relationship, a duty of loyalty and a corresponding duty to disclose information exist between partners and joint venturers. The duty to render complete information arises out of the dependence and vulnerability inherent in the partnership relationship. This aspect of fiduciary obligation is more extensive than the mere duty to supply information upon demand. The duty includes a self-executing obligation to make affirmative disclosure even in the absence of explicit request for information. In a fiduciary relationship, nondisclosure of material fact is actionable fraud.

This exception helps explain, at least in part, Texas Gulf's decision to pay $27 million to settle the lawsuit filed by Royal Trust Company on behalf of the Hendrie Estate. In June 1963 Texas Gulf purchased for $500 an option to explore the estate's land for two years, and the right, during that period, to acquire mining rights to the property for $18,000. If the company discovered a mineable body of ore and exercised the option, which it did, the estate was also entitled to receive a ten percent participation interest in the net profits derived from minerals extracted from its property. This royalty feature was typical in the Canadian extraction industry at the time. In the U.S. it is customary for coal companies to offer landowners a royalty of 6-8%.[21] Participation interests are less common in transactions involving other minerals, including oil and gas, in the U.S.[22]

The sharing of profits from a venture is the definition of a partnership. Having entered into this arrangement, it was a breach of fiduciary duty for Texas Gulf to thereafter negotiate in bad faith in seeking to acquire the net profit interest back from the estate for $57,000 without full disclosure of Texas Gulf's knowledge of its likely value, estimated at the time to be worth more than $100 million. Because these negotiations were unsuccessful, the estate incurred no actual damages. The availability of punitive damages as a remedy for breach of fiduciary duty may have informed Texas Gulf's decision to settle.

Another exception to the silence-is-golden rule exists when a buyer obtains information through improper means. Trespass to the seller's land in the course of performing tests and investigations to determine the presence of mineralization will cost the buyer the right to remain silent. Trespass to land in the course of mineral exploration is hardly a recent or rare occurrence. It has given rise to difficult cases and considerable scholarly commentary. *See, e.g.*, Leon Green, *What Protection Has a Landowner Against a Trespass Which Merely Destroys the Speculative Value of His Property*, 4 TEX. L. REV. 215 (1926).

A buyer's duty to disclose information acquired by wrongful act was first recognized in *Phillips v. Homfray*. 6 Ch. App. 770 (1871). The defendants trespassed on the plaintiff's land, acquired coal from the subsurface, assayed the coal, and thereafter negotiated with plaintiff to purchase the land without disclosing their superior knowledge of its true value. As the court explained, "[B]eing unable to gain access to the coal, the purchasers took advantage of an unlawful access to it in order to test its value, and did not communicate to the vendors the result." The court drew a comparison with the following situation where information wrongfully obtained would trigger a duty to disclose:

> Suppose a picture-dealer, employed to clean a picture, scrapes off a part of the picture to see if he can discover a mark which will tell him who is the artist, and thus finds a mark showing it to be the work of a great artist; that would not be a legitimate mode of acquiring knowledge for the purpose of enabling him to buy the picture at a lower price than the owner would have sold it had he known it to be the work of that artist.

As a consequence, the court refused to order specific performance of the contract of sale.

It would be a mistake to discount the significance of this case as merely an example of a chancellor's refusal to exercise equitable discretion in denying specific performance to a party with unclean hands. The drafters of the *Restatement (Second) of Contracts* take a broader view and base an illustration on its facts:

> A learns of the [presence of] valuable mineral deposits from trespassing on B's land . . . . [A does not disclose this information to B in negotiations leading to contract formation.] A's non-disclosure is equivalent to an assertion that the land does not contain valuable mineral deposits, and this assertion is a misrepresentation.

This illustration is subject to criticism as bootstrapping. Although he is critical of the illustration as being inelegant, Professor Eisenberg concluded that "[T]he Restatement comes to the right result through a rickety back door . . . ." Professor Eisenberg reasoned that:

> [E]ven if the actor is a buyer . . . , disclosure should be required if the information was acquired through improper means . . . . The major rationale for permitting nondisclosure . . . is to provide an incentive for the acquisition of information. This rationale does not hold, or is trumped, when the means used to acquire the information is socially undesirable. [23]

The analysis in the *Restatement*, however, is critical for purposes of crafting a remedy that makes the landowner whole. If the only available remedies are those traditionally granted for trespass, a mineral exploration company may be willing to incur the risk as a cost of doing business. A landowner's actual damages under the circumstances are likely to be nominal. An award of substantial punitive damages and only nominal compensatory damages may not survive appellate scrutiny.

By transforming what would otherwise be trespass into fraud, the panoply of available remedies expands to include not only denial of specific performance in a case like *Phillips v. Homfray* where the seller discovers the truth in time, but also rescission and imposition of a constructive trust. According to the *Restatement (Second) of Contracts* § 161, misrepresentation is grounds for rescinding an otherwise valid contract. A constructive trust is an equitable remedy imposing a trust on property acquired through misrepresentation. Judge Cardozo reasoned that "A constructive trust is the formula through which the conscience of equity finds expression. When property has been acquired in such circumstances that the holder of the legal title may not in good conscience retain the beneficial interest, equity converts him into a trustee." *Beatty v. Guggenheim Exploration Co.*, 122 N.E. 378, 380 (1919).

It is far from certain that a judge, facing a courtroom packed with hopeful miners and their families, would exercise the equitable discretion to grant these potent remedies. There will be equities on the side of a mining company that invested time and resources in acquiring the relevant knowledge. According to Judge Easterbrook, "[T]here would have been no discoveries of ore in Timmins, Ontario, by the Texas Gulf Sulphur Corp. unless the discoverer were allowed to use its hard-won information to appropriate much of the value of the deposits."[24] The collective good may be better served by enforcing consensual agreements giving a fortunate landowner a net profit interest comparable to a finder's share of the value of lost objects under statutes codifying the common law.

Recent developments in technology eliminate the need to physically enter onto land in order to prospect for natural resources. Seismic data recording using the so-called "seisloop" surveying method enables geophysical exploration of land that is inaccessible due to physical conditions (*e.g.*, hilly terrain or dense vegetation) or other factors. Receivers are placed along roads surrounding the area of interest. Seismic sources activated around the periphery cover the area within the loop. When the area is inaccessible because of lack of permission, this method of surveying may constitute unauthorized exploration of the subsurface in violation of the landowner's rights.

Imposing liability for trespass without proof of actual physical entry is problematic. To overcome this obstacle, courts in states rich in natural resources have been persuaded to recognize a new tort variously entitled "wrongful appropriation of the privilege to explore," "geological trespass," or "geophysical trespass." The tort encompasses the conduct of geophysical operations on the land of another without permission or consent. Several jurisdictions recognize versions of this tort.[25]

These two exceptions to the silence-is-golden rule (for parties in a fiduciary relationship and for purchasers with geophysical information obtained by violating the seller's rights) correspond to the disclose or abstain duty in securities transactions. Judge Waterman thought this duty was owed by anyone trading in securities on the basis of material nonpublic information. Subsequent insider trading cases first limited the duty to insiders in a fiduciary relationship with the party on the other side of the transaction. Later cases applying the misappropriation theory extended the duty to traders who violated the rights of the owners of the information.

The primeval urge for wealth sparks investment in the extraction and securities industries. Access to information is the principal driver of profits in both industries. Analytically there is no difference between trading in securities on the basis of material nonpublic information obtained through unlawful means, and acquiring land at a bargain price using wrongfully obtained geophysical information. In either situation, misappropriated information ought not be the basis for gaining a transactional advantage. In July 2016 the SEC issued proposed rules that would require publicly-traded mining companies to disclose exploration results for each of its mining properties that are material to its business or financial condition.[26] Likewise, in the context of a fiduciary relationship, the duty of full disclosure in land sale transactions attaches not only by private morality and the dictates of conscience, but also as a matter of positive law. These exceptions reconcile and unify the duty-to-disclose in the sale of land and securities.

V. Conclusion

Because the Supreme Court twice refused to grant *certiorari* in *Texas Gulf Sulphur*, the Second Circuit would have the last word. Its interpretation of the U.S. law of insider trading has withstood the test of time. At its golden anniversary, *Texas Gulf Sulphur* continues to accurately represent the controlling legal principles that govern the elements of insider trading. It has taken five decades of litigation to sort out the details, but the case would be decided the same way today. Today the SEC would likely refer such an insider trading case for criminal prosecution. However, individual defendants who could prove that they believed in good faith that the discovery was public information by the time of their trades would be exonerated. Texas Gulf's liability would include a penalty based upon the profits made by individual defendants, including tippees who were not company employees.

Texas Gulf, and many of its employees and managers, has borne the stigma of fraud for the past half-century. Viewed from the other side of the border, however, Texas Gulf's legacy is very different. Through the exercise of foresight, dedication, tenacity and hard work, Texas Gulf is credited with saving Timmins and giving the gritty town a new lease on life. For his leadership in discovering the Kidd Creek orebody and its contribution to the nation's economy, Walter Holyk was inducted into the Canadian Mining Hall of Fame in 1997. Although he died broke after he was ordered to restore more than $90,000, including profits made by sub-tippees unknown to him, Kenneth Darke is a local folk hero.

Kidd Creek Mine is scheduled to close in 2022, and Timmins' long-term future is uncertain. Although previously scheduled closing dates have come and gone, the 2022 closing date is based on projections that commodity prices will no longer justify the cost to extract and hoist minerals, and provide the infrastructure necessary for a safe working environment (principally the cost of energy to ventilate and cool air that becomes increasingly dense at lower depths). Although minerals will be left in the ground when the mine closes, it is not considered "ore" by the industry unless it can be extracted responsibly and profitably. Current ownership is averse to allowing another operator to take over the mine (even as part of a joint venture) without indemnification and assumption of liabilities. Although still operating four shifts seven days a week, Kidd Creek Mine has been reducing its work force through attrition.

Reclamation planning is underway to fill the physical void. Reclamation plans include transforming the vast open pit into a man-made lake. Also being considered is a plan to drill holes, pump water and use the earth's natural geothermal energy to operate steam-driven turbines. Letters of credit in the hundreds of millions of dollars have been provided to the Canadian government to secure reclamation of the mine.

Filling the economic void poses a greater challenge. Timmins has always relied upon new discoveries of underground resources. Although it has been more fortunate than most mining towns, Timmins has become dependent upon Kidd Creek Mine for its employment base and philanthropy. In anticipation of the mine's eventual closing, efforts have been made to market Timmins as a tourist destination. The main highway through town was renamed "Shania Twain Way" after the Nashville star who grew up in Timmins. A museum featuring Shania Twain memorabilia, "expected to be the lifesaving tourist attraction Timmins sorely needed," opened in 2001 but closed its doors in 2014 due to lack of interest, and has been bulldozed to the ground.[27] More recent branding of Timmins as "Ontario's best kept secret," targets adventurous travelers seeking a four-season destination for outdoor recreational activities. The descendants of prospectors famous for perpetual optimism and magical thinking now confront a harsh reality: No one has discovered another orebody near Timmins since Texas Gulf in 1963.

Under the securities laws, traders expose themselves to civil and criminal liability by purchasing shares of stock, or recommending the stock to others, without disclosing material nonpublic information. Intentional concealment of relevant information in the purchase of real property has long been considered prudent business conduct. Opponents of insider trading regulation question why it is lawful to profit from informational advantages in the real estate market but not in the stock market. This disparity in duty-to-disclose cases has been invoked by critics as evidence of the intellectual poverty of insider trading regulation. This chapter suggests that these differences may be exaggerated. Loss of the right to remain silent may be a natural byproduct of natural resources extraction.

V

Immaculate Defamation: The Case of the *Alton Telegraph*

I. Introduction

At about the midpoint of its journey, the mighty Mississippi River turns almost due east for a distance of 15 miles before reaching Alton, Illinois, where it joins forces with the Missouri River and resumes its proper course south to the Gulf of Mexico. The Mississippi River derives its name from a combination of the Ojibwa words *misi* (big) and *sipi* (river) and flows 2,350 miles through America's heartland from its headwaters in the north central Minnesota wilderness. Its source, an antler-shaped glacial lake, was discovered in 1832 by Henry R. Schoolcraft, who named it Lake Itasca, derived by combining two Latin words, *veritas* (true) and *capita* (head). It is unclear whether Schoolcraft knew that the lake already had an Ojibwa name, *Omashkoozo-zaaga'igan* (Elk Lake).

The Riverbend, beginning at the confluence of the Mississippi and Illinois Rivers in Grafton, Illinois, is the brand used by Alton and neighboring communities at the southwestern edge of the state to market the region for its natural beauty as a tourist destination. Metro East is the official name for the portion of the St. Louis Metropolitan Statistical Area consisting of the eastern suburbs of St. Louis situated across the Mississippi River. The Metro East is the second largest urban area in Illinois after the Chicago metropolitan area. Riverbend is an apt metaphor for the rule of law in the jurisdiction where these river towns are located. The Madison County judicial system has long been regarded as "bent."

A jurisdiction's lawsuit climate is a significant factor in business owners' growth and expansion plans. According to the Metro East's legal journal, "The reputation we've acquired nationally is a black cloud that hangs over all of us."[1] Based upon a survey of lawyers who represent major employers, the American Tort Reform Association ranked Madison County as the third most unfair litigation environment in the nation in 2013, a slight improvement from its ranking in 2005 as the very worst jurisdiction. Similarly, a national survey of lawyers by the U.S. Chamber Institute for Legal Reform named Madison County as the sixth most unfair and unreasonable jurisdiction in the country in 2012.

Madison County's class action filing rate per capita is about twenty times the national average. Former judge and state's attorney Donald W. Weber explained why Madison County has been such a popular venue for personal injury suits. "Attorneys will do whatever they can to have their cases tried here. [It has] a big pool of laborers, with all the steel companies, barge lines, and railroads that come through here. So the juries are much more likely to be sympathetic to the plaintiff than the big companies."[2] Although their exposure and treatment occurred elsewhere, non-residents have historically filed a disproportionately large percentage of asbestos-related personal injury claims in Madison County, attracted by the reputation of its juries for being generous to working-class plaintiffs. Not unlike Delaware, where corporation franchise taxes are an important part of the state budget, filing fees generated by asbestos lawsuits represent a significant source of income for Madison County government. A 2013 audit of county finances reported an increase in revenue attributable primarily to court filing fees, noting that 1,563 asbestos lawsuits were filed in 2012, compared with 952 in 2011.

Members of the Madison County plaintiffs' bar are actively involved in the highly politicized process by which judges are selected. In one instance of blatant corruption, Circuit Court Judge Barbara Crowder, who formerly oversaw Madison County's asbestos docket, was reassigned in 2011 when it was disclosed that she had granted 82% of 2013 trial slots to three plaintiffs' firms. Just a few days after the docketing decision, lawyers for those firms made at total of $30,000 in contributions to her re-election campaign.

Madison County, along with neighboring St. Clair County, is known as "Plaintiffs' Paradise" for the staggering verdicts awarded by pro-plaintiff juries. Record-breaking jury awards have been blamed for the high malpractice insurance premiums that have resulted in an exodus of physicians from Madison County.

The *Alton Telegraph* has been the principal source of local news for residents of the Riverbend since its founding in 1836. Following a jury trial in 1980, the paper found itself on the wrong side of the largest damage award in the history of U.S. libel law. Although there have since been larger libel judgments against newspapers, the $9.2 million award against the *Telegraph* is the equivalent of $25 million adjusted to constant dollars, placing it among the largest libel verdicts awarded in U.S. history. What makes the *Telegraph* case extraordinary, and one of immaculate defamation, is that the libel was based upon a story that was never published in the paper.

On appeal, the *Telegraph* case would have presented important issues of reporters' privilege, and the rights of citizens to report possible criminal activity to law enforcement officials. Major newspapers and journalism societies raised these issues in *amicus* briefs in support of the *Telegraph.* A pattern of rulings by the trial judge against the *Telegraph* on matters of law and evidence might well have been held to constitute prejudicial error.

What makes the *Telegraph* case tragic is that the trial court decision was never made subject to appellate review. A jury would have the last word after deliberating only five hours following a trial that lasted more than five weeks. The enormity of the judgment against the *Telegraph* dwarfed its net worth. The paper could not afford to post the bond, known as a *supersedeas* bond, necessary to file an appeal. The family that had treated the *Telegraph* as a stewardship through four generations was forced to file for bankruptcy protection to preserve its viability as a going concern.

The *supersedeas* bond has been a little-known feature of appellate practice since colonial times. Following a successful trial verdict, plaintiff becomes a judgment creditor of the defendant, entitled to satisfy the judgment by seeking to execute against defendant's assets. By placing the assets of a bonding company behind the obligation, an appeal bond ensures that money to satisfy the judgment will be available to appellee if the judgment is affirmed on appeal. The parties to an appeal bond consist of the principal (appellant), the obligee or party protected by the bond (appellee), and the surety (typically an insurance company) who agrees to be legally liable to pay appellee if the judgment is affirmed and the principal is unable to satisfy the judgment. The principal signs an indemnity agreement, promising to reimburse the surety if the surety is made to pay. The surety will require the principal to furnish a letter of credit or other form of collateral. The principal pays an annual premium, typically 1-2% of the amount of the bond. Agencies of the federal government are not required to post an appeal bond. FED. R. CIV. P. 62(c).

Posting an appeal bond is technically not a requirement for filing an appeal. Rather, it is a device that stays enforcement of the judgment by execution against defendant's assets during the pendency of the appellate process. *Price v. Philip Morris, Inc.*, 341 Ill. App. 3d 941, 943 (Ill. App. Ct. 2003). In theory, a defendant can appeal without posting a bond, but then the plaintiff would be free to execute on the judgment while the appeal was pending. In *Obsidian Finance Group, LLC v. Cox*, 812 F. Supp. 1220 (D. Or. 2011), after obtaining summary judgment for $2.5 million in damages in a defamation suit against an Internet blogger, plaintiff sought to execute on the judgment by asking the sheriff to seize and sell to the highest bidder (who would presumably be plaintiff) the "intangible personal property" owned by defendant, consisting of defendant's right to appeal. If this novel judgment execution stratagem succeeds, defendant, who could not afford to post a *supersedeas* bond, will lose the right to appeal.

The case, decided by the U.S. Court of Appeals for the Ninth Circuit, raised the issue to be discussed, *infra*, in Part V of this chapter. The court held, as a matter of first impression, that First Amendment defamation rules apply equally to both the institutional press and individual speakers. The court also held that blog posts were protected by the First Amendment as "opinion," and thus were not actionable. Plaintiff was not able to seize defendant's right to appeal.

As a haunting and cautionary tale about the relationship between reporters and their sources in agencies of government, the case of the *Alton Telegraph* is a very good story. It earned plaintiff's counsel a place in the Guinness Book of World Records. For his family's heroic efforts to save the *Telegraph*, the publisher received the prestigious John Peter Zenger Award for Freedom of the Press and the People's Right to Know. The University of Arizona School of Journalism has presented this award, now known as the John Peter and Anna Catherine Zenger Award, annually since 1954 in the cause of freedom of the press and the people's right to know. In 1734 Zenger was charged with seditious libel for publishing news stories critical of royal government officials in colonial New York. His wife continued to publish the *New York Weekly Journal* while her husband was imprisoned for ten months before being brought to trial. Zenger's acquittal by a jury after deliberating for ten minutes established the principle that truth is a defense against libel, and is regarded as helping to lay the foundation for the First Amendment. Paul S. Cousley, the third generation of Cousleys to serve as publisher of the *Telegraph*, was the 1981 recipient of the Zenger Award.

Inspired by subsequent developments in Madison County, the appeal bond process in most states has since been reformed. However, a media organization could still be crippled by the inability to seek appellate review of a sizeable damages award, which is why the *Telegraph* case retains its claim to our attention at its 40th anniversary.

Following the Introduction, Part II of this chapter explores the events leading to the *Telegraph* case. Part III examines the proceedings at the trial court level. Part IV describes the surreal aftermath in which eleven grounds of error were never considered by an appellate tribunal for lack of an appeal bond. Part V argues that, without significant re-imagination, the *supersedeas* bond requirement may violate an emerging right to appeal. Meanwhile, as it applies to organizations engaged in newsgathering and dissemination, the appeal bond process abridges freedom of the press and the people's right to know.

II. Backstory

"Every lawsuit is a potential drama: a story of conflict, often with victims and villains, leading to justice done or denied."[3] In any drama, the place in which events unfold can profoundly influence the outcome. In the *Telegraph* case, the city of Alton itself functions as a principal character.

Alton was named in honor of his firstborn son by Rufus Easton, a prominent lawyer and land speculator who served as the first postmaster of St. Louis. By reason of its proximity to St. Louis, and its location near the confluence of three navigable rivers, Easton perceived the natural advantages of the site as the base for a passenger ferry service. Evidence of Easton's primary reason for his interest in the location is found in the deeds conveying parcels of land in Alton in which he expressly reserved ferry rights for himself and his heirs. By 1818 Easton had acquired much of the land that comprised Alton when it was chartered as a city by the Illinois legislature in 1837.

Easton's vision proved correct, though he did not personally benefit financially from his investment. His heavy speculation in Alton real estate left him in "straightened circumstances for the rest of his life."[4] Alton flourished as a thriving center for transportation and commerce throughout the steamboat era of the 1820s and 1830s. Steamships carried cargo from the Illinois River to the north and the Missouri River to the south to the Port of St. Louis and down the Mississippi River to New Orleans. Alton was the first community outside of Missouri that Samuel Clemens saw when he left home in 1853 at the age of 18 and sailed down the Mississippi to St. Louis. He described Alton as "a dismal little river town full of death, disease, disaster, violence and murder."[5] Although Mark Twain was unimpressed by his visit, Alton's prime location and the region's abundant limestone, coal and timber resources attracted an influx of entrepreneurs and talented craftsmen. Alton attracted immigrants from Scotland, Ireland, England and Germany. The biographer of Mary Easton, Rufus Easton's wife, wrote: "It is hard to believe that at one time in history our city was an industrial mecca."[6]

Prominent among the immigrants to Alton was Lucas J. Pfeiffenberger, who designed dozens of private residences, churches and public buildings of architectural significance, and served four terms as mayor of Alton between 1872 and 1883. Pfeiffenberger stopped in Alton in 1857 en route to the gold rush in California and never left. Pfeiffenberger also served as the first president of Piasa Building and Loan Association, the predecessor to Piasa First Federal Savings & Loan Association ("Piasa"), whose failure was central to the *Telegraph* case.

According to Native American legend, the Piasa bird was a fierce, winged monster dreaded for carrying villagers off one by one to a cave along the riverbank at the site of what would later become Alton, where they would be eaten. Ouatogo, an Illini chief, finally was able to trick the creature into making an attack, whereupon twenty warriors armed with bows and poisoned arrows ambushed and succeeded in killing the giant bird. An image of the Piasa bird is painted on a bluff overlooking the river.

By the middle of the 19th century Alton was one of the most important and enterprising cities in Illinois. Alton boasted four newspapers at the time, including the *Telegraph* which published its first issue on January 15, 1836. It was home to more than 100 industries engaged in brewing, baking and banking among others, and institutions of higher education. Major employers included Laclede Steel, Owens Illinois Glass Company, Standard Oil, and Western Cartridge Company. Alton was growing faster than St. Louis and was almost as large as Chicago. “In 1836, easterners had referred to Alton as the Queen of the West. It vied with St. Louis in importance as a port city.”[7] Alton hosted the final senatorial debate between Abraham Lincoln and Stephen A. Douglas in 1858. On October 15, 1858, after arriving in Alton before dawn aboard the steamship *City of Louisiana,* Lincoln dined with Senator Lyman Trumble in the Christian Hill neighborhood before strolling down the square for his seventh debate with Douglas. The city was also a leading candidate to become Illinois’ state capital. Although Alton received the most votes in a statewide election held in 1834 to choose the capital, its narrow margin over Springfield was deemed inconclusive.

Significant income and wealth disparity was a byproduct of the city’s rapid industrial growth, although even laborers, bricklayers and stonemasons earned an exceptional wage of $1 to $3 daily compared to 40-cents being paid elsewhere. Nonetheless, rapid industrial growth resulted in the sorting of Alton’s residents into sections separated by geography and social class. Historian and lifelong Alton resident Judy Hoffman wrote that, “The majority of Upper Alton’s inhabitants were Northerners from New England and New York. Alton was a city divided by the Upper Town and the Lower Town, by Northern Yankees and Southern sympathizers, by an upper business class and a lower laboring class."[8] Pfeiffenberger and other architects designed magnificent Queen Anne Victorian, Italianate and Georgian Revival mansions built of stone or brick on the bluffs in the Middletown district of the city for the families of steamboat captains and captains of industry. Working-class families settled in neighborhoods of one-story frame houses in the flood-prone low-lying areas closer to the river.

A tragic event threatened Alton's growing prosperity, and enshrined the city in the history of the nation's struggle for freedom of the press a century before the *Telegraph* case. In what has been described as the first battle of the Civil War, the abolitionist Elijah Parish Lovejoy, a Presbyterian minister and editor of the *Alton Observer*, was murdered in Alton. Born in Maine in 1802, Lovejoy moved to St. Louis in 1832 and became editor of the *St. Louis Times*. Lovejoy's strident editorials against slavery prompted a local judge, Luke E. Lawless, to declare the paper a threat to democracy. Lovejoy had previously called Judge Lawless an "Irish papist" for not prosecuting those responsible for lynching a local black cook. Fearing for himself and his young wife, Lovejoy fled St. Louis and relocated across the river to the free state of Illinois in September 1836 where he became editor of the *Alton Observer*. In response to his editorials against slavery in the *Alton Observer*, Lovejoy's printing press had been dismantled and thrown into the Mississippi River by a pro-slavery mob. After this happened for the third time, Lovejoy resolved to defend his property.

On the night of November 7, 1837, an alcohol-fueled mob carrying guns, clubs, stones and torches surrounded the Godfrey, Gilman & Company warehouse on the Mississippi riverfront. One man climbed a ladder up the three-story building intent on setting fire to the premises for the purpose of destroying Lovejoy's fourth printing press, which he had surreptitiously shipped from Cincinnati the previous night. Standing with his supporters on the roof, Lovejoy was killed by shotgun blasts fired from the mob.

News of Lovejoy's death was reported throughout the nation and prompted countless editorials, pamphlets and sermons. The national publicity galvanized public support for the antislavery movement, and left Alton's reputation permanently scarred.

No one was ever convicted of a crime in connection with Lovejoy's murder. His death was an "earthquake" sending shock waves through America and "felt in the most distant regions of the earth."[9] By its mobilization of antislavery sentiment, Lovejoy's martyrdom was a turning point in American history comparable in significance to Harriet Beecher Stowe's publication of *Uncle Tom's Cabin.* John Brown stood up at the end of a memorial prayer meeting in Ohio and announced, "Here, before God, in the presence of these witnesses, from this time, I consecrate my life to the destruction of slavery!"[10] In an address on the centennial anniversary of Lovejoy's death, President Herbert Hoover said, "Since his martyrdom, no man has openly challenged free speech and the free press in America."[11] In Lovejoy's honor, the Thirteenth Amendment to the Constitution abolishing slavery was drafted in Alton, and in 2012, the city honored Lovejoy by observing the 175th anniversary of his martyrdom.

Some historians blame the notoriety of Lovejoy's murder for Alton's long and persistent economic decline. "Alton's prosperity and hopes for the future were gone. The city that was noted for the quality of its citizenry, its benevolence, its men of influence, witnessed a steady exodus of its most progressive and prosperous citizens. Alton was an ostracized city with a devastated economy."[12] Other historians disagree, citing completion of the first railroad to Alton, the Chicago and Alton, as a catalyst in the city's resurgence. "[F]or some years subsequent to 1837, trade was stagnant and prosperity depreciated, while many of the most enterprising business firms met with financial ruin. About the year 1842, business revived again, and from that time on the city has had a healthy, steady and constant growth."[13] Economic conditions in Alton, and the rest of southwestern Illinois, suffered more serious and permanent damage in the 1970s following enactment of the first federal environmental laws, which rendered the region's virtually inexhaustible supply of bituminous coal unmarketable because of its high sulfur content.

Lovejoy is remembered as both the first casualty of the Civil War, and as the first martyr to the cause of freedom of the press. A four-ton bronze statue of Winged Victory on a 93-foot granite column in Alton Cemetery is a towering monument to Lovejoy's memory and the tallest in Illinois. According to an inscription, Lovejoy engaged in "the first armed resistance to the aggressions of the slave power in America." Lovejoy personifies the impact of the abolitionist movement on the evolution of freedom of expression. Before 1837, much of the press had been timid in defense of free speech for abolitionists, who were regarded by many as fanatics. Lovejoy's martyrdom demonstrated how violation of the free speech rights of the unpopular threatened the rights of all. Before 1837, the constitutionally guaranteed freedoms of speech and the press were understood simply as protections against interference by government. Lovejoy's martyrdom demonstrated that, in order to be meaningful, freedom of expression necessarily includes protection from private violence. Lovejoy was an 1826 graduate of Colby College in Maine. Each year since 1952 Colby has conferred the Elijah Parish Lovejoy Award on a journalist whose work upholds the Lovejoy tradition. In his remarks upon receiving the award in 1983, *New York Times* columnist Anthony Lewis described the chilling impact the *Telegraph* case would have on the willingness of newspapers to engage in investigative journalism.

The printing press Lovejoy died defending was carried to a window and thrown onto the riverbank, where it was broken into pieces that were scattered in the Mississippi River. The main frame of the hand-press was recovered in 1915, and resides in a place of honor in the front lobby of the *Alton Telegraph.*

Thirteen years after Lovejoy's murder, John A. Cousley emigrated to Alton from Ulster as part of a mass exodus seeking to escape the Irish potato famine. From 1846 to 1851, during the period known as the Great Potato Famine, it is estimated that as many as 800,000 people died of disease and starvation in Ireland, and close to one million emigrated to the U.S. and Canada. Cousley went to work for the *Telegraph* in 1860 as an apprentice, known as a "printer's devil." By 1891 Cousley had saved enough money to purchase a majority interest in the *Telegraph* from publisher and principal owner Wilbur T. Norton. Cousley was succeeded as publisher by his son, Paul Bliss Cousley, in 1913, and by his grandson, Paul Sparks Cousley, in 1962. By the time of the *Telegraph* case, the paper was one of the oldest family-owned newspapers in the U.S. with a circulation of 38,000.

By the late 1960s the *Telegraph* had earned a reputation for award-winning investigative journalism. University of Georgia journalism professor Conrad Fink wrote that, "Its crusading editors brought home awards and commendations."[14] From 1958 to 1962, the *Telegraph* was cited twenty-two times for its achievements, including for excellence in local news coverage, and exposure of scandal and fraud. "[T]he *Alton Telegraph* had a reputation in its community and throughout Illinois for responsible and significant investigative reporting. Over the years the paper had reported a variety of cases of crime and corruption that might otherwise not have come to light."[15] Investigative journalism conducted by the *Telegraph* in 1969 uncovered a conflict of interest scandal that led to the resignation of two Illinois Supreme Court justices. After Chicago newspapers picked up the story initially reported by the *Telegraph* that the justices were stockholders in a financial institution that was a party to an appeal, the state legislature appointed John Paul Stevens, then a private practitioner, as independent counsel to conduct an investigation, setting the stage for Stevens' appointment to the U.S. Court of Appeals for the Seventh Circuit in 1970 and as an associate justice of the Supreme Court in 1975.

Aggressive investigative journalism also earned the *Telegraph* some powerful enemies. Editor Stephen Cousley speculated that the *Telegraph* case may have been part of an effort by the local Democratic Party political machine to put the paper out of business in response to its long tradition of vigorous investigative reporting.

> We've done a pretty hard-nosed job of reporting on officialdom in the county, digging into things over the years that need digging into. We consider all our reporters to be investigative reporters, and a newspaper that is doing its job will put a spotlight on political officials and judges. Over the years we've made a lot of enemies.[16]

In 1968 *Telegraph* city editor Elmer Broz assigned two reporters, William Lhotka and Joseph Melosi, to investigate rumors that construction trade unions in Madison County had been infiltrated by members of organized crime families with headquarters in Chicago. In multiple conversations with the reporters during the course of their investigation, a

loans. In an effort to correct the deficiencies identified by the Board, Piasa discontinued extending further credit to Green in November 1969.

After the *St. Louis Post-Dispatch* reported that Piasa was under federal investigation for questionable lending policies and practices, and with rumors circulating about organized crime connections, depositors withdrew their savings in a run on the bank. Ultimately the Federal Savings and Loan Insurance Corporation arranged for the merger of Piasa into Illini Federal Savings & Loan Association ("Illini Federal"), which obtained the appointment of a receiver for Green's properties citing dangerously high vacancy rates and arrearages in the payment of rent. The Internal Revenue Service had filed a lien against Green's construction company for failure to withhold payroll and social security taxes. Multiple mechanic's liens had been filed against its properties by trade creditors.

III. Trial

The *Telegraph* case was one of a series of nine lawsuits filed by attorney Rex Carr on behalf of Green to recover damages arising from the loss of his investment properties as a consequence of Piasa's failure. Green was awarded damages of $3 million against Illini Federal as a result of a separate lawsuit filed by Carr. In a complaint against the *Telegraph*, Melosi and Lhotka, filed on July 26, 1977, Green claimed the reporters' memorandum was defamatory, and its transmittal was the proximate cause of his inability to obtain financing for his projects and ultimately for their loss. However, Green made no effort to obtain alternative sources of financing elsewhere.

Because an overwhelming majority of libel suits are decided on motions for summary judgment, the *Telegraph* underestimated the likelihood that the case would ever go to trial. As its lead attorney, the *Telegraph* selected William M. Cox, an inexperienced litigator who had never tried a libel case. The paper retained Stephen Cousely's brother-in-law, Charles Williamson, to represent the reporters. But the *Telegraph* case had been filed in Madison County, whose judges have a reputation for routinely refusing to grant defendants' pre-trial motions, and whose working-class juries are famous for their generosity to plaintiffs injured by corporate defendants.

In motions to dismiss and for summary judgment, the *Telegraph* argued that the reporting of allegations of wrongdoing to law enforcement officials is absolutely privileged, and that Green's suit, which was not filed until eight years after delivery of the reporters' memorandum, was barred by Illinois' one-year statute of limitations for libel. The court denied the paper's motions based on the existence of disputed factual issues.

Trial began on April 28, 1980 and lasted five weeks. On June 3, 1980, after only five hours of deliberation, the jury awarded Green $9.2 million, including $2.5 million in punitive damages, far exceeding the *Telegraph*'s net worth of $3 million. By summarily denying defendants' post-trial motion on November 26, 1980, Madison County Circuit Court Judge Charles Chapman declined the last clear chance to correct the outcome.

From the *Telegraph's* perspective, the case seemed like an easy win. However, Carr remarked: "There is no conceivable way any lawyer could have won their side of the case."[17] Carr could afford to be charitable to the *Telegraph*'s trial counsel, and uncharacteristically modest, in his characterization of the case. Although he was already one of the most successful plaintiffs' lawyers in the country, the *Telegraph* case earned Carr a place in the Guinness Book of World Records. "I do think the case was a lay-down case," Carr wrote in an exchange of correspondence in which the Author suggested that Carr was either being modest or gallant in defending the trial judge whose handling of the case has been criticized by commentators.[18]

Carr's advocacy in the *Telegraph* case illustrates the effectiveness of litigation tradecraft. A classic trial lawyer technique is to identify a familiar image or analogy drawn from everyday life to help make a complex concept more easily understood. Carr convinced the jury that what the *Telegraph* did was no different than allowing one of its delivery trucks to run recklessly over Green, leaving him crippled. Jurors interviewed afterwards said they did not even consider abstract First Amendment issues of press freedom. They deliberated primarily over how much to award Green to compensate for his losses. Jurors interviewed after the trial acknowledged being under the misconception that a public body such as the school district would receive the punitive damage award.

Although they represent an easy target, it would be unfair to blame jurors for the outcome of the *Telegraph* case. As in any trial, the jury reached its judgment based upon the evidence it was permitted to hear and the instructions it received.

Keeping the case simple is a technique shared by the most successful trial lawyers. This technique is especially important in Madison County, where an idiosyncratic selection process screened prospective jurors for level of education, effectively limiting the number of college-educated citizens on the list of eligible jurors. Carr was determined to maintain the focus on the reporters' misconduct in making unfounded allegations in the memorandum about Piasa's involvement with mobsters, which he attributed to a combination of laziness and personal greed. To this end Carr sought and obtained a crucial pre-trial ruling on a motion *in limine* by Judge Chapman that limited testimony about Green's excessive borrowing and other irregularities uncovered by the Board. This evidence was central to the *Telegraph's* key defense that the proximate cause of Green's injury was Piasa's noncompliance with banking regulations, and not the memorandum's allegations about Mafia connections. In support of his motion, Carr argued that such evidence would "unduly complicate this trial and make it extremely difficult for the jury to understand."

It requires a considerable investment of time and energy to know the facts well enough to keep the case simple. By the time the *Telegraph* case went to trial, Carr, by his own estimate, had devoted the better part of one-third of the previous eight years to immersing himself in the details of the federal government's investigation of Piasa. This later proved decisive in Carr's withering five-day cross-examination of Albion Fenderson, General Counsel and Senior Vice President of the Board. Fenderson had testified that the Board's decision to order Piasa to discontinue lending to Green was based solely upon the serious violations of banking regulations disclosed by its audit of Piasa, and not on the allegations in the memorandum about Green's involvement in money laundering. In addition to twice accusing Fenderson of lying under oath, Carr made sure jurors knew that Fenderson was not "one of them." "You are a Harvard grad, aren't you?," Carr asked the witness. Judge Chapman denied defense motions for a mistrial on the two occasions Carr accused Fenderson of lying under oath. A veteran litigator knows when to deviate from the conventional wisdom, such as asking an open-ended question or a question to which the lawyer does not already know the answer. Accusing a witness of lying is generally discouraged because of the risk that jurors may sympathize with a beleaguered witness.

Reminiscent of the public outcry following Elijah Lovejoy's murder, the verdict in the *Telegraph* case was the subject of reports by wire services, major metropolitan newspapers and trade journals. Editor Stephen Cousley drew the comparison: "If we buckled up and rolled over, we'd be giving up the Lovejoy tradition. Somebody has to stand up and fight."[19] Stories about the case appeared in the New York Times, Christian Science Monitor, Chicago Sun-Times, Chicago Tribune, Washington Post, Miami Herald, Los Angeles Times, San Francisco Examiner, Oakland Tribune, Fort Worth Star-Telegram, Editor & Publisher, Arizona Daily Star, and the St. Louis Post-Dispatch, among many others.

Paul Findley, a former journalist and member of Congress representing Madison County, tried to rally support for the *Telegraph.* He wrote letters to dozens of editors and publishers urging creation of a legal defense committee to underwrite the cost of an appeal. "The idea that a newspaper can be sued and possibly driven out of business because of something it didn't print is absurd," Findley wrote in a newspaper column. In an interview, Findley told a reporter:

> In my day I would feel duty bound to present whatever scuttlebutt I picked up. The reporters weren't trying to hang anybody. They were just trying to cooperate. If this becomes precedent, then every citizen, especially reporters is in trouble. They will be reluctant to keep notes and supply leads to law enforcement officials. [This] threatens the very right and obligation of newspapers to gather and disseminate information.[20]

The overwhelming sentiment among the national news media was that of sympathy for the paper, with the notable exception of a story reported by Morley Safer on CBS' *Sixty Minutes* criticizing the *Telegraph* for engaging in substandard practices in investigative journalism. Safer's is a minority opinion. During his time as publisher, Paul S. Cousley earned the respect of his competition for his courage in giving young reporters the freedom to follow their investigative instincts.

IV. Aftermath

The *Telegraph* clearly had not appreciated the gravity of the situation. The paper quickly rejected a pre-trial offer by Carr to settle the case for the $1 million of insurance coverage that was available, in what would have been a record-setting settlement of a U.S. libel case. Carr generally takes a contrarian view of settlement. "A poor trial is *better* than a good settlement, because I've gotten all my business from publicity about me and my cases. You don't get any publicity from a settlement."[21]

Nothing concentrates the mind quite like a seven-figure damages award. If the *Telegraph* had not previously treated the case with the seriousness it deserved, it signaled its intention to pursue a vigorous appeal by retaining the Chicago law firm of Jenner & Block. The case was assigned to Philip W. Tone, who had rejoined the firm in 1980 after serving as a United States District Judge and later as a member of the U.S. Court of Appeals for the Seventh Circuit. Libel specialist David P. Sanders co-signed a 143-page brief filed with the Appellate Court of Illinois on July 28, 1981. At a cost of $100,000, it was surely the most expensive brief never considered by an appellate panel.

The brief led with the argument, which was initially raised by the *Telegraph* in pretrial motions, that disclosures to public officials are absolutely privileged. Although this is an issue on which authority was divided, and was apparently unsettled in Illinois at the time of the *Telegraph* case, there is no doubt that such disclosure was privileged if made in good faith. The evidence of disclosure was a two-edged sword for the plaintiff. On the one hand, it established an essential element required to hold an employer strictly liable on a *respondeat superior* theory: In preparing and transmitting the memorandum, the reporters were actuated by a motive to serve their employer, as opposed to some personal animus. On the other hand, it demonstrated that the reporters, as responsible journalists, were unwilling to go to print without confirmation from federal law enforcement officials of information previously obtained from sources in Madison County government.

The principle that disclosures to public officials are absolutely privileged is further supported by the holding of the New York Supreme Court that the First Amendment precludes liability from being imposed on reporters who rely upon erroneous information from official sources. In *Doe v. Daily News, L.P.*, 660 N.Y.S.2d 604 (Sup. Ct. N.Y. 1997), the trial judge cited absolute reporters' privilege in granting defendants' motion dismissing a libel suit filed by a rape victim who had been falsely accused of perpetrating a hoax by columnist Mike McAlary, the subject of a 2013 Broadway play by Nora Ephron entitled "Lucky Guy." McAlary admitted that he had not interviewed the victim or any witness, and had relied solely upon information provided by sources inside the New York City Police Department. Here, the expectation of a "scoop" proves that the memorandum was a necessary part of the reporters' newsgathering process prior to publication.

The authors of the *Telegraph's* brief are not alone in believing that the trial judge should have directed a verdict in favor of the *Telegraph* on this point. No response to the brief was ever filed on behalf of Green. In an exchange of correspondence with the Author, Carr rejected the

> . . . argument that there was a freedom of the press privilege protecting this information not published but given to the [federal government] by a reporter seeking a story . . . . Freedom of the press to malign and slander others is limited to articles published in the paper in good faith, not to information published privately to law enforcement agencies for the purpose of getting a story.[22]

As evidence of the reporters' lack of good faith, Carr stressed their expectation of a "scoop" as a *quid pro quo* for their information. Carr believes that he also succeeded in casting doubt on Melosi's credibility by challenging his testimony that a local contractor, whose name Melosi insisted he could not recall, had implicated Green and DeGrand in the use of Mafia money.

> He said he could not remember the name of the source because he made himself forget the name because he knew he might be asked to identify his source. I suggested to him that he concentrate on forgetting the name of 'Rex

> Carr' and see how successful he might be. The jury visibly reacted to the question.[23]

Without explicitly accusing him of bias, the brief catalogued Judge Chapman's consistent pattern of rulings adverse to the *Telegraph* on matters of law and evidence, and errors in his instructions to the jury. It has not gone unnoticed that Judge Chapman, himself a former plaintiffs' lawyer, presided over the *Telegraph* case while serving the balance of his term as a lame-duck following his defeat in a judicial election in which he had sought unsuccessfully to obtain the *Telegraph*'s endorsement. Although the brief avoided direct personal criticism of Judge Chapman, the argument section began by blaming trial court error as having "resulted in the outrageous spectacle now to be reviewed by this Court."[24]

Among the most damaging of Judge Chapman's rulings was his refusal to permit evidence to be introduced that Green had already recovered $3 million from Illini Federal in recoupment for the same losses claimed in his libel suit against the Telegraph. Judge Chapman's pre-trial rulings on the reporters' privilege and statute of limitations issues were cited as grounds for reversal or remand for a new trial, as were his refusals to grant a mistrial on the basis of misconduct by plaintiff's counsel. Among Judge Chapman's questionable instructions was advising the jury that damages could be awarded for lost future profits. Illinois courts have long held that lost profits must be established with certainty in order to constitute an element of damages. *TAS Distributing Co. v. Cummins Engine Co.*, 491 F.3d 625, 632 (7th Cir. 2007). Even in Madison County, a properly instructed jury might have regarded lost future profits in a field as competitive and market-sensitive as real estate development to be too speculative to be provable with certainty.

In reading the 4,000-page trial transcript, Philip Tone, a strong proponent of courtroom civility, likely would have been more outraged by Carr's riffs than someone more familiar with the rough-and-tumble standards of practice in Madison County. Of the eleven separate grounds for error, the argument portion of the brief devoted a disproportionately large amount of space (25%) to the claim that the *Telegraph* had been denied a fair trial by reason of juror passion and prejudice, kindled by Carr's pervasive gross misconduct in the jurors' presence. Fenderson was not the only witness Carr accused of lying under oath in the presence of the jury. As part of his impeachment of Melosi, Carr asked whether the witness had studied in journalism school "how Goebbels of the Nazi Party made the science of the big lie a real skill and a real science."[25] Carr would similarly invoke the name of the Nazi propaganda minister, and reference to the "big lie," during closing argument in 1987 on behalf of a class of plaintiffs in a toxic tort case against the Monsanto Company. Carr's accusing witnesses of lying under oath in the presence of the jury was the brief's principal example of attorney misconduct. However, it cited no binding precedent for the proposition that it is prejudicial error in Illinois to deny a motion for a mistrial on this basis in a civil suit, and research has disclosed no Illinois case to this effect.

Damage awards against newsgathering organizations for defamation are among the most likely to be reversed on appeal, or substantially reduced. One law review article found that seventy percent of libel judgments against publishers are reversed on appeal.[26] Even when verdicts are upheld, damages are often reduced substantially. According to former CBS News division president Richard S. Salant,

> Juries routinely award . . . extravagant punitive damages of millions, sometimes tens of millions of dollars. Just as routinely, the appellate judges reduce the punitive damages, or simply remove them. It is a senseless ritual in which only the attorneys win. All the publicity centers on the original award, and that encourages other libel litigations.[27]

Former Miss Wyoming Kim Pring was awarded $26.5 million in damages in February 1981 after Penthouse published a fictional account of the bizarre sexual behavior of a thinly disguised Miss Wyoming. The jury verdict was reversed on appeal. *Pring v. Penthouse Int'l., Ltd.*, 695 F.2d 438 (10th Cir. 1982), cert. denied, 462 U.S. 1132 (1983) (recognizing that obvious fantasy is not actionable as defamation). In *Guccione v. Hustler Magazine, Inc.*, 800 F.2d 298 (2d Cir. 1986), cert. denied, 479 U.S. 1091 (1987), the court reversed a $1.6 million defamation judgment. In *Morsette v. Final Call*, 764 N.Y.S.2d 416 (N.Y.App. Div. 2003), the court reduced by more than one-half a $13 million libel verdict against Nation of Islam newspaper. Contemporaneously with the incipient appeal of the Telegraph case, the Ohio Court of Appeals overturned a $40 million judgment against *Hustler* magazine on the grounds that the "enormous excessiveness of the verdict coupled with the repeated appeals to passion and prejudice can lead to no other conclusion but that the verdict of the jury was one influenced by passion and prejudice." *Guccione v. Hustler Magazine, Inc.*, No. 80AP-375, 1981 WL 3516 at 40 (Ohio App. 1981).

Besides the possibility that it was generated by juror passion and prejudice, the award of $2.5 million in punitive damages in the *Telegraph* case was reversible on other grounds. At the time of the case, Illinois followed the so-called "complicity rule," by which an employer is not strictly liable for punitive damages based on the tortious misconduct of employees. In order to recover punitive damages a plaintiff must prove culpability on the part of managerial personnel or ratification of employee misconduct. There was no evidence that any *Telegraph* editor ever saw the memorandum or knew of its contents.

Second, under the interpretation of the First Amendment guarantee of freedom of the press adopted by the United States Supreme Court in *Gertz v. Robert Welch, Inc.*, punitive damages are awardable only if plaintiff proves by clear and convincing evidence that the defamatory statements were made with actual malice or with reckless disregard for their truth or falsity. There was no evidence other than that the reporters believed the contents of the memorandum to be true.

The compensatory damages portion of the award was likewise vulnerable to substantial reduction on appeal. Almost half of the $6.7 million in compensatory damages consisted of lost future profits from uncompleted projects, based upon conjecture regarding their success. As we will see in chapter VII, commercial real estate development involves an inherently high level of market risk because of the infinite variety of things that can and will go wrong, making estimates of future profitability highly speculative. In addition, the *Telegraph* was prejudiced by another of Judge Chapman's questionable orders *in limine*, preventing defense counsel from mentioning that Green had already obtained a $3 million verdict in a lawsuit against Illini Federal in compensation for his inability to obtain financing and loss of his properties, the same losses Green claimed in the *Telegraph* case.

"I was very worried that the verdict might be overturned by the Appellate Court," Carr has acknowledged; "I thought there was at least a 50/50 chance of that occurring or a sizable reduction."[28] Although Carr's worries about the verdict surviving appellate review were understandable, they turned out to be unnecessary. In order to appeal a civil judgment, the Illinois court rules governing appellate practice required a defendant to post a *supersedeas* bond equal to 150% of the damage award, including punitive damages. With a net worth of only $3 million, the *Telegraph* lacked the resources to secure a $13.8 million appeal bond. The *Telegraph* sought a relaxation of the bond requirement, claiming that the enormity of the judgment made it a practical impossibility to comply. Both the intermediate appellate court and the supreme court of Illinois refused, citing the absence of any flexibility under the rules or interpretative cases.

In order to protect its assets from immediate seizure and preserve its status as a going concern, the *Telegraph* was forced to file a Petition under Chapter 11 of the Bankruptcy Code on April 10, 1981. The Cousleys erroneously believed that the bankruptcy filing would shelter the *Telegraph's* assets against execution by Green, while at the same time enable the paper to appeal the award without having to post a bond. The federal bankruptcy court held on January 22, 1982 that it had no jurisdiction to consider the merits of the *Telegraph*'s state court appeal. The Appellate Court of Illinois held on April 7, 1982 that the state courts no longer had jurisdiction over the case once the *Telegraph* was involved in bankruptcy proceedings. Finding itself in a Catch-22 situation, the *Telegraph* agreed to settle the case in June 1982 for $1.4 million, of which one million dollars came from the paper's insurer paying the policy limit. The *Telegraph* by then had paid more than $600,000 in attorneys' fees.

Once aggressive in its news coverage, the *Telegraph* turned cautious, even passive, in the wake of the case. "A chill descended on the *Telegraph*. Salaries were frozen. Newsroom vacancies went unfilled. Cautious editors barred the use of anonymous sources; reporters often destroyed notes after use lest they be subpoenaed in any future lawsuit."[29] The *Telegraph* began subjecting reporters' contacts with outside sources to supervision by editors. Editor Stephen Cousley described the *Telegraph* as being like "a tight end who hears footsteps."[30] He also remarked, "Wouldn't you be gun-shy if you nearly lost your livelihood and your house?"[31]

New York Times columnist Anthony Lewis, accepting Colby College's annual award in 1983 in memory of Elijah Lovejoy, described the chilling effect of the *Telegraph* case on the paper's tradition for investigative journalism. "Inside the paper, there are all kinds of cautionary rules to ward off heavy libel damages in the future. . . . When someone recently said there was misconduct in a sheriff's office, the editor decided against investigating the story. 'Let someone else stick their neck out this time,' he said."[32]

The *Telegraph* was sold to a newspaper chain controlled by Ralph M. Ingersoll in 1985. Stephen Cousley resigned as editor in September 1986.

V. An Appeal for Appeal Bond Reform

Entitlement to an appeal is thoroughly engrained in the popular imagination, and is taken for granted by many law-trained people. However, the right to appeal is without basis in constitutional law. The Fourteenth Amendment guarantee of due process of law has not been held to include a constitutional right to an appeal. *U.S. v. MacCollom*, 426 U.S. 317, 323 (1976). The Supreme Court has declined petitions for *certiorari* seeking to persuade the Court to recognize a constitutional right to appeal in both civil and criminal cases. There is a persuasive argument for recognizing a constitutional right to appeal as a fundamental element of procedural fairness. It is based upon the structural need for a reliable appellate check on trial court decision-making, not only in places like Madison County with its reputation for having "magnet courts." Concern about judicial bias is not limited to states like Illinois where elected judges are subject to political pressures. "Sometimes the bias may be unconscious; judges are, after all, subject to the same cognitive biases as everyone else."[33]

Trial and appellate court judges experience the trial drama from very different perspectives. Unlike their appellate court counterparts, trial judges personally confront the victims and villains of the drama in their courtrooms, evaluating their demeanor and credibility, or perceived lack thereof. Under the circumstances, it is foreseeable that trial judges' emotional impulses may influence their judgment. "[J]udges, like everyone else, have two cognitive systems for making judgments – the intuitive and the deliberative – and the intuitive system appears to have a powerful impact on judges' decision making."[34]

We will revisit this dynamic in chapter VI which explores a bench trial of a lawsuit filed by magazine publisher Penthouse against Dominion Federal Savings & Loan for breaching a commitment to participate in a $97 million loan to finance a casino-hotel project in Atlantic City. Dominion's share of the loan was twice the maximum amount it could lend to a single borrower under the same federal banking regulation that Piasa violated in its loans to Green. When a sub-participant backed out of the deal too late to find a replacement, Dominion desperately needed a way out of its commitment without incurring liability. Judge Kevin Duffy found that attorney Phillip Gorelick was retained to serve "as Dominion's hatchet man," to "bully and intimidate" Penthouse by making an endless series of unreasonable demands until the commitment expired and Dominion was released from its obligation. *Penthouse Int'l., Ltd. v. Dominion Fed. Sav. & Loan Ass'n.*, 665 F. Supp. 301, 307–08 (S.D.N.Y. 1987). Judge Duffy found incredible Gorelick's testimony that he could not have acted in bad faith for the purpose of destroying the deal because his client had never made him aware of its dilemma. Driven literally to the point of distraction by what he perceived as Gorelick's perjury, Judge Duffy held the members of Gorelick's law firm jointly and severally liable for damages by reason of their partner's fraudulent conduct in the sum of $130 million, the lion's share of which represented lost future profits from a hypothetical Penthouse casino-hotel. All of Judge Duffy's factual findings were categorically reversed on appeal as clearly erroneous, together with all of his conclusions of law. *Penthouse Int'l., Ltd. v. Dominion Fed. Sav. & Loan Ass'n*, 855 F.2d 963 (2d Cir. 1988), cert. denied, 490 U.S. 1005 (1989).

Misplaced confidence in the certainty of access to appellate review has a liberating, but not necessarily beneficial, influence on trial court behavior. Mindful of the availability of an appellate corrective, trial judges may be tempted to access their inner-Solomon, be empowered to strike a blow for morality or intuitive fairness, lash out against what they perceive as disrespect or social injustice, or yield to such powerful forces of human nature as empathy, indignation and outrage.

In *Popov v. Hiyashi*, No. 400454, 2002 WL 31833731 (Cal. Super. Ct. Dec. 18, 2002), Judge Kevin McCarthy might have awarded ownership of Barry Bonds' single-season homerun record baseball to Patrick Hyashi, in whose hands (and then pocket) the loose ball came to rest in the right-field stands at San Francisco's PacBell Park on October 7, 2001. But first in time the ball had briefly been in the webbing of a glove worn by Alex Popov, who tried to catch the ball in flight only to lose it after being tackled, roughly jostled and kicked (and perhaps bitten) in the ensuing scrum. Judge McCarthy concluded that a zero-sum decision awarding the ball to either party on these facts would be unfair to the other. He convened a session of court at the University of California, Hastings College of Law to hear a panel of law professors participate in a forum on the law of possession. When the professors predictably disagreed, Judge McCarthy found himself "left with something of a dilemma." He used his equitable discretion to craft a novel but personally satisfying remedy: By ordering that the baseball be sold and the proceeds divided equally between the claimants, Judge McCarthy secured a place in first-year Property casebooks for his opinion, and the sobriquet of Solomon-like for himself. Whether the decision would have survived appellate review will never be known. The ball sold at auction for only $450,000. Popov's share was insufficient to pay his legal fees, let alone finance an appeal. Attorney Martin Triano sued his former client to collect $473,530 in unpaid legal fees. Hyashi's lawyer presumably had agreed to take the case on a contingency fee basis.

Montgomery County, Maryland Circuit Court Judge James S. McAuliffe was refreshingly candid in announcing his decision from the bench in a lawsuit filed by a client of the author seeking to enforce a two-page letter of intent for the purchase of a $13 million shopping center. Letters of intent under the circumstances are routinely held by courts to be unenforceable for lack of commercial certainty, as the trial judge acknowledged before granting declaratory judgment in favor of the purchaser. Judge McAuliffe expressly noted the strong probability of appeal as a consideration in deciding the case according to his personal sense of justice. "I think it not unlikely that there will be cross appeals filed in this case . . . finding their way along Route 50 to this state's capitol," he opined adding, "I am not so much concerned about the winning and the losing. . . . [R]egardless of the winning and losing, I am going to sleep at night." Order, *Gorlitz v. Montgomery Village Associates II L.P.*, Civil No. 13856 (Cir. Ct. Md. May 23, 1986), at 6 (on file with author).

Judge Kathleen McHugh of the Broward County Circuit Court in Florida was prepared to accept football player Chad "Ochocinco" Johnson's plea bargain until he gave a playful slap on the backside to his lawyer during a hearing. Judge McHugh rejected the bargain and sentenced Johnson to thirty days in jail, perhaps punishing him for spectators reacting with laughter in her courtroom.

For no apparent good reason, Miami-Dade County Circuit Court Judge Valerie Schurr in the summer of 2009 granted a request by Joseph and Blanca Doyle for continuance of Republic Federal Bank's residential mortgage foreclosure of their 8,300 square foot home with an assessed value of $2.6 million. "I was trying to make everybody happy," Judge Schurr explained in her opinion.

> We have so many foreclosures here and I give continuances on these sales. I just do. . . . [Y]ou know, people are having a hard time now. They are having a difficult time. Everybody knows it. Businesses are failing. People are losing money in the stock market. You know, employment is high. It's just everybody knows that we are in a bad time right now and I hate to see anybody lose their home.

The Florida Court of Appeal rebuked Judge Schurr for "abuse of discretion in the most basic sense of that term." *Republic Fed. Bank v. Doyle*, 19 So. 2d 1053, 1054 (Fla. Dist. Ct. App. 2009). Although granting continuances generally is within the trial judge's discretion, "no judicial action of any kind can rest on such a foundation." The sternly worded unanimous opinion quoted Justice Cardozo's admonition that a judge "is not to yield to spasmodic sentiment, to vague and unregulated benevolence."

A Long Island couple was left debt-free as a result of a Suffolk County judge's indignation after hearing testimony by the regional manager for IndyMac Bank. The lender's intransigent refusal to restructure the couple's sub-prime loan, or otherwise cooperate in avoiding foreclosure was, according to Judge Jeffrey Spinner, not only "harsh, repugnant, shocking and repulsive," but also "inequitable, unconscionable, vexatious and opprobrious." *IndyMac Bank v. Yano-Horoski*, 890 N.Y.S.2d 313, 319 (N.Y. Sup. Ct. 2009). Noting that "Suffolk County is in the yawning abyss of a deep mortgage and housing crisis with foreclosure filings at a record high rate," Judge Spinner *sua sponte* invoked his equitable jurisdiction to void the mortgage, erasing the $290,000 principal balance and an additional $235,000 in accrued interest and penalties.

By providing a check on both the perception and the reality of biased, corrupt or simply misguided trial court decision-making, access to appellate review encourages confidence in the rule of law. Appellate decision-making is widely considered as enjoying the benefits of deliberation, including the exchange of viewpoints and information, inherent in the dynamics of the appellate process. If nothing else, the appellate courts' claim to superior judgment is based upon the larger panel of deciders, on the theory that "three heads are better than one."

The statistical probability of a successful appellate outcome demonstrates the harshness of an inflexible appeal bond requirement, especially in the context of large- verdict defamation cases. The reversal rate of state court cases on appeal is only 33%. But the rate increases to 42% when a defendant appeals a judgment for plaintiff, and to 48% when the amount of the judgment exceeds $1 million. The rate of reversal or reduction of punitive damage awards in libel cases is higher than 70%. Salant attributes the high rate of reversal in libel cases to sympathetic juries. "When juries decide punishment in libel cases, their natural sympathies tend to lie with the damaged plaintiff with whom they can identify far more easily than with the powerful and sometimes arrogant news organizations."[35] Considering the likelihood of success on the merits, the *Telegraph*'s inability to seek appellate review of a multi-million dollar defamation award for want of a *supersedeas* bond was highly prejudicial.

The appeal bond process in many states has been reformed since 1980, inspired by tobacco litigation tried in Madison County. A lawsuit filed in 2000 by Sharon Price, on behalf of herself and a class of smokers, alleged that Philip Morris, manufacturer of Marlboro Lights and Cambridge Lights cigarettes, among other brands, had violated the Illinois Consumer Fraud Act by engaging in materially false and deceptive representations in using the descriptor of "Lights" in the branding of both cigarettes, and the phrase "Lowered Tar and Nicotine" on both cigarette packaging labels. Following a bench trial in Madison County Circuit Court in 2003, Philip Morris was ordered to pay $7 billion in compensatory damages, $3 billion in punitive damages to the State of Illinois, plus attorneys' fees.

In order to stay execution under Rule 305 of the Illinois rules governing appellate practice, Philip Morris was required to post a $12 billion *supersedeas* bond to cover the entire judgment, interest, and costs of appeal. The manufacturer claimed it could not post a bond of that magnitude and make a $2.6 billion payment due under a national agreement that resolved lawsuits between cigarette makers and several states. Accordingly, Madison County Circuit Court Judge Nichols Byron reduced the size of the bond, allowing Philip Morris to make cash payments of $800 million and to deliver a $6 billion interest-bearing promissory note. Elizabeth Warren, then a Harvard University law professor specializing in bankruptcy and currently a U.S. Senator from Massachusetts, testified against the reduction of the amount of the bond and the substitution of a promissory note as being too small and too risky to protect the judgment creditor.

The plaintiffs appealed the revised bond arrangement. The Appellate Court of Illinois held that Rule 305 was unambiguous, and the trial court had no authority to deviate from its requirements. It remanded the case to the Madison County Circuit Court to recalculate the amount of the appeal bond.

Philip Morris appealed to the Supreme Court of Illinois. In the exercise of its supervisory authority, the supreme court reinstated Judge Byron's modified appeal bond requirement for Philip Morris. Madison County earned $17.6 million in interest from the bond which was used to discharge virtually all county debt, pay for administration and criminal courts buildings, establish an early retirement program for county employees, and install a state-of-the-art 911 dispatch system. In addition, exercising its rule-making authority governing appellate practice, the supreme court amended Rule 305, "to give the courts discretion in a money judgment case to approve a bond or other form of security that covers less than the entire amount of the judgment plus anticipated interest and costs." ILCS S. CT. RULE 305 (Commentary) (Revised Jan. 15, 2004).

"Appeal bond reform began in earnest in about 2000,"[36] and since *Philip Morris*, most states have amended their appeal bond statutes to make the process less onerous for appellants. The Arizona Chamber of Commerce & Industry published a summary of the appeal bond requirements in all 50 states.[37]

Five northeastern states do not require a bond at all. They are Connecticut, Massachusetts, New Hampshire, New Jersey and Vermont. In Maine, execution of judgments is stayed pending appeal, but the court has discretion to order the judgment debtor to post a bond in an amount determined by the court to compensate for the delay, loss of interest and cost of appeal. Me. R. Civ. P. 62(c) (2013). In Minnesota, trial courts have discretion to waive an appeal bond, although the state supreme court has instructed that this discretion is to be exercised sparingly. Minn. R. App. P. 108.02 (Advisory Committee Comment 2009 Amendments). Other states impose caps on the amount that must be bonded, exclude the punitive damages portion of the award entirely, or limit the amount of punitive damages required to be bonded.

There are few states remaining, such as Alabama, Alaska and Washington, that require full-judgment appeal bonds. Many states have caps that are set at such high levels as to be virtually meaningless. The caps in the following states range from $25–100 million: Arkansas, Colorado, Florida, Georgia, Indiana, Iowa, Kentucky, Michigan,

Mississippi, North Carolina, Ohio, Oklahoma, Rhode Island, South Dakota, Tennessee, Virginia, West Virginia, and Wisconsin.[38]

In Kansas for judgments exceeding $1 million, upon proof that requiring a bond in the full amount of the judgment will result in "a denial of the right to an appeal," the court may reduce the size of the bond to $1 million plus 25% of the amount of the judgment in excess of $1 million.[39] Arizona, Nebraska and Texas have caps of 50% of appellant's net worth.[40] Hawaii and Wyoming have caps for small business appellants based upon number of employees.[41]

Even if a statute or appellate court rule appears mandatory on its face, some courts, both federal and state, have been receptive to equitable arguments seeking an interpretation that allows for the exercise of discretion.

A *supersedeas* bond in the full amount of the judgment, plus interest and costs, is required to stay execution of a federal court judgment. Fed. R. Civ. P. 62(d). Notwithstanding its literal language, some federal court judges have interpreted Rule 62(d) as providing room for flexibility. For example, Judges Richard Posner and Frank Easterbrook have taken the position that a federal court may limit the required amount of the appeal bond to compensatory damages, and substitute alternative forms of security, such as forbidding the payment of dividends or other cash distributions by the judgment debtor during the pendency of an appeal. *Olympia Equip. Leasing Co. v. Western Union Tel. Co.*, 786 F.2d 794, 797 (7th Cir. 1986); *see also Texaco, Inc. v. Pennzoil Co.*, 784 F.2d 1133, 1152-55 (2d Cir. 1986) (upholding reduction of $12 billion bond requirement to $1 million), *rev'd on other grounds,* 481 U.S. 1 (1987); *Northern Indiana Public Service Co. v. Carbon County Coal Co.*, 799 F.2d 265, 281 (7th Cir. 1986) (court has discretion to require appellant to provide periodic reports to facilitate monitoring in lieu of bond).

Several state courts have come to similar conclusions: *See, e.g., Polar Equip., Inc. v. Brunswick Corp.*, No. 3AN-87-3826 CI (Alaska Sup. Ct. Apr. 23, 1992) (refusing to order bonding of punitive damages portion of award so long as appellant maintained a net worth equal to ten times the unbonded amount of the judgment); *Midkiff v. de Bisschop*, 574 P.2d 128, 131 (Haw. 1978) (amount of bond discretionary with trial court); *Scott*

River Sand & Rock Co. v. Dunevant, 213 P.3d 251, 253 (Ariz. Ct. App. 2009) (court has discretion to reduce bond or substitute alternate security); *Shanghai Inv. Co v. Alteka Co.*, 993 P.2d 516, 538 (Haw. 2000) (court has discretion to allow alternative forms of security in lieu of appeal bond).

Judge Frank Easterbrook's reasoning in *Olympia Equipment* in favor of judicial discretion in setting *supersedeas* bonds is the most analytically satisfying: By placing the assets of a bonding company behind the obligation, an appeal bond assures that money to satisfy the judgment will be available to appellee if the judgment is affirmed on appeal. As a practical matter, a defendant who would be rendered insolvent by a damages judgment will be unable to secure a bond. Even if such a defendant could obtain a bond, the result would be a windfall to the judgment creditor, who would then be placed in a preferred position over unsecured creditors of the judgment debtor. What a judgment creditor can reasonably expect under such circumstances is that its position will be protected against erosion during its period of jeopardy (*i.e.*, while the right to enforce its judgment is stayed pending completion of appellate review).

If and when there is a constitutional right to an appeal, the constitutionality of non-discretionary appeal bond rules and statutes will be subject to challenge in situations like the *Telegraph* case, where posting a bond in the full amount of the judgment would force the judgment debtor into bankruptcy. One commentator believes that requiring an appellant to post a *supersedeas* bond without judicial discretion to provide for alternative forms of security "denies an appellant's due process right to an effective appeal."[42]

Whether or not a constitutional right to appeal is ever recognized generally, for media defendants the right to appellate review is an essential buttress of explicit constitutional guarantees protected by the First Amendment. Freedom of the press has long been held to occupy a preferred position among the constitutional values, in light of journalists' role in keeping people informed as citizens. "[T]he First Amendment rests on the assumption that the widest possible dissemination of information . . . is essential to the welfare of the public, that a free press is a condition of a free society." *Gertz v. Robert Welch, Inc.*, 418 U.S. 323, 398 (1974) (White, J., dissenting). Journalism professor Michael Killenberg wrote:

> Journalists play an indispensable role as surrogates for citizens too busy, too tired, too infirm or too unqualified to govern for themselves. Reporters act on the public's behalf when they scrutinize candidates for elected office; request judicial records at the courthouse; investigate the expenditure of municipal tax dollars; attend meetings of the school board; interview prisoners held in the county jail; or stand watch over a limitless range of issues and conditions that touch the lives of citizens. As they serve the public, journalists expose corruption, sound alarms, question public policy, demand accountability and expose injustice.[43]

Supreme Court decisions recognize that access to independent appellate review ensures that protected expression will not be inhibited by protecting media defendants against the existential threat of potentially crippling damage awards. The Supreme Court has recognized the uniqueness of libel suits in establishing a heightened standard of review for malice in order "to ensure that protected expression will not be inhibited." Appellate judges "must exercise independent judgment and determine whether the record establishes actual malice with convincing clarity." *Bose Corp. v. Consumers Union of U.S., Inc.*, 466 U.S. 485, 505, 514 (1984). The Court has also required that appellate courts engage in *de novo* review of punitive damages awards.

Without the certainty of access to appellate review, the prospect of staggering libel judgments can chill the exercise of First Amendment rights, as the Court in *Gertz* predicted, especially by small publications which are a principal source of minority and unpopular points of view.

> If the press could be faced with possibly sizable damages for every mistaken publication injurious to reputation, the result would be an unacceptable degree of self-censorship, which might prevent the occasional mistaken libel, but would also often prevent the timely flow of information that is thought to be true but cannot be readily verified. *Dun & Bradstreet v. Greenmoss Builders, Inc.*, 472 U.S. 749, 770 (White, J., concurring).

Newsgathering organizations that seek to raise First Amendment defenses in appealing a punitive damages judgment are constitutionally entitled to independent appellate review, even if they cannot afford a *supersedeas* bond for the full amount of the judgment. In such cases, a judgment creditor is entitled to protection against the possibility that appellant's financial condition may take a turn for the worse during the appellate process, and against the specter of appellant dissipating assets or placing assets beyond the reach of execution.

The legitimate interests of both parties may be accommodated by alternative forms of security in lieu of a *supersedeas* bond. As a condition of appeal, the trial court may require the judgment debtor to (a) take all steps necessary to maintain the value of its assets (*e.g.*, carry adequate insurance); (b) not make payments to third parties except debts to trade creditors in the ordinary course of business; (c) freeze salaries; (d) suspend bonuses, dividends and other cash distributions; (e) refrain from incurring further indebtedness or pledging existing assets as collateral for antecedent indebtedness; and (f) afford inspection and audit rights to the judgment creditor. The alternative security package is similar to the typical financial covenants for the protection of creditors included in commercial loan agreements designed to assure that debtors will maintain their financial status and refrain from conduct that would adversely affect their condition. The constant tension between lenders and borrowers closely resembles that between judgment creditors and debtors.

Additional conditions may be imposed depending upon the particular circumstances. For example, in *Obsidian Finance Group, LLC*, appellee complained that appellant was causing further harm to appellee by continuing to post defamatory comments on appellant's websites. Under such circumstances, it would be appropriate to condition relaxation of the appeal bond requirement upon appellant suspending further comment about appellee pending the outcome of the appellate process. This and certain other elements of an alternative security package may constitute an abridgment of speech. That certain burdens on the press result in incidental abridgment of speech does not render them impermissible. If partial or incidental abridgement of speech is justified by valid governmental interests, constitutional rights have not been denied. *American Communication Ass'n v. Douds*, 339 U.S. 382, 399 (1950). Accelerated oral argument should be made available in such cases to reduce the period of time during which appellee is at risk and — when a condition of relaxation of the appeal bond limits appellant's rights — during which appellant is at risk. Accelerated oral argument was part of the package of alternative security crafted by the Seventh Circuit in *Olympia Equipment.*

Since colonial times, the *supersedeas* bond has been understood as a means of ensuring that, if affirmed on appeal, the judgment will be satisfied. It is time to re-imagine the concept of an appeal bond in a more fundamental way than occurred during the first generation of reforms inspired by *Philip Morris.* For media defendants at least, the appeal bond should properly be understood as a device to preserve the *status quo* and protect the constitutional right to appeal.

VI. Conclusion

Located near the confluence of three major rivers, the city of Alton became the place where the exercise of freedom of the press and the right to appeal intersected in the historic case of the *Alton Telegraph.* The paper that helps perpetuate the memory of Elijah Lovejoy, the first martyr in the cause of a free press, was forced to file for bankruptcy after losing a record judgment in a libel suit. The irony is that the suit was based upon a story that never appeared in the paper. The tragedy is that the jury verdict was never subject to appellate review because the *Telegraph* lacked the resources to post a bond of the magnitude required to stay enforcement of the judgment pending appeal.

Forty years after the *Telegraph* case, the inability to seek appellate review of a crippling damages award in a libel suit still presents an existential threat to all but the largest media organizations. By its chilling effect on newsgathering and its adverse impact on the people's right to know, the appeal bond requirement abridges First Amendment freedoms. A re-imagination of the *supersedeas* bond requirement, at least as it applies to media defendants seeking to raise First Amendment protections, will reconcile their constitutional right to appeal and the legitimate interests of their judgment creditors.

VI

The Art of Breaking the Deal: The Case of the Penthouse Casino

I. Introduction

On the Boardwalk in Atlantic City, adjacent to the Trump Plaza Hotel and Casino, sits a vacant parcel of prime real estate. Intended by magazine publisher Robert Guccione as the site of a $200 million Penthouse Hotel and Casino, the property remains undeveloped save for minimal landscaping and a driveway for parking the stretch limousines used to transport high-rollers from the Philadelphia and New York metropolitan areas. A wholly-owned subsidiary of Penthouse International, Ltd. ("Penthouse") ran out of money after spending $70 million on the project. It suspended construction in 1980, leaving a half-completed structure of rusting steel girders. Construction never resumed. In the litigation that followed to assign blame, a prominent attorney was held personally liable for $129 million in damages for helping to extricate an institutional lender from a commitment to provide financing that it could not fulfill.

For its central role in Penthouse's financial collapse, its links to the FBI's tragicomic ABSCAM sting operation and the epic pornographic film *Caligula*, and with cameo appearances by real estate magnates Harry Helmsley and Donald Trump (not to mention former Miss America Vanessa Williams), the case of the Penthouse casino at its 35th anniversary is a very good story. *Penthouse Int'l, Ltd. v. Dominion Fed. Sav. & Loan Ass'n. (Penthouse I)*, 665 F. Supp. 301 (S.D. N.Y. 1987), *rev'd*, 855 F.2d 963 (2nd Cir. 1988) *cert. denied*, 490 U.S. 1005 (1989) (*Penthouse II*).

On another level, *Penthouse* dramatically illustrates the role and function of lawyers in sophisticated transactional practice, a context that deserves more attention than it receives in professional responsibility scholarship. Transactional real estate practice generates a greater proportion of legal malpractice claims than any other field (twenty-five percent). Personal injury practice runs a close second with twenty-four percent. The most common causes of client complaints against real estate lawyers are counseling outside of their areas of expertise, failure to advise of business risks (e.g., not advising a landlord against signing a lease with the shell subsidiary of a credit-worthy parent who had not signed or guaranteed the lease), and multiple representation of clients with conflicting interests.

Daunting in its length and complexity, the case is haunting in depicting how an experienced attorney can find himself accused of perjury and cast in the unenviable role of appellant as a consequence of his choices and actions. Doctrinally, the *Penthouse* case straddles at least seven substantive areas of law, including Contracts, Torts, Land Finance Law, Banking Law, Federal Courts, Remedies and Legal Profession. *Penthouse* has been described as "the real capstone" by the authors of a Real Estate Transactions casebook in which it appears as the final case. "The entire course comes together in this case. . . . [I]t includes all of the elements of a commercial real estate project and illustrates almost every point covered . . . in the book."[1]

Context is critical to a full understanding of most legal disputes. Part II of this chapter explores the seemingly trivial circumstances and inter-contingent events leading to the *Penthouse* case. Part III describes the proceedings at the trial court level, which might best be characterized as bizarre. Part IV analyzes the appellate court's categorical reversal of virtually every finding of fact and conclusion of law. Perhaps more than facts and legal doctrine, the historical moment in which the appeal in *Penthouse* was heard goes a long way toward explaining, if not dictating, the outcome. The appellate court avoided the specter of a casino, bearing the name of a sexually explicit magazine, being constructed in Atlantic City with public financing at taxpayers' expense. Part IV also examines the decision by the Supreme Court to deny *certiorari*, based upon information only recently made publicly available. A cautionary tale about professional responsibility in transactional practice, *Penthouse* exposes the risks an attorney incurs in zealously promoting a client's strategic business objectives. Part V recommends that the scope of the common law litigation privilege be expanded to shield transactional lawyers from civil liability to third parties for practicing the art of breaking the deal.

II. Backstory

Soon after gambling was legalized in New Jersey in 1977, Guccione, the President of Penthouse, conceived the idea of developing a casino-hotel complex on the Atlantic City Boardwalk. The advent of casino gambling in Atlantic City sparked a resurgence of construction on the Boardwalk, making it one of the nation's hottest commercial real estate markets. "Though [Guccione] knew nothing about gambling, he figured it would be easy to open a casino."[2] Penthouse assembled five contiguous parcels of land along Missouri Avenue adjacent to the Boardwalk, three of which it owned in fee simple. The other two parcels were the subject of long-term ground leases, including one which was leased from an entity controlled by New York real estate magnate Harry Helmsley (the "Helmsley lease"). Vera Coking, an adjacent property owner, refused a reported offer from Guccione of $1 million to sell her narrow lot. So Penthouse built a steel frame around her house in an effort to force her out, creating a must-see photo op for tourists. "Her modest house would be surrounded by that metal superstructure like a caged dollhouse, creating an almost iconic image of the city's struggle to revitalize itself."[3]

Initially unsuccessful in obtaining outside financing, Penthouse (through its wholly-owned subsidiary, Boardwalk Properties, Inc.) commenced construction using internal resources. By intending to finance construction without the involvement of institutional lenders, Penthouse was following a long tradition in the gaming industry. "Nevada developers had always relied on the Mafia for financing, because legitimate banks refused to give casinos construction loans." It was not until the 1950s that the Bank of Las Vegas "saw the lack of credit as a business opportunity and began giving casinos access to clean capital."[4] Before cable and pay-per-view eroded the market, and the Internet made pornography readily available without cost, so-called men's magazines like *Playboy* and *Penthouse* were capable of producing vast streams of revenue. The notion that Penthouse could finance development of a casino-hotel solely with retained earnings, although it seems unlikely with the benefit of hindsight, would have been entirely rational at the time of its conception.

While *Playboy's* overall circulation, including subscriptions, was always higher, *Penthouse* overtook *Playboy* in highly profitable newsstand sales in 1978, selling an average of 4.3 million copies in the U.S. and Canada alone. "*Forbes*, in announcing the news, said *Penthouse* 'may be the single most profitable magazine in publishing history save perhaps *TV Guide* or *Readers Digest.*'"[5] The September 1984 issue of *Penthouse*, featuring grainy black-and-white nude photographs of Miss America Vanessa Williams, sold out a press run of six million copies on the day it was released. Priced at $4 per copy ($1 above the usual newsstand price), it was the most profitable issue of a magazine ever published. Penthouse had paid photographer Tom Chiapel $100,000 for the set of photographs, including pictures of Williams in sexually suggestive poses with another nude female model. Amid mounting pressure from pageant officials and sponsors, Williams resigned her title. Public reaction tended to support Williams and portray Guccione as the heavy, in part for not waiting another two months, when Williams' reign as Miss America would have been over, to publish the pictures. Chiapel had previously tried to sell the photographs to *Playboy* but Hugh Hefner considered both the price and litigation risk excessive. In a Today Show interview with Bryant Gumbel, Hefner did not miss the opportunity to claim the high moral ground in criticizing his competitor. "When one is publishing a magazine that has erotic content, if you don't approach the business that you're in with a set of moral values, then we're in a lot of trouble."[6] Williams claimed she never consented to commercial use of the photographs, and ultimately sued Chiapel but not Penthouse.

The financing of its Atlantic City casino depended heavily upon the box-office success of *Caligula*, an historo-pornographic epic produced by Penthouse. The first century Roman emperor Caligula was one of Guccione's personal idols. *Caligula* began filming in Rome in 1976 amid great expectations as the first major motion picture to feature eminent actors (including Sir John Gielgud, Helen Mirren and Peter O'Toole) and hard-core pornographic imagery. Delayed by quarreling over artistic differences, and contractual litigation with screen-writer Gore Vidal and others, *Caligula* was finally released in 1979. The title was originally to have been "Gore Vidal's Caligula." After viewing twelve minutes of additional scenes that Penthouse added to the film to increase its hard-core sexual content, Vidal demanded to have his name removed. Penthouse ultimately consented in exchange for Vidal's agreement to forego a 10% share of profits to which he was entitled by way of compensation, in addition to the more than $200,000 he received for writing the script.

The film turned out to be a critical disaster, and a financial catastrophe for Penthouse which had invested $17.5 million in production costs. Film critic Roger Ebert walked out of the movie early, giving Caligula zero stars and describing it as "sickening, utterly worthless, shameful trash." Victor Canby, movie critic for The New York Times, described it as "remarkably repulsive." Although a heavily-sanitized version was available on DVD, the uncut version of *Caligula* was banned in the United Kingdom for nearly three decades. The British Board of Film Classification did not allow the complete version to be released until 2008. Most distributors shunned the film on account of its sexually explicit imagery and graphic violence. So, Guccione rented a theater on Third Avenue in Manhattan and opened it himself. Public antipathy to the film was in part a reaction to Guccione's decision to charge the then-exorbitant ticket price of $7.50.

The failure of *Caligula* to generate anticipated revenue forced Penthouse to seek alternative sources of financing. In a lawsuit filed against Penthouse and Guccione, Marjorie Lee Thoreson, who had been the 1975 Penthouse Pet of the Year and who performed the scenes in *Caligula* to which Vidal objected, claimed that she had been coerced in 1980 into providing sexual favors to a furniture manufacturer from Milan as a *quid pro quo* for providing construction financing. *Thoreson v. Penthouse Int'l, Ltd.*, 563 N.Y.S.2d 968 (N.Y. Sup. Ct. 1990). The trial court awarded $4,060,000 in damages, which was reduced to $60,000 on appeal. *Thoreson v. Penthouse Int'l, Ltd.*, 606 N.E.2d 1369 (N.Y. 1992) (vacating punitive damages award because statute at issue did not authorize such relief).

It was during this period that Guccione was approached by Melvin Weinberg, who claimed to represent Arab interests with virtually inexhaustible sums of cash to invest in U.S. business opportunities. In fact, Weinberg was a convicted felon who, in return for a sentence of probation, had agreed to cooperate with the FBI in "ABSCAM," the undercover investigation of suspected criminal activity by public officials in the fledgling Atlantic City gaming industry. "ABSCAM" was the code word given by the FBI to the sting operation it conducted from 1978 to 1980. It was derived by combining the first two letters of "Abdul Enterprises, Ltd.," a fictitious organization purportedly backed by extremely wealthy Arab sheiks that Weinberg claimed to represent, with the word "scam." *United States v. Myers*, 692 F.2d 823, 829 (2d Cir. 1982), cert. denied, 461 U.S. 961 (1983). Meetings between FBI agents, posing as representatives of the sheiks, and public officials who, in return for money, were willing to use their influence with the government on the sheiks' behalf, were monitored with concealed videotape cameras and microphones. *See also United States v. Silvestri*, 719 F.2d 577, 579–80 (2d Cir. 1983). Weinberg told Guccione that his principals would be willing to lend Penthouse $150 million so it could resume and complete construction, conditioned upon receipt of a casino license.

Weinberg tried to induce Guccione to offer to pay a $300,000 bribe to New Jersey casino regulatory officials in return for issuing a license. Guccione refused, asking Weinberg, "Are you out of your mind?" Weinberg then orchestrated a campaign to increase the pressure on Guccione to compel his participation in the sting operation, and later punish Guccione for his refusal to cooperate, by maligning him in statements to legitimate prospective lenders, influential politicians and business associates. Weinberg's attempts to manipulate Guccione were detailed in a report by a United States Senate Committee titled "Final Report of the Select Committee to Study Undercover Activity of Components of the Department of Justice." S. REP. NO. 97-682 (1982) ("Senate Report"). According to the Senate Report, Weinberg circulated rumors about Penthouse's unlikely prospects for obtaining a casino license as a result of its ailing financial condition and Guccione's organized crime connections. As a result of the ABSCAM probe, six members of the House of Representatives and the mayor of Camden, New Jersey were convicted of various offenses related to corruption of public office. Senator Harrison Williams of New Jersey was convicted of bribery. Facing certain expulsion from the Senate, he resigned his seat in 1982.

Although the government was successful in securing convictions, media reports of the trials of public officials from 1980 to 1982, including a series of nationally syndicated columns by Jack Anderson, exposed the outrageousness of Weinberg's techniques and the FBI's failure to properly supervise his activities. The Senate Report, released in January 1983, excoriated the FBI for the ABSCAM operation and particularly for the targeting of individuals such as Guccione. According to the report, Weinberg's attempted entrapment of Guccione

> . . . provides a glaring example of the risks posed to innocent citizens by the government's reliance upon unsavory informants and dishonest middlemen, when they are given wide latitude to develop scenarios and select targets of their investigation. . . . Because of the risks to innocent citizens illustrated by the costs imposed on Guccione . . . the Select Committee has recommended . . . the creation of a statutory entrapment defense applicable in such circumstances and the codification of threshold standards for offering an individual an opportunity to commit a crime.

After the Senate Report was issued, the FBI strengthened its controls on undercover operations with a view toward avoiding harm to the reputations of innocent third parties.

The Senate Report confirmed that Guccione had no organized crime connections, and had engaged in no wrongdoing. "Because I was a pornographer Italian-American Sicilian," he told a reporter years later, "they assumed I was Mafia. But I was clean. I've always been clean."[7] Buoyed by his public exoneration, Guccione later filed suit against the United States for negligent supervision and control of Weinberg's undercover activities on behalf of the Federal government, enabling Weinberg to commit defamation and tortious interference with Penthouse's attempt to secure construction financing. Judge Constance Baker Motley of the U.S. District Court for the Southern District of New

York dismissed the complaint as barred by sovereign immunity. 670 F. Supp. at 537. Guccione, represented by Alan Dershowitz, appealed to the Second Circuit, which affirmed unanimously. *Guccione v. United States*, 847 F.2d 1031, 1033 (2d Cir. 1988), *reh'g denied*, 878 F.2d 32 (2d Cir. 1989), *cert. denied*, 493 U.S. 1020 (1990).

National press coverage of ABSCAM extensively reported that the FBI had been interested in Guccione's potentially illegal Atlantic City activities. News articles, including one in The New York Times, described an affidavit of a government prosecutor linking Guccione with ABSCAM targets. Following the suspension of construction in 1980, Penthouse was unable to obtain financing for its casino project for the duration of the ABSCAM investigation.

Litigation would also have been a significant source of distraction for Penthouse. The period marked "a career apex in controversy" for Guccione, who has been described as "one of the most litigious men in America, and one of the most often sued."[8] Former Miss Wyoming Kim Pring was awarded $26.5 million in damages in February 1981 after Penthouse published a fictional account of the bizarre sexual behavior of a thinly disguised Miss Wyoming. The jury verdict was reversed on appeal. *Pring v. Penthouse Int'l., Ltd.*, 695 F.2d 438 (10th Cir. 1982) (obvious fantasy not actionable as defamation or invasion of privacy), *cert. denied*, 462 U.S. 1132 (1983). Reverend Jerry Falwell sued to enjoin publication of the March 1981 issue containing an interview he had granted to two freelance journalists that was subsequently sold to Penthouse. Judge James Turk, a Federal district court judge sitting in Lynchburg, Virginia (Falwell's hometown and the center of his evangelistic broadcasting activities), ruled in Penthouse's favor. Cher was more successful. Her $200,000 judgment against Penthouse for printing an unauthorized interview and likeness in the March 1981 issue of *Penthouse Forum*, a subsidiary publication, was affirmed on appeal. Penthouse spent $20 million defending a libel suit filed by Moe Dalitz (an associate of mobsters Lucky Luciano and Bugsy Siegel) and his investment partner Mervyn Adelson, chief executive officer of Lorimar Television, arising from publication of a story claiming that their development of Rancho La Costa, a luxurious resort in La Jolla,

California, had been financed by a questionable $250 million loan from a Teamsters pension fund and was a favored hangout for members of organized crime. Adelson told Guccione that Barbara Walters had refused to marry him until he refuted the charges in the story. (The couple eventually did marry but divorced, and subsequently remarried and divorced again.) A jury verdict in favor of Penthouse in 1982 was reversed by the trial judge, and the case was later settled with Penthouse apologizing to Adelson but not Dalitz.

In any event, the dramatic spike in interest rates to record high levels would have made the cost of borrowing prohibitive. The interest rate charged by construction lenders typically fluctuates with changes in the prime rate of interest. Between the time Penthouse commenced construction in 1978 and the time it suspended construction in 1980, the prime rate doubled from 8.5% to 17%. Prime reached a record high of 21-1/2% in December 1980, and hovered at about 17% until February 1982.

It was not until June 1983 that Penthouse finally managed to obtain a commitment for a $97 million loan from Queen City Savings & Loan Association of Plainfield, New Jersey ("Queen City") to complete construction and provide permanent financing. The term of the loan was 10 years. The interest rate was fixed at 14-7/8% for the first five years, and 15-3/8% thereafter. A rather small bank inexperienced in transactions of this nature, Queen City organized a syndicate consisting of a dozen financial institutions. Loan participation is the term used to describe the arrangement by which a lender sells portions of its interest in a loan to a consortium of other lenders, while still controlling the administration of the loan. The original lender (Queen City) is referred to as the "lead lender" and the lenders who purchase interests in the loan are referred to as "participants." Loan participation is commonly used to spread the risk and exposure of funding a loan to finance a project of uncertain viability because of the property's location or the identity of the borrower.

The syndicate organized by Queen City included Dominion Federal Savings & Loan Association ("Dominion"). Founded in 1974 by William L. Walde, McLean-based Dominion was the largest savings and loan in Virginia. Walde, who served as chairman of the board of directors, was known as "Mr. Northern Virginia." Federal banking regulators gave him the less complimentary nickname of "Wild Bill" for his penchant for making risky mortgage loans. In November 1983, Dominion agreed to provide $35 million to the Queen City syndicate and received a $175,000 commitment fee in return. Because this was twice the maximum amount that Dominion could legally lend to a single borrower under Federal banking regulations, Dominion arranged to sell half of its participation to Community Savings & Loan Association of Bethesda, Maryland ("Community") by the terms of a written agreement dated December 2, 1983.

Dominion bore a risk by agreeing to lend above its regulatory limit without conditioning its obligation to lend on its ability to sub-participate its interest. By early February 1984, that risk manifested itself. Dominion became aware that Community had begun to show some reticence with serving as a sub-participant in a casino loan, ostensibly for moral reasons. Finding itself in the awkward position of having committed to lend far more than the amount it was legally permitted to lend, Dominion desperately needed to find an exit strategy without breaching its commitment. Penthouse had been dropped as a listed borrower on Dominion's internal Commitment Participation Report for February 1984. The trial judge would later describe this "as almost conclusive proof" that Dominion's officers had decided to breach its commitment by that time. *Penthouse I*, 665 F. Supp. 301, 306 (S.D.N.Y. 1987). On February 8, 1984, less than a month before the scheduled closing date, the president of Dominion called Philip Gorelick, a member of the Washington, D.C. law firm of Melrod, Redman & Gartlan, P.C. ("the Melrod firm") asking him to attend a pre-closing meeting scheduled in New York the following day, and thereafter to serve as lender's counsel. Founded in 1965, the Melrod firm consisted of 45 attorneys during this period. Gorelick, a 1966 graduate of Harvard Law School, was sixth in seniority. The Melrod firm's principal practice areas were banking and commercial real estate law.

At the pre-closing meeting, Gorelick complained about the quality of Queen City's loan documents, describing the existing drafts as "idiotic." He insisted that "everything presented was unacceptable" and had to be completely redrafted by his law firm. The paperwork was clearly inadequate. Documentation for a $97 million loan had been prepared using a standard, "plain language" mortgage published by Blumberg Legal Forms imprinted with the warning, "Consult your lawyer before signing this mortgage — it has important legal consequences." *Penthouse II*, 855 F.2d 963, 969 (2d Cir. 1988). While Gorelick's complaints about the paperwork may have been well founded, he never prepared more than rough drafts of certain loan documents, none of which were sent to anyone for review. Moreover, his other complaints and demands were obstreperous. He demanded that Penthouse commit to pay his firm a $150,000 bonus fee upon closing for clearing his desk in order to give priority to the loan, but Gorelick later declared the loan as not being "in a position to close at any time." *Penthouse I* at 307. He never disclosed this fee arrangement (later characterized by the trial judge as "extortion") to Dominion, an obvious breach of the fiduciary duty owed by an agent to a principal. *Id.* at 306 n.1.

In addition to numerous requests for additional information, Gorelick demanded as a condition of closing that: (1) Dominion replace Queen City as lead lender; (2) Penthouse hire Sigal Construction Company as general contractor; (3) a hotel management agreement be in place prior to closing; and (4) Penthouse obtain a series of proposed amendments to the Helmsley lease. Only the last of these demands arguably was a pre-closing condition under the terms of the loan commitment. Under questioning at trial, Gorelick admitted that much of the additional information for which he made numerous requests (described by one witness as "never ending") was not essential for closing the deal, and was not required by the commitment. *Id.* at 308.

Gorelick told Penthouse that he was still in the process of revising various closing checklists as late as February 29, 1984, but the Melrod firm's demands proved too onerous. The March 1 closing deadline came and went. Accused at one point in the Penthouse transaction of not acting in good faith, Walde replied, "Screw good faith. We're going to do it our way because we're the co-leader." *Id.* at 306. Reading between the lines of the trial court opinion, it is possible to sense the clash of egos in the description of the tense meetings between Walde and Guccione that took place in March 1984 at Guccione's townhouse on Manhattan's East Side and at Walde's office in an effort to hold the syndicate together as the financing commitment expired without the loan closing. The terms of the loan became less attractive to at least one of the participants after the prime rate of interest rose from 11% to 11-1/2% on March 19, 1984. Eventually the loan syndicate unraveled, and the deal fell apart.

III. Trial

The Honorable United States District Judge Kevin Thomas Duffy presided over a bench trial of the lawsuit filed by Penthouse against Dominion for anticipatorily breaching the commitment. Trial lasted three weeks, from May 11, 1987, until June 1. The central issue in the case was whether Dominion had clearly and unequivocally refused to fund the loan and, if so, whether its refusal was due to legitimate concerns about the borrower's compliance with the commitment, or illegitimate concerns about the loss of its sub-participant.

Bubbling not far below the surface was the issue of whether Gorelick's tactics constituted fraudulent lawyering for which Dominion could be held responsible under the developing doctrine of bad faith lender liability. Beginning in the 1980s, a series of cases held institutional lenders liable for causing harm to commercial borrowers and third parties on expansive common law theories, including breach of the implied covenant of good faith and fair dealing. The seminal case was *State National Bank of El Paso v. Farah Manufacturing Co.*, 678 S.W.2d 661 (Tex. App. 1984), holding a lender liable to a borrower for breach of fiduciary duty. By the time of the *Penthouse* case, lender liability law was regarded as an emerging growth market for law firms interested in improving profitability by expanding their areas of practice.

Gorelick was called as a witness. He denied having been told anything about the problems Dominion was experiencing with Community. Judge Duffy found "totally incredible" Gorelick's testimony that he could not have acted in bad faith for the purpose of destroying the deal because his client had never made him aware of its dilemma. During morning recess on the day cross-examination of Gorelick began, Judge Duffy summoned defense counsel to join him in his robing room. Without comment the judge handed counsel a volume of the Federal Supplement, directing his attention to the first line of a 1974 opinion by Judge Duffy, which read, "John Spurdis is a liar." Counsel tried to explain that Gorelick may have been obnoxious or aggressive, but was not a liar. "Judge Duffy simply shrugged expressively." *Penthouse II* at 973. According to the court, "The inferences to be drawn from Gorelick's outrageous perjury are often the exact opposite of what he said." *Penthouse I* at 306–07. The court further detailed his intent to commit perjury:

> Gorelick took the stand and attempted brazenly to lie to the court. During cross-examination, the crucible of truth, Gorelick continuously shifted uneasily in the chair, sweated like a trapped liar, and the glaze that came over his shifty eyes gave proof to his continuing perjury. His total lack of veracity was shown not only by his demeanor but by the shady practices he seemingly reveled in. *Penthouse I* at 306 n. 1.

The robing room incident was later cited by defendants in their motion for a new trial. Defense counsel claimed that Judge Duffy misinterpreted Gorelick's demeanor during cross-examination; that it was a reaction to anxiety generated by the report Gorelick by then would have received from counsel about the robing room incident. Judge Duffy's response was that much of the testimony that he found totally incredible was on direct examination. "Gorelick's demeanor was that of a liar during his direct examination when questioned regarding those things about which he had decided to perjure himself." *Penthouse Int'l, Ltd. v. Dominion Fed. Sav. & Loan Ass'n* (Penthouse III), 678 F. Supp. 61, 62 (S.D.N.Y. 1987). As to the effect on Gorelick's demeanor of hearing about the robing room incident, Judge Duffy was skeptical that "this conversation might have so damaged Gorelick's 'fragile psyche' . . . . Am I to believe this of the man who was chosen by the officers of [Dominion] to break up a loan closing by bullying the other participants?" *Id.*

The court found Gorelick was retained to "bully and intimidate" Penthouse by making an endless series of unreasonable demands until the commitment expired and Dominion was released from both its obligation and its dilemma. *Penthouse I* at 307. In particular Judge Duffy found "totally unreasonable and arbitrary" Gorelick's demand that Penthouse hire Sigal Construction Company. "There is nothing to show that Sigal had any special expertise to recommend it as a builder or consultant for a major project other than a personal relationship between Sigal and the partners of the Melrod firm." *Id.* at 311. "Recognizing the potential liability they were incurring, [Dominion's officers] sought a cover-up," Judge Duffy wrote. "In this plot they found a willing tool in Gorelick." Labeling him a "hatchet man intent on destroying the deal," the trial judge described Gorelick's dilatory tactics as "deliberate efforts to sabotage the deal." According to Judge Duffy, "Gorelick brought about its demise."

Judge Duffy agreed with Penthouse's claim that Dominion had engaged in bad faith, and had anticipatorily breached the mortgage commitment. The court assessed damages against Dominion and the Melrod firm, jointly and severally, in the sum of $128.7 million! Damages were based upon unchallenged expert witness testimony estimating the profits likely to be generated by Penthouse's entry into a highly competitive industry and market. *Penthouse II* at 983. In retrospect, defendants' trial strategy on the damages issue appears over-confident. Expecting to prevail on the liability issue, they called no witnesses to rebut the proof of damages Judge Duffy allowed Penthouse to introduce into evidence. Penthouse had not sought damages from the Melrod firm in its proposed judgment. Judge Duffy added the award against the law firm *sua sponte* on the grounds of fraud. In a post-trial order filed September 30, 1987, Judge Duffy explained his rationale as follows:

> [T]he firm did not disclose the true nature of the agency which it undertook; and the actions of the firm through its partner constituted active fraud. The analogy that comes to mind . . . is that of a hoodlum enforcer for a loan shark . . . . In this case the Melrod firm did not disclose the true nature of its agency, *i.e.*, to scuttle the deal . . . . *Penthouse II* at 984.

Because the Melrod firm's malpractice insurance would be expected to cover some of the damages, Judge Duffy's order was reported as good news for Dominion.

Defendants moved for a new trial on the basis of newly discovered evidence and prejudicial error by the trial judge. The newly discovered evidence consisted of the defamation and tortious interference lawsuit

Guccione filed in 1987 against the Federal government arising from the ABSCAM investigation. Defendants claimed that, had they known about this lawsuit at the time of trial, they would have raised the defense of preclusion or insisted upon a division of damages. *Penthouse III* at 63.

Citing the robing room incident described above, defendants based their motion for a new trial in part on their claim that Judge Duffy clearly had made a determination as to Gorelick's credibility before he had finished testifying. According to Judge Duffy, he had only made a preliminary determination at the time of the incident, and intended the robing room meeting to serve as "[a] word of advice to save a colleague from an embarrassing situation." *Id.* at 62.

> After watching and listening to Phillip [sic] Gorelick testify for perhaps a total of four hours, I thought that much of what he had said was intentionally untrue. I knew that if this was not corrected by the witness I would have to find that he was a liar and that he had committed perjury. I thought that such a finding by a district court could have an adverse impact on him professionally and perhaps even personally. . . . Because I have not given up the ideals of my past, I decided to inform his counsel that if I found Gorelick to be a liar I would be obligated to articulate that finding. *Id.*

According to Philip M. Horowitz, who served as chair of the Melrod firm's real estate practice group and was a member of its management committee, the court rejected the firm's argument that it had been denied a fair trial by the court's *sua sponte* decision to hold the firm jointly and severally liable for all of the damages, rather than the much smaller amount for which the firm originally thought it might potentially be liable.[9] "Melrod's claim apparently, however, is not that they were unprepared to meet the allegations of the complaint as amended, but rather that they are now unprepared to pay the sum of money for which they have been held liable." *Penthouse III* at 64.

In a published order denying the motion, Judge Duffy took advantage of the opportunity to continue his rhetorical assault on Gorelick: "It seems that I come from another generation. It was once thought that the law was one of the highest of callings that a person could have, and a court was regarded as a temple of justice not to be desecrated by a lawyer telling lies." *Id.* at 62. Judge Duffy concluded that

> . . . it is clear from any fair reading of the record that Gorelick lied in many places. . . . Gorelick's lies constituted knowing, willful perjury. . . . Did he really expect me to believe that the people at the Dominion Federal Savings & Loan Association made up their mind to 'screw good faith' and break up the deal but did not tell him of that fact when they retained him as replacement counsel only one day before the preclosing conference? *Id.* at 63.

IV. Appeal

By the time *Penthouse* reached the U.S. Court of Appeals for the Second Circuit, it was clear that the savings and loan ("S&L" or "thrift") industry was in the process of dramatic upheaval. The first signs of the impending crisis had begun to appear publicly in early 1987, but the stark reality of its magnitude could not have been apparent to Judge Duffy at the time of trial. The panic began in the Sun Belt and spread across the country: during the first three months of 1987, depositors withdrew a record $14 billion from S&Ls in what regulators were nervously calling a silent run. In March 1987 the Government Accounting Office released a report estimating that the Federal Savings and Loan Insurance Corporation ("FSLIC") — the organization which insured deposits in savings and loans in much the same way the Federal Deposit Insurance Corporation insures bank deposits — was insolvent by at least $4.2 billion.

By summer 1987 a steady stream of alarming headlines accompanied the growing crisis in the S&L industry. Following a decade of lax supervision by bank regulators, risky lending practices, and outright fraud and misconduct by S&L officers, many institutions were insolvent. At the time of the *Penthouse* appeal, the S&L crisis had become a major national embarrassment, the resolution of which would require massive consolidation, shrinkage and restructuring of the thrift industry.

The loss expected to be borne by taxpayers was then estimated at $100 billion and rising daily. Congress sought to restore public confidence and some semblance of order by creating the Resolution Trust Corporation

("RTC") in 1989 to replace the FSLIC and act as conservator of failed savings and loans. Before the crisis was over, fully one-third of the S&L industry would be liquidated or sold, including Dominion itself. The total cost of funding the industry's bailout would approach $200 billion. By way of comparison, the loss borne by taxpayers as a result of the S&L crisis far exceeded the total cost of the financial system bailout (including the Troubled Asset Relief Program) in 2008–09.

Thousands of depositors withdrew more than $125 million from Dominion following the trial court decision. The value of its stock declined by more than half. In order to pursue an appeal to the Second Circuit, Dominion was required to post a $50 million appeal bond. Nothing focuses the mind quite like a nine-figure damages award. Arthur Liman, a self-described "big trouble" lawyer, was retained to represent Dominion on appeal. Liman was a partner in the litigation department at Paul, Weiss, Rifkind, Wharton & Garrison, one of New York City's largest law firms. His previous high-profile clients included financiers Carl Icahn and Michael Milken. He represented Harry Helmsley's wife, Leona, in connection with Federal charges of tax evasion in the 1990s. As chief counsel for the Senate select committee appointed to conduct the Iran-Contra investigation, Liman had recently achieved celebrity status as a result of his questioning of Lt. Col. Oliver North and other witnesses over the course of forty days of televised hearings during the spring and summer of 1987.

Within the Melrod firm, the magnitude of its potential liability had not been apparent before Judge Duffy's ruling.[10] For purposes of appeal the firm retained separate counsel. The Federal Home Loan Bank Board was recruited by appellants as *amicus curiae.*

In an opinion by United States Circuit Judge Frank X. Altimari, the Court of Appeals for the Second Circuit categorically reversed all of Judge Duffy's findings of fact as being clearly erroneous, together with all of his conclusions of law. Dominion's stock price rose by $3 per share on the day of the decision, closing at $10.25. Judge Duffy's calculation of damages was hard to explain and easy to reverse as speculative. *Penthouse II* at 983. One authority has described the trial court's calculation of damages as "zany."[11]

As to Dominion's alleged anticipatory breach, the Second Circuit found there was never a clear and unequivocal declaration by Dominion that performance would not be forthcoming. Of Gorelick's four demands, the only one that occurred before the March 1 closing date was his insistence on amendments to the Helmsley lease. The Second Circuit held Judge Duffy's finding that this demand gave rise to an anticipatory breach clearly erroneous. Instead, the Second Circuit regarded Gorelick's demands made after March 1 to be irrelevant once the commitment had expired. Furthermore Judge Duffy was clearly erroneous in finding that Penthouse was in a position to fully comply with all of the pre-closing conditions before the loan commitment expired on March 1, a requirement of a claim for anticipatory breach of contract. The commitment included a myriad of conditions, requiring, among other things, approval of plans and specifications, access to utilities, receipt of governmental approvals, and a license to operate from the New Jersey Casino Control Commission. In order to close the loan, Queen City had been willing to waive compliance by Penthouse with the unmet pre-closing conditions. These included several of the most essential conditions of the commitment, such as unresolved title issues, and the absence of construction plans and specifications, utility arrangements, and a casino license.

Relying on Federal regulatory policy articulated by *amicus curiae*, the Second Circuit held that Queen City did not possess authority to unilaterally waive so many critical pre-closing conditions without consulting with its participants. According to *amicus curiae*, Queen City's unilateral waiver of key pre-closing conditions was "completely at odds with" and "seriously undermines" the Federal Home Loan Bank Board's "supervisory policies concerning safe and sound underwriting." *Penthouse II* at 981. The inherent risk to participants of making a mortgage loan without the ability to control its administration contributed to the failure of many lending institutions during the S&L crisis. This is yet another example of a risk that Dominion bore. A loan participation agreement typically requires the consent of a majority in interest of the participants before closing conditions may be waived by the lead lender. "If a lead lender has this authority," the government urged, "the FSLIC fund is exposed to inordinate risk." *Id.*

The Second Circuit reversed Judge Duffy's holding that the Melrod firm had committed fraud by reason of Gorelick's falsely representing to Penthouse that Dominion intended to fulfill its obligations under the loan commitment at a time when it was no longer willing or able to perform. The panel noted the absence of testimonial evidence, and that the trial court had failed to make specific findings on each element of the fraud cause of action.

The Second Circuit substituted its own interpretation for Judge Duffy's finding that Gorelick was engaged in a deliberate effort to sabotage the deal. The panel concluded that, by the time Gorelick joined the negotiations, it was apparent that Queen City's attorney was in over his head. The court cited expert testimony supporting Gorelick's position that the loan was not in a position to close any time in the near future based upon legitimate concerns about the borrower's compliance with the commitment. It found that Gorelick had fulfilled his role "to ensure that the interests of his client were protected. In so doing, he insightfully observed serious problems with the transaction and promptly raised his objections." *Penthouse II* at 979. The Second Circuit reversed the trial court's perjury finding as not based upon clear and convincing proof.

The Second Circuit opinion is subject to criticism, particularly regarding its emphasis on the March 1 expiration date. First, in the absence of express documentary language, time is not of the essence in real estate transactions in New Jersey unless it is clear from an examination of the circumstances that the parties so intended. *Paradiso v. Mazejy*, 69 A.2d 15, 17–18 (N.J. 1949); *Gorrie v. Winters*, 518 A.2d 515, 516–17 (N.J. Super. Ct. App. Div. 1986). The loan commitment between Queen City and Penthouse, by its terms, was governed by New Jersey law. So, *Penthouse* should have been remanded for the trial court to make such a determination. Ordinarily in the Federal system the appellate court remands to the trial court from which the review has been taken. Remand to a different district judge is appropriate if the record reflects personal bias or other unusual circumstances. Second, it is clear that negotiations continued past March 1 without an extension of the closing date. Both parties forged ahead in their respective efforts for several weeks (still seeking to close the loan, in the case of Penthouse; perhaps not so much, in the case of Dominion) as if the March 1 date was not significant. *Penthouse II* at 972. Although the Second Circuit acknowledged that the parties' conduct in continuing to negotiate may be consistent with an implied extension of the March 1 deadline, it did not remand for trial court determination of the highly fact-dependent issue of waiver.

The Second Circuit decision has been criticized for usurping the fact-finding prerogative of a Federal district court judge. Federal Rule of Civil Procedure 52(a)(6) states that "Findings of fact . . . must not be set aside unless clearly erroneous, and the reviewing court must give due regard to the trial court's opportunity to judge the witnesses' credibility." The presumption that a trial judge's findings of fact are correct is especially strong when the findings rest in large measure on the credibility of witnesses, and when the trial is as long and complex as in *Penthouse.* In *Bose Corp. v. Consumers Union of U.S., Inc.*, the Supreme Court held "the likelihood that the appellate court will rely on the presumption tends to increase when trial judges have lived with the controversy for weeks or months instead of just a few hours." 466 U.S. 485, 500 (1984).

Since the appellate court in *Penthouse II* found that the trial court failed to make specific factual findings on each element of the fraud cause of action, and that the holding that Gorelick committed perjury was not based on sufficient proof, it should have remanded the case with appropriate instructions to give the trial court the opportunity to expand the record by developing additional facts. According to one authority, "appellate courts must appreciate judicial constraints, and termination of proceedings should not be left to the unfettered discretion of the appellate tribunal."[12]

The opinion relies upon the panel's independent fact-finding for a critical element of its internal logic. As in the case of contracts generally, an implied duty of good faith and fair dealing arises from a loan commitment. There is some divergence of opinion on the extent to which this duty applies to commercial loan transactions, absent a special relationship between the parties or specific language in the loan agreement.[13] But it is generally accepted that the principal duty imposed by a commitment is good faith negotiation of the details left open by the commitment. Making negotiations depend upon a party's acceptance of new terms unexpressed in the commitment, or on terms inconsistent with the commitment, may violate the duty of good faith.

Penthouse cited four demands by Gorelick that were not authorized by the commitment. Three of these occurred after the March 1 expiration date making them irrelevant under the court's analysis. Before March 1, however, Gorelick had insisted upon Penthouse obtaining a series of amendments to the Helmsley lease as a condition of closing. Gorelick had described each of these lease amendments as being "required," although it is undisputed that some were not required by the terms of the commitment. Unless the Helmsley lease was amended, the closing of the loan would constitute an event of default. Because the commitment required that there be no lease violations, it was clear that some amendments to the Helmsley lease were necessary. However, Gorelick's list of proposed amendments went beyond what was required to satisfy the commitment. *Penthouse II* at 978. If the list of proposed amendments represented Dominion's final position on the matter, Gorelick's stubborn insistence may well have constituted not only bad faith, but also the clear and unequivocal declaration of nonperformance that is the precondition for a claim of anticipatory breach of contract.

The Second Circuit gave considerable weight to a letter sent to Penthouse by Gorelick's law partner, Louis J. Trotter, Jr., accompanying the list of proposed lease amendments. Trotter's cover letter described the enclosed list as "a nearly final version of what the lender will be looking for and [would] certainly provide you with a jumping off point for your discussions with Helmsley." *Id.* at 970. The appellate court interpreted this language in the cover letter as Trotter's softening the adamancy of Gorelick's demands, which might otherwise have evidenced Dominion's bad faith and anticipatory breach. "Thus, Gorelick's statements that the proposed amendments were required clearly were qualified by the statements made in Trotter's cover letter." *Id.* at 978.

Trotter's name appeared once in passing in the trial court opinion. *Penthouse I* at 308. His cover letter was not mentioned at all. Subject to cross-examination on remand, it is far from obvious that Trotter would have supported the Second Circuit's interpretation of his letter. First, Trotter would need to explain away the inconvenient title of the enclosure:

"Amendments Required to the Helmsley Lease." Although the cover letter is discussed at length at two different points in the Second Circuit's opinion, *Penthouse II* at 970, 978, the title of the enclosure was conspicuously absent. Second, Trotter would surely be challenged as to the meaning of the ambiguous phrases "jumping off point" and "nearly final version of what the lender will be looking for." Gorelick's requests are described elsewhere in trial testimony as being "never ending." *Penthouse I* at 309. Viewed in context, the Second Circuit's interpretation of the Trotter cover letter is strained. The more plausible reading is that Trotter was hedging against the possibility that Penthouse was somehow able to obtain from Harry Helmsley all of the amendments on Gorelick's initial list. In that event, Gorelick would come up with new and additional requirements for Helmsley lease amendments. Finally, having the fact-finding advantage of observing the decade in seniority that separated Trotter and Gorelick (Gorelick was a 1966 Harvard Law School graduate while Trotter graduated from Yale Law School in 1976), it might seem less likely to the trier of fact that Trotter would have authority to over-ride his senior partner by converting his demands into proposals.

The decision to terminate the *Penthouse* case by outright reversal was outcome-driven. Liman had made it abundantly clear during oral argument that, unless the district court judgment was reversed, Dominion would be rendered insolvent and forced to liquidate. According to an article written by nationally recognized litigator Helen Davis Chaitman and published in the *New Jersey Law Journal* in November 1988, "In today's economy, with the federal savings-and-loan bailout estimated at tens of billions of dollars, no court is going to want to create another failed institution." Dominion's reported net worth was $74 million at the time. Reversal by the Second Circuit would postpone, and might even avoid, the rescue of yet another financial institution at taxpayers' expense. To a Federal appeals court mindful of the deepening financial crisis, further proceedings below would have been considered futile as a practical matter, even if they would not have been futile as a matter of law. Law professor Michael Berch wrote "The appellate court should take it upon itself to enter judgment without additional proceedings only after deciding that further proceedings would be futile — that is, the appellate court should enter judgment when *as a matter of law* [a party] would, under any circumstances, ultimately prevail."[14] Judicial efficiency was served in *Penthouse*, but at the cost of orderly procedure and perhaps justice as well.

Penthouse made these arguments in its petition to the U.S. Supreme Court for a writ of *certiorari*. Until relatively recently, the Court's decision to grant or deny *certiorari* was non-transparent and somewhat mysterious. Justice Felix Frankfurter's is an often-repeated formulation of the conventional wisdom. "[A]ll that a denial of a petition for a writ of *certiorari* means is that fewer than four members of the Court thought it should be granted . . . ." *Maryland v. Baltimore Radio Show*, 338 U.S. 912, 919 (1950). A law review article published in 1953 and coauthored by Yale Law School Professor Fowler V. Harper and then Yale Law student and future United States Circuit Judge for the Second Circuit George Pratt noted that "[t]he Court has succeeded in cloaking its *certiorari* behavior in such a shroud of mystery that any explanation of what happens is the sheerest of guesswork."[15]

In his retirement, the late Justice Harry Blackmun executed a deed of gift conveying all of his personal and official papers to the Library of Congress as of the fifth anniversary of his death, which turned out to be March 4, 2004. Harold Hongju Koh, one of Justice Blackmun's former clerks, described the Blackmun papers as "a treasure trove, the ultimate legal archaeological dig."[16] Professor Lee Epstein helped create a digital archive of Justice Blackmun's papers. The archive includes preliminary ("pool") memoranda from the 1986–1993 terms. Since its roll-out in Fall 2007, the archive has opened a fascinating window into the internal decision-making process by which the Court determines which cases it will consider. During Justice Blackmun's tenure, eight of the nine justices used a "*certiorari* pool" to facilitate consideration of the more than 7,000 *certiorari* petitions received by the Court each term. Clerks from different chambers collaborated in reading the requests and preparing memoranda evaluating them. (In 1989 only Justice John Paul Stevens did not participate in the pool.) The resulting pool memorandum summarized the arguments for and against review, and analyzed the legal issues. It concluded with the writer's recommendation. In handwriting at the end of the memorandum are comments by Justice Blackmun's "elbow" clerk, who reviewed the memorandum for the Justice.[17] Discussing the unprecedented breadth and depth of the Blackmun papers, Laura Kalman, Professor of History at the University of California, Santa Barbara, wrote: "some justices destroy their papers. They believe the less the public knows about the Supreme Court, the more easily the illusion is preserved that our system is based on the rule of law, rather than men and women."[18]

Thanks to the extraordinary work of Professor Epstein and her colleagues, the current generation of law students is the first that will not have been taught the conventional wisdom that it is impossible to know why the Supreme Court denies *certiorari.*

A Preliminary Memorandum, now contained in the Blackmun Archive, dated March 23, 1989 was circulated among the justices for their review in advance of a conference held on March 31 to decide whether to grant or deny *certiorari* in *Penthouse.* According to the memorandum, "Prominence was assured in this case because of the sums awarded and the rigorous legal battling of all parties, including District Judge Kevin Duffy." Ultimately the memorandum concluded that the *Penthouse* case was not "certworthy." The pool memo writer in the *Penthouse* case was Stephen Higginson, one of Justice Byron White's clerks. In 2011 President Obama nominated Higginson to fill a vacancy on the U.S. Court of Appeals for the Fifth Circuit. He was confirmed unanimously by the Senate. Justice Blackmun's clerk annotated the Pool Memorandum to note that the author was Justice White's clerk, had graduated from Yale Law School, and had previously clerked for Judge Patricia Wald of the U.S. Court of Appeals for the D.C. Circuit. Justice Blackmun's clerk further annotated the memorandum to indicate concurrence with the author's conclusion that the issues were not certworthy.

The memorandum characterized the Second Circuit decision as "a forceful reiteration in lender liability caselaw that parties will be strictly held to written agreement terms." *Penthouse I* may have represented the high-water mark in lender liability caselaw and was certainly the largest lender liability judgment. *Penthouse II* was hailed by lenders as marking a reversal of the tide in lender liability law. The general counsel of the California Bankers' Association commented that lenders will "heave the greatest sigh of relief" over the Second Circuit's decision.[19] On this issue, however, there was no split of authority among the circuits that might require Supreme Court intervention; and, in any event, the issue was not one of Federal law. The Preliminary Memorandum similarly rejected as a state law matter Penthouse's argument based on time not being of the essence. According to the memorandum, Penthouse was "unconvincing in its effort to characterize as certworthy" the argument that the Second Circuit overstepped its review authority by making *de novo* factual determinations.

With the Supreme Court's denial of *certiorari*, the Second Circuit had almost the last word. It would be a mistake to construe the Supreme Court's decision to deny *certiorari* in the *Penthouse* case as an endorsement of the Second Circuit decision. The Rehnquist Court did not regard its principal function to be the correction of errors in cases where the lower courts may have reached an incorrect result, but which did not involve unsettled questions of Federal constitutional or statutory law of general interest. The market of institutional lenders, by contrast, may be said to have unanimously affirmed the *Penthouse* case. It is fair to draw a negative inference about the quality of the credit from the fact that, after the Queen City deal so spectacularly fell through, Penthouse was never able to secure replacement financing for its project from any other lender. On the other hand, funding for new construction in general became virtually non-existent in the early 1990s in the climate of fear, if not panic, that followed in the wake of the S&L debacle.

V. Euchre

Euchre is a four-person trick-taking card game that was brought to the United States in the 19th century by German immigrants and that remains popular on Midwestern college campuses. Used as a verb, the word means to outwit or deceive someone, *e.g.* "they euchred Congress out of $50 billion."

Loan closing negotiations routinely begin with an exchange in the nature of a bonding exercise. Borrower's counsel seeks reassurance from lender's counsel, asking in a hopeful tone of voice, "We're not going to live and die by the commitment, right?" To which lender's counsel replies, "No, we're not going to live and die by the commitment." That having been said, the attorneys get down to the business of negotiating the terms of the final loan documents in a spirit of reasonableness and good intentions. In the Author's experience, as in *Penthouse*, negotiations with Gorelick followed a different routine.

Gorelick was a "go-to" choice as lender's counsel in commercial loan transactions. Bank clients likely interpreted his unyielding tenacity and combativeness as evidence of his dedication and undivided loyalty. Counsel for borrowers, however, dreaded loan transactions with Gorelick, who could be abusive and demeaning. *Penthouse I* at 307. The Author recalls a former law partner describing a transaction in which a borrower client specifically requested that a lender's promise not to retain Gorelick be made a term of the loan commitment. The Author recalls another former law partner describing a client, a prominent real estate developer in the Washington, D.C. suburbs of Northern Virginia, being taken to the hospital complaining of chest pains after hearing Gorelick insist that a construction loan was in no position to close. The Author recalls personally hearing Gorelick express the opinion that all of the Author's documents had to be completely redone.

In the dynamic environment of real estate transactions, circumstances or market conditions may change between the time of commitment and closing. This can take the form of sub-participant remorse, as in *Penthouse*, or, more commonly, the fluctuation of interest rates. By agreeing to make a long-term loan at a fixed rate of interest, a lender is betting that interest rates will not rise precipitously during the commitment period. If this turns out to be a losing bet, a lender may be tempted to scrutinize the terms of the commitment in search of an escape route.

Under the dominant contemporary understanding of contract law, promisors enjoy significant freedom to change their mind. According to legal ethics Professor Stephen Pepper, "[a]lthough it is unclear whether the law regards intentional breach of contract as normatively wrong . . . it is clear that the message of the law is that breach of contract is not prohibited" nor is it "contrary to law."[20] Contracts scholar Allan Farnsworth wrote,

> Commitment is not a matter of yes or no but a matter of degree, enforced by a cascading array of remedies, some specific and some substitutional. . . . There remains much truth in the assertion of Oliver Wendell Holmes that "the duty to keep a contract at common law means a prediction that you must pay damages if you do not keep it — and nothing else."[21]

Of course, the exercise of this freedom may come at a high price to be paid in compensatory damages. Damages for breach of an agreement to lend money are measured by the additional interest the borrower would be required to pay based on the market rate of interest at the time of breach, plus compensation for additional foreseeable expenses resulting from the breach. For this reason, one bound by a promise that turns out to be unfavorable will benefit greatly from a failure by the other party to satisfy conditions that would release the promisor from an onerous obligation. The party on the more favorable side of the deal must be careful to fully comply with every condition, or be subject to the claim of breach and loss of bargain.

In his influential treatise, *Contract as Promise*, Professor Charles Fried describes the elaborate jockeying for position that occurs in these situations: "This maneuvering becomes downright comical in the case where the party claiming the benefit of the release by virtue of a breach of condition would himself have been unwilling or perhaps even unable to perform. Such a party must hope that the other party will breach before he does."[22] Judge Duffy found that Dominion, not content to simply hope, retained Gorelick specifically in order to euchre Penthouse into breaching first.

Declining mortgage interest rates present the mirror-image situation. By April 1984, as rates began to ease, lenders encountered reluctance on the part of new borrowers to close loans previously committed at higher rates. Similarly, existing borrowers sought to prepay their high interest rate loans in order to derive the benefit of refinancing at lower rates.

Substantial penalties have long been a standard feature of institutional loans to deter borrowers from repaying indebtedness ahead of schedule. Lenders worry that borrowers might be tempted to evade the prepayment penalty by intentionally defaulting for the purpose of forcing the lender to accelerate the indebtedness. To prevent this strategic behavior, lenders include a provision in mortgages making any tender of payment after default and acceleration (*i.e.*, redemption) conclusively presumed to be evasive, and subject to the prepayment penalty.

In September 1982 Teachers Insurance & Annuity Association ("TIAA"), the largest provider of retirement savings vehicles for universities and other educational institutions, committed to lend One City Center Associates ("OCCA") $20 million for 35 years at a fixed interest rate of 14.25% to finance a high-rise office building in Sacramento, California. Closing was scheduled for April 30, 1984. The final loan documents submitted to OCCA for review included a default prepayment presumption clause. OCCA refused to go forward with the loan, ostensibly for the reason that this provision did not appear in the commitment and was unacceptable. OCCA waited until four days before the scheduled closing date to object to the default prepayment provision.

TIAA filed suit against OCCA seeking to recover damages for breaching the loan commitment. TIAA claimed that OCCA had failed to negotiate in good faith, and was seeking to sabotage the transaction because the intervening decline in interest rates had made the loan commitment unattractive. In his opinion the trial judge noted that loan documents generally include provisions not contained in the commitment, but necessary to implement its terms. Citing the testimony of witnesses that the default prepayment fee was consistent with industry practice, and evidence of OCCA's communication with various lenders and brokers in attempting to obtain alternate financing on more favorable terms, the court characterized OCCA's refusal to negotiate with TIAA concerning the default prepayment provision as "simply a last ditch attempt to scuttle the loan agreement." *TIAA v. Butler*, 626 F. Supp. 1229, 1235 (S.D.N.Y. 1986). The court found that:

> When they were unable to persuade Teachers [TIAA] to lower the interest rate agreed to in September 1982 and when they realized that Teachers was serious about living up to its commitments, defendants engaged in an eleventh hour comparison of the closing documents to the

> Commitment Letter to come up with an ostensible reason for not going forward with the loan. *Id.* at 1236.

Similarly, in another case involving TIAA, a court held the borrower liable for breach of its loan commitment because borrower took a negotiating stance designed to alter or scuttle the transaction after a decline in interest rates rendered the agreement less advantageous to borrower. *TIAA v. Ormesa Geothermal*, 791 F. Supp. 401, 415 (S.D.N.Y. 1991).

In *TIAA v. Butler*, the court awarded TIAA damages of $3.4 million. The court measured damages by calculating the difference, discounted to present value over the 35-year term of the loan, between the contract interest rate of 14-1/4%, and the prevailing market rate of interest at the time of breach of 12-1/4%. Thus the court placed TIAA in the same position it would have been in had the borrower performed its obligation under the loan commitment.

A lender or borrower who seeks to extricate itself from a loan commitment due to a change in market conditions, or other circumstances, during the commitment period engages in a form of transactional misbehavior. More commonly described as "opportunistic behavior," transactional misbehavior may be subtle in character, easily masked as legitimate conduct, and inherently difficult to detect. Defined as seeking to modify the dynamics of a deal after the deal has been struck, transactional misbehavior is predictable when real estate transactions are properly understood in their market context. *Penthouse* exposes the unacceptable risk a lawyer faces in assisting a client engaged in transactional misbehavior: The lawyer presents a tempting target for civil liability to vengeful adversaries whenever a business transaction falls apart.

Many if not most lawyers feel free to give advice and recommend conduct which may facilitate breach of contract, secure in the knowledge that professional privilege shields lawyers from liability while acting within the scope of the attorney-client relationship. According to legal ethics Professor Stephen Pepper, "it would probably be malpractice to fail to give it when relevant to the client's situation or to advise that breach of contract is prohibited by law."[23] Pepper draws an ethical distinction between legal advice which is likely to lead to conduct prohibited by law, as opposed to advice that is likely to lead to conduct to which the law only attaches a cost or penalty. Similarly, the Restatement (Third) of the Law Governing Lawyers provides that: "A lawyer who advises or assists a client to make or break a contract . . . is not liable to a nonclient for interference with contract or with prospective contractual relations or with a legal relationship, if the lawyer acts to advance the client's objectives without using wrongful means." § 57(3).

In fact, outside the litigation context, only a qualified privilege protects transactional lawyers from liability to nonclients. Advising and assisting in a client's breach of contract within the context of a professional representation has been held not to result in liability so long as an attorney does not act solely out of self-interest, or employ wrongful means. Decisions further qualify the scope of the privilege by making fraud, malice, bad faith, and improper motive grounds for loss of the privilege. Notwithstanding the existence of a qualified privilege, lawyers have been held liable to third parties for assisting a client to break a contract based on tortious interference with contractual relationships, aiding and abetting breach of fiduciary duty, and other theories. "Breach," wrote two George Washington legal ethics professors, "remains a choice for the client, but it is clearly a wrongful act that — *prima facie* — the morally sensitive lawyer may not encourage and may not thereafter assist."[24]

By Judge Duffy's lights, Dominion retained Gorelick to act as an instrument for its will to euchre Penthouse into breaching the commitment before Dominion would be forced to admit its inability to perform as a matter of Federal banking law. Although the Second Circuit was not persuaded, Judge Duffy's findings convinced a leading authority on the law of mortgage commitments that, after Community backed out, Dominion tried to find a way to get out of the transaction by attempting to impose conditions on the borrower in addition to those in the commitment.[25] Perhaps fearful that this could be perceived as fraudulent lawyering, Gorelick chose instead to deny knowledge of Dominion's predicament.

The appellate court acknowledged that, as the trier of fact in a non-jury case, it was the trial court's prerogative to view Gorelick's testimony as incredible. In other words, the Second Circuit conceded that Gorelick may well have lied under oath about why Dominion had retained him and what he had been instructed to do on its behalf. It is a nearly inescapable conclusion that the Second Circuit believed that the part of Gorelick's testimony that literally drove Judge Duffy to distraction was immaterial. By not remanding the case for further fact-finding, the Second Circuit in effect held that assisting in a negotiating strategy designed to scuttle a transaction, even if it could be proven, does not expose an attorney to liability for fraud.

By way of contrast with the qualified professional privilege for transactional lawyers, an absolute privilege shields litigators from civil actions brought by third parties for statements as well as conduct occurring before, during and after judicial proceedings. The common law origin of the lawyer's litigation privilege is a matter of dispute. Some authorities trace its roots to the 16th century English case of *Buckley v. Wood*, 76 Eng. Rep. 888, 889 (K.B. 1591) (holding attorney immune from suit for defamation for filing a document with the court describing the plaintiff as "a maintainer of pirates and murderers" even if the characterization was false). Arising initially from cases protecting against suit for defamation, the litigation privilege has been expanded to include a broad variety of torts, including intentional infliction of emotional distress, invasion of privacy, malicious prosecution, abuse of process, and statutory violations. Modern cases extend the litigation privilege beyond tort claims to encompass causes of action for breach of contract and breach of fiduciary duty, and beyond the litigation context to include administrative and alternative dispute resolution settings.

Created by common law in most states, the litigation privilege may be expanded by judicial decision. The privilege derives from common law in 42 states, and is codified by statute in six others. Georgia and Louisiana recognize a more qualified immunity by statute. *Penthouse* may be read to extend the lawyer's litigation privilege to protect an attorney acting in the scope of professional representation from civil liability for advising and assisting a client engaged in transactional misbehavior. An attorney acting in a legitimate effort to advance the interests of a client deserves to be protected against civil claims arising from zealous representation.

The rationales for the litigation privilege support expansion of its scope to include transactional practice. Litigators, by virtue of their "hired gun" or mercenary role, may be more frequent targets of revenge-seeking lawsuits by their clients' adversaries. The emphasis placed on winning in the adversarial system pressures litigators to engage in more zealous, and perhaps questionable, forms of advocacy with the potential for harming nonclients and instilling a desire for revenge. However, high-stakes business negotiation is adversarial and often combative. Office practitioners deserve no less protection than litigators against retaliatory legal actions by disgruntled nonclients when a business deal ends badly. Like their litigator counterparts, transactional lawyers do not typically make sympathetic defendants, and will be tempted to settle to avoid the adverse reputational consequences of a trial.

The administration of justice can best be achieved if contracting parties as well as litigants have full access to legal advice and assistance. The Missouri Court of Appeals articulated the rationale for protecting zealous advocacy:

> The rationale for the privilege granted to an attorney representing a client is the attorney's fiduciary duty to the client, and the public policy that attorneys be able to discharge that duty by freely using those procedures that are necessary to competently represent their clients unfettered by fear of personal liability. *Macke Laundry Serv. Ltd. v. Jetz Serv. Co.*, 931 S.W.2d 166, 177 (Mo. Ct. App. W.D. 1996).

Regardless of practice area, a lawyer should not be discouraged from representing clients with appropriate vigor.

Recasting the litigation privilege as a broader professional privilege would represent an important step toward achieving the goal of a unified code of professional responsibility. Treating attorneys engaged in the office practice of law differently from litigators perpetuates a basic misconception of the importance of the role played by transactional lawyers in shaping the law, and leads to inconsistency in sanctioning comparable acts of misconduct. Law professor Daniel Bogart argues:

> Transactional lawyers — not just litigators, legislators, and judges — make law. To some, this may seem a novel thought. The regimen of law school study, and the manner in which the law, courtrooms, lawyers, and judges are portrayed in the media, sometimes distort our view of how "the law" is created, renewed, and destroyed. Even lawyers are subject to these misperceptions. Lawyers, too, often envision the law as resulting solely from enactments of legislatures, or from courtroom battles where two or more sides argue their positions and a judge renders an opinion.
>
> Those of us who have practiced "telephone law" know the fallacy of this view, however. We also "make" law. We make law when we convince our opponents to concede a point where the case law underlying the negotiation is unclear and unresolved. And when enough similarly situated attorneys arguing on behalf of their clients about a contractual provision convince some adequate number of opponents, also similarly situated, that the "law" is on their side, at some point negotiations cease and custom or practice takes over. This transactional law is conveyed in its unique way, across jurisdictional boundaries, as one lawyer incorporates the innovation of another in his or her own contracts and documents.[26]

It may be argued that there should be no absolute professional privilege because of the lack of effective means of control by a tribunal over the transactional lawyer's conduct. It is true that a range of disciplinary measures can be imposed within the litigation context pursuant to the rules of civil procedure, and the court's inherent contempt power.

Protection against civil liability does not mean immunity from consequence and punishment for misconduct by transactional lawyers. Codes of professional responsibility limit how far a lawyer may go in zealously promoting a client's business objectives. Gorelick's conduct implicated multiple rules of professional responsibility. First, his committing Penthouse to pay a $150,000 bonus fee without Dominion's authorization violated Model Rule of Professional Conduct ("MRPC") 1.5(b) (any changes in the basis or rate of the fee shall be communicated to the client), and MRPC 1.8(f) (prohibiting a lawyer from accepting compensation from one other than the client without the client's consent).

Second, his belittling opposing counsel by describing his draft loan documents as "idiotic" violated MRPC 4.4(a) (prohibiting the use of means that have no substantial purpose other than to embarrass), and MRPC 1.3 cmt. [1] ("The lawyer's duty to act with reasonable diligence does not require the use of offensive tactics or preclude the treating of all persons involved in the legal process with courtesy and respect.") Third, Gorelick's insisting on redrafting loan documents yet failing to do so within a reasonable period of time violated MRPC 1.3 (requiring that a lawyer act with reasonable diligence and promptness). Finally, his insisting that Penthouse supply extensive information not essential to close or required by the commitment violated MRPC 4.4(a) (prohibiting the use of means that have no substantial purpose other than to delay or burden).

Disciplinary proceedings, which evaluate an attorney's conduct in light of the relevant jurisdiction's code of professional responsibility, subject transactional attorneys to potential loss of livelihood in the form of temporary or permanent license revocation, and are relevant subjects of inquiry in any subsequent malpractice litigation. Thanks to the Internet, even a public censure or reprimand will permanently tarnish the sterling reputation which is an attorney's stock-in-trade.

A disciplinary proceeding involving legal ethics expert David T. Austern's illustrates the consequences of assisting a client in transactional misbehavior. A highly respected real estate lawyer, Austern wrote an ethics column for the Association of Trial Lawyers of America. Following his public censure for assisting a client in perpetrating a fraud, the ethics course he had taught for 19 years as an adjunct at Georgetown University Law School was delisted. Interestingly, the D.C. Court of Appeals held that Austern's assisting a client in perpetrating a fraud while serving as escrow agent was comparatively less serious than a litigator's misrepresentation of facts to a court. *In re Austern*, 524 A.2d 680, 683 (D.C. 1987).

VI. Conclusion

"Every lawsuit is a potential drama: a story of conflict, often with victims and villains, leading to justice done or denied."[27] It was with a sense of drama that Arthur Liman, who successfully argued the appeal in *Penthouse*, proclaimed that a contrary result "would have had a chilling effect on the whole financial system of the United States." At the very minimum, the trial court judgment left unreversed would have rendered yet another financial institution insolvent in a time of crisis. The unacceptable end result would have been a Penthouse Hotel and Casino on the Boardwalk in Atlantic City constructed with the benefit of public financing at taxpayers' expense.

The Second Circuit's decision in *Penthouse* was highhanded and outcome-driven, which is not to say that the result was wrong given the historical moment in which the case was decided. Commercial real estate development has always involved a high level of market risk. Beginning in the early 1980s, lenders faced an additional risk category arising from novel and expansive theories of lender liability. It would take the S&L debacle in the late 1980s to trigger an increased concern for the health of the nation's lending institutions. *Penthouse* presented the Federal courts with a timely and high-profile case to signal the swinging of the pendulum back against lender liability claims.

With remarkable prescience, Guccione's chief financial officer told The Washington Post in April 1982 that Guccione's obsessive quest to build a Las Vegas-style casino on Atlantic City boardwalk could well be his downfall. The project ultimately cost more than $200 million, consisting mostly of attorneys fees and interest. Coinciding with a precipitous decline in circulation for sexually explicit print media, his gamble on Atlantic City was a major factor that led to Guccione's loss of control of Penthouse. *Penthouse* reported a 33% decline in circulation from 1997 to 2001. Desperate to raise cash, Guccione was forced to incur junk bond financing. Penthouse posted a $10 million loss in 2001 and was sold to creditors in 2003. Guccione resigned as chairman in 2004. He died of cancer two months before his 80th birthday in 2010.

Penthouse sold its property on the Boardwalk to Donald Trump in 1993 for $44 million. Trump demolished the steel skeleton of Penthouse's unfinished casino, releasing Vera Coking's home (described in Part III of this chapter) following a decade-long encagement. He integrated a portion of the former Penthouse property into his adjoining Trump Plaza Hotel and Casino. After negotiations to purchase the Coking parcel failed, Trump tried unsuccessfully to have Atlantic City acquire title by exercise of eminent domain. A New Jersey court held that the city's vague and open-ended agreement with Trump for the use of the property as a parking lot for limousines of the casino's high rollers "for a reasonable period of time," without any constraints on its ultimate use, did not satisfy the public use requirement of the Fifth Amendment. *Casino Redevelopment Authority v. Banin*, 727 A.2d 102 (N.J. Super. 1998). The Coking property was sold to billionaire Carl Icahn for $583,000 in 2014. Penthouse opened a casino in Dublin in May 2012.

Judge Duffy went on to distinguish himself by presiding ably over the high-profile criminal trial of the four principal perpetrators of the 1993 World Trade Center bombing. The Second Circuit commented: "Judge Duffy carefully, impartially, and commendably conducted the two lengthy and extraordinarily complex trials from which these appeals were taken. The fairness of the proceedings over which he presided is beyond doubt." *United States v. Yousef*, 327 F.3d 56, 173 (2d Cir. 2003). He was selected to act as the mediator in the Enron shareholder and bankruptcy proceedings. Judge Duffy's frustration with lawyers who did not satisfy his standards for professionalism would continue to draw criticism from the Second Circuit. Judge Duffy was sharply rebuked in 1996 for making disparaging and prejudicial comments directed at attorneys in two separate cases, once referring to defense counsel as a "junkyard dog." *Rivas v. Brattesani*, 94 F.3d 802, 805 n. 1 (2d Cir. 1996); *Santa Maria v. Metro-North Commuter Railroad*, 81 F.3d 265, 275 (2d Cir. 1996). He has been described as "one of the most often reversed judges in the Second Circuit."[28] Judge Duffy assumed senior status in 1998.

Even with the reversal in *Penthouse*, it would only be a matter of time before Dominion joined the long roster of failed S&Ls. Citing negative publicity from the *Penthouse* case, Roanoke-based Dominion Bankshares Corporation sued Dominion for causing confusion among its customers and damage to its reputation. By way of settlement, Dominion agreed in 1989 to change its name to Trustbank Federal Savings Bank. Trustbank was declared insolvent and placed in conservatorship with the RTC on January 25, 1991, ending Walde's tenure as chairman. The RTC tried unsuccessfully to recover $20 million in damages from Walde, blaming him for Trustbank's failure and accusing him of gross negligence and breach of fiduciary duty. *RTC v. Walde*, 856 F. Supp. 281 (E.D.VA. 1994) (suit dismissed as being barred by statute of limitations). The RTC also accused Walde of fraudulently shifting ownership of three homes worth $5 million to his wife, and hiding millions of dollars in other assets. Queen City changed its name to First Atlantic Savings & Loan Association in 1986. It was declared insolvent and taken over by the RTC in 1990.

The trial court decision in *Penthouse* left the Melrod firm suspended in a state of limbo pending the outcome of the appellate process.

> For nearly two years, from August 1987 to August 1989, the judgment hung over the firm like a Damoclean sword. If the full judgment were ever upheld, there was no way the firm could survive. And that, in turn, made it hard for the firm's lawyers to drum up business.[29]

The firm ultimately dissolved in 1993, sharing the fate of so many members of its clients' industry.

At its 35th anniversary, *Penthouse* is regarded as a capstone decision in land finance law, dramatizing the potential liability a lawyer incurs for zealous advocacy in promoting a client's strategic business objectives. A lawyer's conduct on behalf of a client engaged in transactional misbehavior is governed by the code of professional responsibility. An attorney acting within the scope of client representation should not be exposed to claims by vengeful adversaries. The litigation privilege should be expanded to shield transactional lawyers from civil liability for practicing the art of breaking the deal.

VII

Tools of Ignorance: An Appraisal of Deficiency Judgments

I. Introduction

The national pastime, perhaps more than any other sport, has a rich and colorful language. Likewise, cases arising out of the baseball context tend to inspire colorful rhetorical flourishes. Justice Blackmun described baseball as a "fine sport and profession, which brings surcease from daily travail and an escape from the ordinary to most inhabitants of this land." *Flood v. Kuhn*, 407 U.S. 258, 266–67 (1972). The Supreme Court of Missouri waxed poetic about "the joy that comes with being close enough to the Great American Pastime to smell the new-mown grass, to hear the crack of 42 inches of solid ash meeting a 95-mph fastball, or to watch a diving third baseman turn a heart-rending triple into a soul-soaring double-play." *Coomer v. Kan. City Royals Baseball Corp.*, 437 S.W.3d 184, 188 (Mo. 2014) (en banc).

Baseball fans of a certain age will remember when announcers and color commentators used the phrase "tools of ignorance" to describe the catcher's face mask, oversize mitt, chest protector, shin guards, and other padding and bumpering. The thought was that no sensible athlete would choose a position that required wearing an extra 10 pounds of equipment and sitting in a crouch for nine innings during the dog days of summer. It was also a reminder that, by the premature end of his playing career, the typical major league catcher had broken most of the bones in both hands at least once, and suffered post-concussion syndrome from foul balls and flying bats ricocheting off his mask, and collisions with base runners determined to reach home plate ahead of his tag. When it became apparent that the catcher's position produces a disproportionate number of major league managers, the phrase fell into desuetude.

The roster of former catchers who became Major League Baseball managers includes Yogi Berra (Yankees and Mets), Bruce Bochy (Giants), Mike Scioscia (Angels), Jeff Torberg (multiple teams), and Joe Torre (Cardinals and Yankees). In the 1901–1981 time period, among managers who were former players, ex-catchers comprised a larger percentage (21.6%) than any other position. Legendary play-by-play announcer Joe Garagiola and color commentator Tim McCarver were former catchers. As the only position player who can see the entire field, the catcher functions as an unofficial on-field member of the coaching staff, making decisions on every play. "It is a thinking man's position," according to one former catcher turned television analyst.[1] "The brain of a catcher is like a hamster running on a wheel: It's going all the time."[2]

Mike Matheny, four-time Gold Glove-winning catcher and manager of the St. Louis Cardinals and Kansas City Royals, is the most recent example of this phenomenon. Matheny had earned a career salary of more than $18.5 million as a player with the Cardinals in the early 2000s. He built a 10,000 square foot, 17-room house on 11 acres in the St. Louis suburb of Wildwood, containing an indoor batting cage, four-car garage, five fireplaces, home theater, a pool with a water slide, a private lake with a floating island golf green, and a treehouse wired for electricity. A scoreboard next to a baseball diamond on the property bears the name "Field of Dreamers."

But by 2010 the Mathenys had been evicted from their home and were sharing his in-laws' 2,500 square foot house in Chesterfield. Matheny was unable even to take along keepsakes from his playing career.[3] By the time he succeeded Tony LaRussa as the Cardinals' manager in 2012, Matheny had lost his personal fortune to a deficiency judgment as a result of the 2008 financial crash. He had been held personally liable for a $4.2 million deficiency judgment following a mortgage foreclosure of commercial property he was unable to develop or market during the Great Recession. Matheny's failure to succeed in real estate was the proximate cause of his return to major league baseball as a manager. "I wouldn't be a manager now," Matheny told the St. Louis Post-

Dispatch in 2013, "if he hadn't lost it all on three lots in the Chesterfield Valley."[4]

A deficiency judgment is a judgment rendered in favor of a creditor for the difference between the unpaid balance of a debt secured by a mortgage and, under the traditional common law approach, the amount paid by the high bidder at a public sale of the mortgaged property conducted for the satisfaction of that debt. After obtaining a deficiency judgment, the lender is in a position as an unsecured creditor to levy against its debtor's other assets to satisfy that personal judgment. A deficiency judgment is obtained as part of the original proceeding following judicial foreclosure. Where foreclosure is by power-of-sale, however, the mortgagee obtains a deficiency judgment by filing a separate lawsuit against the mortgagor.

"Every lawsuit is a potential drama: a story of conflict, often with victims and villains, leading to justice done or denied."[5] Commenting on the value of narrative in legal scholarship, law professor Jean Love argued that students learn from narratives in ways they cannot learn from objective analyses and traditional scholarly presentations.

> Stories and counterstories, to be effective, must be or must appear to be noncoercive. They invite the reader to suspend judgment, listen for their point or message, and then decide what measure of truth they contain. . . . [T]hey offer a respite from the linear, coercive discourse that characterizes much legal writing.[6]

Besides being a good story, Matheny's is a haunting and cautionary tale for those who would seek to parlay success in an unrelated field into a second career in real estate development. It will be painfully familiar to the transactional practice attorneys who represent clients engaged in one of the riskiest of businesses.

A legacy project is a capstone to a successful career in an unrelated field. Penthouse Magazine publisher Robert Guccione is an example of this phenomenon. In chapter VI we saw how Guccione lost control of his company as a consequence of his obsessive quest to build a casino-hotel on the Boardwalk in Atlantic City. The story of Michael J. Fuchs provides another example. The founder and former chairman of the board of Home Box Office invested nearly $100 million of his own money, and borrowed an additional $70 million from a syndicate of lenders, including the Bank of Hawaii, to develop 65 acres of coastal land in Hawaii for luxury housing including amenities consisting of a 5.5 acre park with freshwater pond, pools, hula mound, jogging trail, and courts for basketball, tennis and sand volleyball. Fuchs was only able to sell 14 of the 59-lot subdivision before the Hawaii real estate market collapsed in 2007. Fuchs defaulted on the loan in 2008. The lender initiated foreclosure proceedings in 2009 which resulted in a $21.6 million deficiency, for which Fuchs was held personally liable. Fuchs subsequently filed a class action suit challenging the constitutionality of the arithmetical method for calculating deficiency judgments as a violation of due process. The court granted the lender's motion to dismiss the complaint with prejudice on procedural grounds. *Agbannaoag v. Honorable Judges of Circuit Court*, Civ. No. 13-00205 BMK, 2013 BL 253342 (D. Haw. Sep. 20, 2013), *rehearing denied,* 2013 BL 311543 (Nov. 8, 2013).

Commercial real estate development is accomplished through the use of other people's money, typically by borrowing from an institutional lender. By entering into a mortgage transaction, a property owner incurs a dual risk — the risk of loss of title to the property through foreclosure, and the risk of personal liability for the deficiency in the event the property sells at foreclosure for less than the remaining balance of the debt. A commercial borrower may be able to protect against this latter risk by negotiating for a non-recourse mortgage, whereby the borrower is exculpated from personal liability, although this is generally available only for post-construction loans secured by improved property that is already under lease.

Deficiency judgments have long been recognized as the greatest obstacle to devising a mortgage foreclosure process that accommodates the legitimate interests of lenders and borrowers, along with the public interest in judicial efficiency and access to affordable credit. Sadly, but predictably, it takes a severe economic downturn like the Great Recession to focus attention to the problem of calculating deficiency judgments.

Deficiency judgments were a frequent consequence of foreclosures in the period following the Great Depression of the 1930s, when fully half of home mortgages went into default. Foreclosing mortgagees made nominal bids at auction sales at which there were few buyers at any price, acquired their borrowers' property, and claimed deficiency judgments for virtually the full amount of the debt. The mortgagee's presence at the sale tended to discourage other bidders who would know that the mortgagee was unlikely to permit the collateral to be sold to bargain hunters. Other bidders were thus discouraged from making any bid at all.

Contemporary mortgage lenders seldom pursue deficiency judgments for the reason that they are unprofitable. Most borrowers in foreclosure have very few financial resources. According to a recent federal government study, the recovery rate on deficiency judgments was one-fifth of 1%.[7] Deficiency judgments are generally pursued only against investors, repeat defaulters and non-hardship cases. Lenders recently have become more aggressive in pursuing deficiency judgments against so-called "strategic defaulters" (*i.e.*, borrowers who have the financial ability but elect not to pay). A rarity since the Great Depression, deficiency judgments returned with a vengeance to the dismay of investors like Matheny who borrowed to finance land development during the period before the bubble in property values, inflated by subprime mortgages, burst so spectacularly and unexpectedly in 2008.

The Great Recession began in December 2007 with the bursting of the housing bubble and subsequent mortgage market meltdown. Securities backed by subprime mortgages (for example, mortgages based upon fraudulent appraisals and approved without any documentation of the borrower's income) led to both the housing boom and its collapse. "Due to securitization, investor appetite for mortgage backed securities (MBS) and the tendency of rating agencies to assign investment-grade ratings to MBS, loans with a high risk of default could be originated, packaged and the risk readily transferred to others."[8] In an effort to minimize their risk to subprime mortgage lenders, these mortgages had been packaged and sold to mutual funds, pension plans, and other investors. When the housing price bubble burst in 2008, mortgage-backed securities plunged in value triggering a financial crisis that pushed the economy into the worst recession since the 1930s. A worldwide tightening of credit paralyzed the housing and construction markets. The unemployment rate spiked to 10% in October 2009, its highest level in 30 years. Venerable financial institutions like Bear Stearns and Lehman Brothers failed. Municipal and state government budgets dependent upon property tax revenues were squeezed.

As used in the title of this chapter, the phrase "tools of ignorance" is intended as a metaphorical critique of existing methods for calculating the size of deficiency judgments. Mike Matheny's story provides a backdrop for examining the method by which deficiency judgments are calculated. Under traditional common law, a deficiency judgment is derived mechanically by subtracting the price for which the property sold at foreclosure, less the expenses of sale (including attorney's and trustee's fees, expenditures for the protection of the security, publication and court costs), from the outstanding mortgage indebtedness. No consideration is given to evidence of higher property valuations. Nor does the borrower receive credit for a higher purchase price realized at a subsequent sale by the foreclosing mortgagee or its affiliate. The net foreclosure sale price conclusively determines the extent to which the value of the property is below the outstanding debt.

In theory, through the application of competitive market forces, the property's fair market value will be realized by foreclosure, any equity in the property above the outstanding mortgage debt will be returned to the mortgagor, and, in the event the sale proceeds are insufficient to satisfy the debt, the sale price is used to establish the mortgagor's deficit. In practice, the dynamics of the open cry auction format penalizes borrowers by discouraging competitive bidding. Real estate does not trade freely in an auction market even under the best of circumstances. Foreclosure sales are not well attended. They are advertised in the classified columns of legal newspapers with limited circulation. The mortgagee is frequently not only the winning bidder but also the only bidder attending the sale. The foreclosing mortgagee enjoys inherent advantages. It bids by way of a credit against the mortgage debt while other bidders are required to pay cash or its equivalent. And most real estate buyers are unaccustomed to all-cash purchases. The mortgagee has an informational advantage over third-party purchasers having thoroughly evaluated the property as part of the loan underwriting process. A third-party purchaser must commit resources to due diligence without knowing its chances of being the high bidder. Potential bidders may find it difficult to inspect the premises prior to sale. Mortgagors who are about to lose their property through foreclosure understandably are reluctant to cooperate. As the party with the most to gain from increasing the purchase price, such behavior is self-destructive. But borrowers facing foreclosure may not be thinking clearly enough to act in their economic best interest. An auction sale is particularly ineffective during the periods of economic depression and collapsed real estate values in which large numbers of foreclosures occur. As a result, the lender, behaving opportunistically, will be the high bidder at an artificially low price in the vast majority of foreclosure sales.

Courts in states that follow traditional common law grant exceptions only in cases where the mortgagor can prove that the foreclosure process was defective, or that the sale price was unconscionable or so inadequate as to raise an inference of fraud or unfair dealing. Illinois law, for example, provides exceptions only in the following circumstances: (1) proper notice was not given; (2) the terms of the sale were unconscionable; (3) the sale was conducted fraudulently; or (4) justice was otherwise not done. *Resolution Trust Corp. v. Holtzman*, 618 N.E.2d 418 (Ill. App. Ct. 1993). Missouri requires a sales price that both raises an inference of fraud and shocks the conscience. *In re Russell*, 2013 WL 1868346 (Bankr. W.D. Mo. May 3, 2013). Applying this standard, Missouri courts have refused to set aside sales that resulted in prices that were only 20% to 30% of fair market value. *First Bank v. Fischer & Frichtel, Inc.*, 364 S.W. 3d 216, 217 (Mo. banc 2012) (refusing to modify a sales price that was "barely more than 50% of the fair market" because the "lender gave cogent reasons for its lower bid due to the depressed real estate market and the bulk nature of the sale"). A Louisiana court held that "[D]efendant's sole argument is that he is entitled to an extra credit . . . representing the gain realized by plaintiff from the sale of the property to a third party after the sheriff's sale. The law simply does not provide such a remedy for defendant." *Capital One, N. Am. v. Nicoll*, 113 So. 3d 1158, 1161–62 (La. Ct. App. 2013). In one rare instance, however, a Missouri court refused to award a $6,000 deficiency judgment to a lender who bid $21,000 after having contracted to immediately resell foreclosed property for $29,000. *Reg'l Inv. Co. v. Willis*, 572 S.W.2d 191, 193 (Mo. Ct. App. 1978).

Some commentators propose "[t]here is no reason to distinguish between profits realized on a resale and a surplus produced at a foreclosure sale."[9] But this arithmetical method for calculating deficiency judgments has come under attack by judges and commentators as unjust and overdue for reform. Even in a stable market, a forced sale normally will not yield a price that reflects the intrinsic value of property if it were marketed by an owner not under distress. The United States Supreme Court has observed the price-suppressing tendency of the forced sale of property at foreclosure. "No one would pay as much to own such property as he would pay to own real estate that could be sold at leisure and pursuant to normal marketing techniques." *BFP v. Resolution Trust Corp.*, 511 U.S. 531, 539 (1994). During severe economic downturns, mortgaged property is sold "under the hammer" at substantially depressed prices.

In the wake of the Depression, states enacted remedial legislation to prevent perceived lending abuses, and to moderate the economic dislocation caused by declining property values. Statutes circumscribing the ability of lenders to obtain deficiency judgments benefit some defaulting mortgagors, but not without a tradeoff: The unintended consequences of Depression-era measures impose costs on a larger pool of borrowers by increasing the expense and reducing the supply of financing for land acquisition and development. One commentator argued that "anti-deficiency legislation inappropriately shifts the risk of market fluctuations from the owner to the lender, who must absorb losses but forgo gains in the value of the property. Efficiency and fairness dictate that the fluctuation of value must remain with the borrower as owner."[10]

The most common form of debtor-protection is the so-called "fair value" limitation on deficiency judgments. Embodied in statutes in many jurisdictions and the common law of others, the fair value approach is recommended by the Restatement of Property. While not prohibiting a lender from seeking a deficiency judgment, fair value limitation offers a more debtor-friendly alternative to the arithmetical method. The Restatement states in relevant part on this point:

(a) If the foreclosure price is less than the unpaid balance of the mortgage obligation, an action may be brought to recover a deficiency judgment against any person who is personally liable on the mortgage obligation in accordance with the provisions of this section.
(b) Subject to Subsections (c) and (d) of this section, the deficiency judgment is for the amount by which the mortgage obligation exceeds the foreclosure sale price.
(c) Any person against whom such a recovery is sought may request in the proceeding in which the action for a deficiency is pending a determination of the fair market value of the real estate as of the date of the foreclosure sale.
(d) If it is determined that the fair market value is greater than the foreclosure sale price, the persons against whom recovery of the deficiency is sought are entitled to an offset against the deficiency in the amount by which the fair market value . . . exceeds the sale price.

RESTATEMENT (THIRD) OF PROP.: MORTGAGES §8.4 (1997) (Foreclosures: Action For A Deficiency) (Professors Grant Nelson and Dale Whitman served as co-reporters).

This chapter argues that the Restatement approach is hollow at its core — the meaning of fair value is vague, subjective and unquantifiable. A more structured alternative to the traditional common law method of calculating deficiency judgments requires legislative action. The statutory variation proposed in this chapter is informed by experience in transactional practice and alternative dispute resolution. It would more fully involve appraisal professionals in a quasi-judicial capacity. By offering a more structured alternative to the Restatement, the proposal seeks to accommodate the interests of borrowers, lenders, and the public.

II. Toughest Man Alive

Hall-of-Fame manager Tony LaRussa, who preceded Mike Matheny as manager of the Cardinals, managed for eight seasons with the Chicago White Sox and ten seasons with the Oakland Athletics before becoming manager of the Cardinals in 1996. Although he never practiced law, LaRussa graduated from Florida State University School of Law in 1978 and was admitted to the Florida bar in 1980. "The best degree a baseball manager can get is a J.D.," LaRussa has said. "The law degree taught me how to study, how to think, and how to develop and implement a strategy."[11] LaRussa was the second lawyer to serve as Cardinals manager. Branch Rickey, who managed the Cardinals from 1919 to 1925, earned a law degree from the University of Michigan while serving as its baseball coach from 1910 to 1913.

LaRussa once described Matheny as the only one of LaRussa's players he would have allowed one of his daughters to marry. (Matheny's being already happily married at the time would not have diminished the sincerity or intended magnitude of LaRussa's compliment.) That this public expression of favoritism by their manager never seemed to offend Matheny's teammates is evidence of the way they felt about him. Matheny acquired the nicknames, "Toughest Man Alive" and "Mad Dog Matheny" for his hard-nosed style of play. After being struck square in the face by a 96 mile-per-hour fastball during an at-bat in 1998, he caught an entire 10-inning game the following day with a puffy face and a couple of missing teeth. Matheny, according to Cardinals announcer Rick Horton, "was kind of a cross between Clint Eastwood and John Wayne in a baseball uniform."[12]

Michael Scott Matheny grew up in Reynoldsburg, a suburb of Columbus, Ohio. He was drafted by the Milwaukee Brewers out of the University of Michigan, where he was co-captain of the baseball team. Matheny played three seasons for the Wolverines from 1989–92 before leaving to pursue a professional career. Vin Scully, long-time play-by-play announcer for the Los Angeles Dodgers, recounts an anecdote describing how a defecating pigeon affected Matheny's decision to attend Michigan instead of signing a professional contract with the Toronto Blue Jays directly after high school. After calling the Blue Jays on his first day of class to decline their offer, Matheny stepped out onto West Quad. Immediately, a "turkey-sized pigeon" rained down poop from the sky, completely covering Matheny's head. Because he had to shower and change, Matheny arrived 20 minutes late for class and just in time to meet what he described as a "hot blonde" named Kristin, who was on the field hockey team. Mike and Kristin Matheny have been married since 1993 and have five children. The Michigan Daily's account of the incident is available at https://www.michigandaily.com/sports/trading-blue-gold-mike-mathenys-path-and-michigan.

Matheny's coach and mentor during his final two years at Michigan was Bill Freehan, an 11-time all-star catcher for the Detroit Tigers. Freehan was hired by Michigan athletic director Bo Schembechler to replace Bud Middaugh who resigned after the 1989 season amid allegations he had diverted funds to baseball players from the sale of football game programs. It was Freehan who foresaw Matheny's potential not only as a major league catcher, but also as a manager. Freehan encouraged Matheny to take Spanish courses in order to better communicate with Latin players. "He (Freehan) called me into his office one day and said, 'If you're going to be in this game for a long time, even after your playing days, you need to change all your electives to Spanish,'" Matheny recalled.[13] Matheny returned to Ann Arbor during each of his first two off-seasons as a minor league player to complete the final 42 credits required to earn his degree in sports management and communications, with a minor in Spanish.

Matheny played for Milwaukee from 1994–1998 and for Toronto in 1999. After being released by the Brewers and Blue Jays, Matheny achieved success over the course of the next five seasons with the Cardinals. The Cardinals played in the post-season during four of his five years with the team, including the 2004 World Series. Matheny himself missed the 2000 post-season as a result of a freak accident. During the final weekend of the regular season, Matheny severed two flexor tendons and a nerve on the ring finger of his right hand upon opening a box containing a hunting knife that he received as a 30th birthday present.

Matheny was considered one of baseball's best defensive catchers. He set major league records for catchers by playing in 252 games without committing an error from August 1, 2002 to August 4, 2004, and by fielding 1,565 consecutive chances without an error in 2004. He is one of only three major league players to catch at least 100 games in a single season without committing an error. He was adept at blocking balls in the dirt and throwing out base-runners attempting to steal. He was a master of the psychology of handling pitchers. Matheny won the Rawling's Gold Glove, awarded to the best defensive player in each position, in 2000, 2003 and 2004 with the Cardinals, and in 2005 with the Giants. When it became apparent that the Cardinals were grooming Yadier Molina as his replacement, Matheny signed a three-year $10.5 million contract with the San Francisco Giants in 2005. Molina has since won nine Gold Gloves, in 2008–2015 and in 2018. Suffering from the effects of post-concussion syndrome, Matheny retired from baseball in 2007 with one year remaining on his contract.

A year after retiring as a player, Matheny agreed to coach his son's little league team, the TPX Warriors. The Warriors wear maize-and-blue uniforms, the iconic color scheme of Matheny's alma mater. During a flight from New York to St. Louis in 2009, Matheny took out his laptop and wrote from scratch a five-page, 2,556-word letter to parents of team members describing his coaching philosophy and expectations. The letter went viral after being posted online, and has become known as "The Matheny Manifesto." Matheny says it is rare that he visits a city and is not asked about the manifesto. In the letter, Matheny described a team without parental intrusion, and a distinctly faith-based emphasis on character development with 30 minutes of each practice devoted to character study. It instructs parents to watch games silently, limiting themselves to clapping, because even shouting encouragement puts too much pressure on their children. Players are instructed never to question authority figures, either coaches or umpires.

Parents were required to read and sign the letter. It concluded by noting that it "may not be the right fit" for everyone, and some parents declined to sign after reading it. Matheny makes no apology for the Christian influence, and players of all denominations are welcome on the Warriors, although "potential coaches must make a testimony of faith." Matheny has co-authored a book based on the letter, entitled *The Matheny Manifesto* that was published by Random House in 2015. He was in the Dominican Republic on a service trip with the Warriors in Fall 2011 when his cellphone rang with a call from Cardinals general manager John Mozeliak offering him the job of manager.

The winningest manager in Cardinals history, LaRussa would have been a tough act to follow for anyone. The Cardinals had won the World Series the year before Matheny succeeded him as manager in 2012. His 2,728 wins ranks third among managers in major league history behind only Connie Mack and John McGraw. (LaRussa's decision to return to baseball as manager of the Chicago White Sox at the age of 76 was almost entirely motivated, at least in part, by the likelihood of surpassing McGraw early in the 2021 season.) He was chosen manager of the year four times and won 12 division titles, six pennants and three World Series titles as manager of the Chicago White Sox, Oakland Athletics and Cardinals. He was enshrined in the National Baseball Hall of Fame as a member of the Class of 2014. Further complicating Matheny's task in succeeding the legendary LaRussa was the loss of star player Albert Pujols, who left the Cardinals to join the Los Angeles Angels following the 2011 season.

The choice of Matheny over more obvious candidates was greeted with skepticism. "During an autograph-signing . . . a woman approached to tell [Matheny], 'I thought they were crazy for hiring you, but I guess it's going OK.'"[14] Matheny himself described his hiring as a "parting-of-the-Red-Sea, walking-on-water type of miracle."[15] At the time of his selection, Matheny was the youngest manager in major league baseball. Besides some limited experience serving as a minor league instructor and adviser to the Cardinals, he had no prior full-time professional coaching experience in any capacity. The Cardinals ownership was persuaded that Matheny's presence and other intangible qualities, and his innate leadership ability derived from 13 seasons behind the plate, outweighed his lack of formal managerial experience. The Cardinals' ownership was aware of the pending litigation at the time of Matheny's selection as manager. "He was very upfront and candid about it from the start of our process," a spokesman for the Cardinals told a reporter.[16]

Matheny had been preparing for his new role by reading books about leadership and consulting with captains of industry. His study of the subject led Matheny to adopt the so-called "servant leadership" model, an organizational structure in which the pyramid is flipped upside down. Characterized by humility and loyalty, servant-leadership is a concept that suits his personality. Matheny publicly proclaims his Christian faith and its central role in his life. He is active in the Fellowship of Christian Athletes. He subscribes most autographs with a citation to the New Testament (John 3:16 or John 3:17). He credits his religious faith with influencing his business and coaching philosophy. Matheny is self-reflective and chronicles his life in a blog. Mikematheny.com. The servant leadership model is also one that Matheny finds familiar. "It struck me that I had done some of this as a leader in a catching role," Matheny has said. "My whole point of being in that uniform was to make my pitchers' job easier and to make them better."[17] Matheny was considered a master of the psychology of handling pitchers. "He knew some guys needed to be yelled at (like Matt Morris), and he knew that some guys needed to be handled differently (like Garrett Stephenson)."[18]

Matheny led the Cardinals back to the post-season in his rookie year as manager. The Cardinals lost to the San Francisco Giants in the 2012 National League Championship Series (the final playoff round before the World Series). They reached the World Series the following year, although they lost the 2013 World Series to the Boston Red Sox in six games. Matheny is one of only ten major league managers in baseball history to lead a team to the postseason in his first two seasons as manager. "He's a rock star in the heartland and revered around the game for his humble leadership qualities."[19]

Matheny had demonstrated the ability to inspire others during his playing career. When pitcher Darryl Kile, a close friend, died suddenly of heart failure during a road trip, Matheny is credited with helping teammates cope in the wake of tragedy to reach the 2002 National League Championship Series. As a coach, Matheny tries to inspire and encourage players by positive reinforcement, rather than exert control by scolding. According to Cardinals pitcher Adam Wainwright, the team played with confidence as a result of Matheny's calming influence:

> "Mike has a way with words. . . . He's an uplifter. He's an encourager. From a moment of weakness where you begin to doubt your ability or question your role on the team, then you have the guy who is putting out the starting lineup every day telling you that you have a place and that you don't have anything to worry about. All of a sudden, you're confident and get right back in a rhythm.[20]

Matheny is said to be particularly adept at handling younger players. A baseball fundamentalist, Matheny fully subscribes to his predecessor's emphasis on the importance of playing the game "the right way." However, he has been more sensitive than LaRussa to the negative perception created by over-use of the phrase, "Cardinal Way." Intended by LaRussa as short-hand for professionalism and respectfulness, the phrase was perceived by some outside the clubhouse as sanctimonious, and perhaps boastful. The Cardinals under Matheny's leadership discouraged use of the phrase, at least for purposes of public consumption.

Along with other former catchers, Matheny successfully lobbied Major League Baseball to adopt new rules that require base-runners and catchers to avoid collisions at home plate. Matheny has compared the catcher in this situation with a punt returner in football, except without the punt returner's protective equipment. "Just do a risk-reward assessment of the situation. What's the reward? The reward is, the fans come to their feet. You may get a little rise out of your team because your catcher stuck his nose in there. But what's the risk? The risk is injury to both players."[21] The rules, which went into effect in the 2014 season, leave open the possibility of collisions under certain circumstances. Matheny had advocated a stronger, less ambiguous version of the new rules. He is apologetic for waiting so long before making public his struggle with post-concussion syndrome, and feels guilty that other catchers likely suffered similar issues as a result of his not coming forward sooner.

Matheny had already begun to prepare for his second career in real estate during his time as an active player. He has described enduring grief from teammates for doing correspondence course homework on road trips. Matheny has acknowledged being thrilled by the challenge of chasing real estate deals, in which he experienced early success. He acquired 370 acres of farmland in central Illinois with former Cardinals teammates Jason Isringhausen and John Mabry. He purchased 250 acres of land in Jefferson County, Missouri with Mabry. He bought a 400-acre farm in West Virginia, his childhood home in Ohio, and an interest in a Long Island real estate project.

In September 2005 Matheny formed MPD Investments, LLC ("MPD") with former St. Louis indoor soccer players Daryl Doran, a neighbor of Matheny's, and Brett Phillips. The entity bought and quickly sold a block in the WingHaven development in St. Charles, Missouri, realizing a $2.4 million profit in six months. As Matheny described the market before 2008, "You could throw a dart at any kind of real estate and you were going to do well."[22]

The bursting of the housing bubble and subsequent mortgage market meltdown were unexpected when Matheny retired from baseball in 2007 and began his second career in real estate. Near the peak of the bubble, the chief economist for the National Association of Realtors published a book entitled, *Why the Real Estate Boom Will Not Bust — And How You Can Profit from It*. In December 2007, Nobel Prize winning economist Gary Becker wrote: "The vast majority of economists, including me, were surprised by the extent of the subprime mortgage crisis."[23] Matheny could not have picked a worse time. The greatest financial downturn since the Great Depression suddenly appeared seemingly out of nowhere in mid-September 2008 when Lehman Brothers, one of the oldest investment firms in the country, filed for Chapter 11 bankruptcy protection. Real property of all kinds experienced dramatic declines in value. A wave of foreclosures disrupted the lives of millions of borrowers, including Mike Matheny's. The years leading up to Matheny's return to baseball as a manager took turns, "threatening to bankrupt him, evicting him, challenging him, and ultimately providing an opportunity he would have rejected if not for the tribulations preceding it."[24] Following an historical digression on the history of foreclosure and deficiency judgements in Part III of this chapter, Matheny's brief career in real estate, and how it led to his return to baseball as a manager, will be the topic of Part IV.

III. An Historical Digression

The introduction of foreclosure in 17th century England was a remarkable innovation in the history of jurisprudence, and the most significant reform in the evolution of land finance law. Oliver Wendell Holmes identified the court of equity's creation of foreclosure as "one of the most splendid instances in the history of our jurisprudence."[25] It is ironic that the modern cause of action for a deficiency judgment, unknown to early English common law, was an unintended consequence of that reform. "The deficiency judgment problem resulting from the foreclosure sale of property for less than the balance due on the mortgage was a perplexing phenomenon of the drastic decline in realty prices during the period from 1929 to 1934."[26]

The Anglo-American mortgage originated as a device to circumvent the biblical prohibitions against usury. The Book of Leviticus 25:36–25:37 commands: "Do not take interest or any profit from them, but fear your God, so that they may continue to live among you. You must not lend them money at interest or sell them food at a profit." Deuteronomy 23:20–23:21 forbids charging fellow Israelites interest, and Luke 6:35 commands "lend to your enemies without expecting to get anything back." Landowners could not borrow money and pay interest in a straightforward mortgage transaction. This presented a challenge for lenders seeking to earn a profit from money-lending in a form that would not be deemed interest. Christian lenders believed that it was necessary to take possession of the land in order to collect income from rents and profits. "The pious Christian lender was forced to take possession of the property so that he could reap the rents and issues as recompense for his money lent."[27] Usury was punishable by excommunication or other censure by the ecclesiastical courts during the medieval period. "[D]uring the medieval period fear of excommunication or other censure by the ecclesiastical courts was a greater deterrent than was the civil penalty of confiscation of all of the property of the usurer . . . ." *In re Mich. Ave. Nat'l Bank*, 2 B.R. 171, 174 (Bankr. N.D. Ill. 1980). A loan transaction thus necessarily involved not only the transfer of title to the property from the borrower to the lender, but also the transfer of possession.

Jewish law did not require creditors to possess the land. Accordingly, for hundreds of years until the 13th century, borrowers found it comparatively more advantageous to transact with Jewish lenders. Their superior product became unavailable with the banishment of the Jews from England by Edward I in 1290.

By the 15th century, the law of estates and future interests had sufficiently evolved to create the "modern" mortgage in the form of a fee simple subject to condition subsequent. The property owner conveyed defeasible title to the lender, subject to the condition subsequent that would revest title in the borrower upon repayment of the debt. The word "mortgage" was an amalgam of the French word for "dead" and "gage," an Anglo-Saxon term which roughly translates as "pledge." According to a leading authority on the history of the law of property, the device was called a "mortgage" because "it is doubtful whether the [borrower] will pay . . . ; and if he doth not pay, then the land which is put in pledge upon condition for the payment of the money is taken from him forever, and so dead to him . . . . And if he doth pay the money, then the pledge is dead as to the [lender]."[28]

A creditor would lend no more than it thought the land was worth, or would be worth at the end of the term of the loan. Because the length of a typical mortgage loan was only six months, the risk that the property might decline in value was minimal. There was no personal liability on the part of the borrower if the value of the land happened to be less than the amount of the debt, nor was there any surplus payable to the borrower if the value of the land exceeded the debt.

Time was of the essence of mortgages prior to the 17th century. Payment was required to be made on one day and one day only, known as "Law Day." There was no right to prepay. To this day, the traditional view persists: unless expressly granted in an agreement, borrowers do not have the right to prepay.[29] A mortgagor who failed to repay the indebtedness during regular business hours on the appointed day for any reason forfeited all interest in the mortgaged premises to the mortgagee, a process that came to be known as strict foreclosure. Regardless of how much of the debt had been repaid, a borrower who failed to discharge the obligation in full on Law Day lost title to the entire property. These rules were strictly enforced by the courts of law.

The deficiency judgment was unknown to early foreclosure practice. Strict foreclosure meant that the mortgagee took title to the property in full satisfaction of the debt. Not until the 18th century would it become the rule that, if the value of the land was insufficient to fully compensate the lender, it might maintain an action at law for the balance as a personal obligation of the mortgagor after foreclosure. In the 18th century, the size of the deficiency was ascertained by estimate based on proof of the value of the property, usually based on reports from appraisers. *See Amory v. Fairbanks*, 3 Mass. 562, 562–63 (1793). This chapter, *infra* Part V, proposes a return to a similar model.

Forfeiture of title was repugnant to the notion of equity. By the 17th century the English Courts of Chancery began to intervene to protect borrowers against forfeitures resulting from harsh common law rules. Chancellors created exceptions in cases of accident, mistake and special hardship. Soon courts were routinely granting equitable relief, compelling mortgagees to reconvey property to mortgagors upon repayment of the principal, with interest and costs, even if Law Day had long since passed. Use of the term "equity" to describe the extent to which the fair market value of the property exceeds the amount of indebtedness secured by the property and, therefore, the net value of a borrower's ownership interest, "pays linguistic homage to the generations of chancellors who have been moved to protect debtors from overreaching moneylenders."[30]

As a consequence of the creation of the borrower's equity of redemption, a lender's title was clouded (*i.e.*, rendered unmarketable) for an indefinite period of time by the possibility that a defaulting borrower might seek and obtain relief in equity notwithstanding the terms of the mortgage. It was impossible for a lender to know with any degree of certainty when or whether it would be free to use or sell the land. Accordingly, the lender was given the right to petition for a decree of foreclosure, meaning that the chancery court would set a date certain when the borrower's equity of redemption would finally terminate if the default persisted. Lenders' inevitable response was to include a waiver of the equity of redemption as a standard provision in mortgages. The chancery courts responded to these attempts to circumvent equitable jurisdiction by creating a prohibition against contemporaneous clogging of the equity of redemption. Foreclosure thus became the only method for extinguishing the mortgagor's equity of redemption. The impact of cutting off the equity of redemption was to grant indefeasible title to the mortgaged property to the mortgagee, regardless of the value of the property in relation to the outstanding indebtedness. The only effect of foreclosure was to terminate the mortgagor's right of redemption. It did not cause a sale of the property, and it did not establish a deficiency.

The unfairness of strict foreclosure would later be mitigated by providing for open cry public auction of the mortgaged property to the highest bidder, either as a result of a judicial proceeding, or under a power-of-sale contained in the mortgage. All states allow mortgagees to file a civil action seeking judicial foreclosure. If the court finds that the mortgagor has defaulted under the terms of the loan, the court will order that the property be sold at a public foreclosure sale. If the mortgagor fails to exercise the right of redemption prior to the sale of the property, the collateral will be sold to the highest bidder at the foreclosure sale. The purchaser takes title to the property free of any liens, or other interests or encumbrances, subordinate to the foreclosed mortgage. About half the states by statute permit power-of-sale foreclosure as an alternative to judicial foreclosure if the mortgage contains a power-of-sale clause. The ability to foreclose without resorting to a judicial proceeding is comparatively more advantageous to mortgagees in terms of time, expense, and transaction costs incurred in order to comply with the formalities of judicial foreclosure.

The foreclosure sale price, net of expenses, provided the basis for an unsatisfied lender to pursue the borrower for a deficiency. The movement away from strict foreclosure and toward public sale was surely not intended to affect the debtor adversely.

> It was probably assumed that, at the time of the sale, the property would usually bring more than the mortgage. The assumption was doubtless well founded in a period of rising land values; but the technique did not afford sufficient protection to the debtor in depression times . . . . In these times, the technique of sale made bad matters worse for the debtor.[31]

Of course, foreclosures were more common during times of declining real estate values. The modern cause of action for a deficiency judgment was an unintended consequence of the reform of the foreclosure process designed to relieve debtors from the harshness of strict foreclosure.

During the Great Depression, absence of competition at foreclosure sales enabled mortgagees to behave opportunistically by bidding a nominal amount, obtaining title to the property, and then seeking a judgment for the artificially high difference between the purchase price and the remaining amount of the debt. When market conditions stabilized, lenders were able to resell foreclosed property at a profit, for which the borrower did not receive credit. Lenders realized what amounted to a windfall, because the double recovery collectively exceeded the mortgagee's debt. Borrowers suffered not only the loss of title to their property but also liability for a substantial deficiency.

Measures for the relief of debtors are the inevitable product of depression periods in which large number of foreclosures occur, eliciting the concern of voters and legislators. To counter unjust enrichment of mortgage lenders and the oppressive effect of economic conditions on borrowers, many states codified protections in the form of statutory rights of redemption, anti-deficiency statutes, and fair value legislation. Many states enacted temporary moratoria on foreclosures. These statutes were designed to give debtors an opportunity to refinance once market conditions stabilized or, at least, delay foreclosure until the economy improved with the passage of time and competitive bidding might be expected to resume. The constitutionality of moratoria statutes was upheld in *Home Building & Loan Ass'n v. Blaisdell*, 290 U.S. 398 (1934). Most of these statutes expired by their own terms or by additional legislation after the Depression ended.

Statutory rights of redemption exist in approximately three-fifths of the states. They afford the mortgagor a second opportunity to redeem, and thereby avoid the loss of title to the property, during a specified period following the foreclosure sale. Most of these statutes permit the mortgagor to remain in possession during the redemption period. The period of time during which the mortgagor can exercise its statutory right of redemption ranges from three months in Wyoming to two years after the sale in South Dakota. Allowing mortgagors to remain in possession during the redemption period eases the disruption of foreclosure, especially in states that permit power-of-sale foreclosure which may be accomplished in a matter of weeks. Statutory redemption encourages purchasers at foreclosure sales to bid up to the fair market value of the property by affording the mortgagor the opportunity to repurchase the property at the price paid by the buyer at the foreclosure sale. The statutory right of redemption, therefore, affords mortgagors some protection from an unfair price on foreclosures sales.

Anti-deficiency statutes are the most efficacious of the debtor-protection measures. In the wake of the Depression, the Commissioners on Uniform State Laws had called for the elimination of deficiency judgments entirely, believing such elimination was "urgent" and would materially benefit both mortgagors and mortgagees. Although no state forbids deficiency judgments in all cases, California's is considered the most pervasive because its protections extend to commercial borrowers.

It is also the most complex, frequently creating bewilderment among attorneys in other jurisdictions. In one case, a California neurosurgeon was held personally liable for a $4 million deficiency judgment following foreclosure of two mortgages encumbering apartment buildings in Missouri in 1989. He sued the Missouri real estate lawyer who had represented him in the loan transactions, claiming that it was legal malpractice not to inform him that Missouri law did not protect against deficiency judgments. The suit was settled after the Author testified that a Missouri real estate lawyer should be expected to warn a client about the significant differences between Missouri and California law on this subject. *Resolution Trust Corporation v. Mohammad Alul, et al.*, Cause No. 4:92CV768, *consolidated with* 4:92CV2029.

Enacted in 1933, the California statute was intended to prevent future real estate recessions from spiraling into depressions. Discussing the statute, the Supreme Court of California explained that if defaulting purchasers were burdened with large personal liability, it would aggravate any general or local economic downturn. *Cornelison v. Kornbluth*, 542 P.2d 981, 989 (Cal. 1975). The statute prohibits a deficiency judgment following any foreclosure by power-of-sale. CAL. CIV. PROC. CODE § 580(d) (West 1976). This provision is in the nature of a trade-off in return for the borrower not having a statutory right of redemption following power-of-sale foreclosure. The statute also prohibits deficiency judgments following foreclosure of any mortgage given to the vendor of property to secure the unpaid balance of the purchase price. § 580(b). The rationale for this provision is to protect against sellers' natural tendency to overvalue real property for which there is no independent check when the vendor is also the lender. This rationale has been criticized as highly dubious. The statute prohibits deficiency judgments following foreclosure of a purchase-money mortgage on a dwelling containing not more than four families, regardless of the method of foreclosure and the identity of the mortgagee. § 580(b).

Although the scope of protection is less extensive and more ambiguous than California, several other states similarly prohibit lenders from pursuing borrowers for deficiency judgments under certain circumstances when foreclosure yields proceeds of sale that are insufficient to cover the amount of the debt.

Fair value legislation, while not prohibiting lenders from seeking deficiency judgments, is a significant substantive limitation on their size. New York's fair value statute was the first of its kind. It was upheld by the United States Supreme Court as enforceable against a constitutional challenge that it violated the contract clause. The Court held that a lender's contractual rights were not impaired by calculation of a deficiency based upon a lower court finding that the fair value of mortgaged property was $25,318, notwithstanding that the lender had acquired the property at a foreclosure sale for $7,500. *Honeyman v. Jacobs*, 306 U.S. 539 (1939).

Fair value statutes exist in twenty-nine states in various forms,[32] although it is not always possible to identify and classify a statute with complete confidence. For example, Florida's deficiency statute has been characterized as "unique and ambiguous."[33] The statute appears to give trial courts the flexibility to choose between the foreclosure sale price and the market value of the foreclosed real estate in a deficiency judgment proceeding. The statute reads: "[T]he amount bid at the sale may be considered by the court as one of the factors in determining a deficiency under the usual equitable principles." FLA. STAT. ANN. §45.031(8).

These statutes create what is considered to be a fairer method than the traditional common law mechanism for assessing the debtor's personal liability upon default. They typically limit the deficiency to the difference between the remaining mortgage debt and the fair market value of the collateral at the time of foreclosure, or the price paid by the foreclosure sale purchaser, whichever is greater. Depending on the statute, a trial court or a jury is responsible for determining fair value. In New York, fair value is a question of law, and in Minnesota, it is a question of fact. *Compare* N.Y. REAL PROP. ACTS. LAW § 1371(2) (McKinney 2011) *with* MINN. STAT. ANN. § 582.30 (West 2012). Fair value statutes reflect the position embodied in the Restatement of Property. RESTATEMENT (THIRD) OF PROP.: MORTGAGES § 8.4 cmt. a (1997).

Except for West Virginia in 2014 and Hawaii coincident with the pandemic in 2000, no state court has followed the Restatement recommendation to adopt the fair value approach through exercise of its equity jurisdiction. In fact, when the Missouri Supreme Court declined to a adopt a fair value approach, it pointed out that states do not adopt the fair value approach to deficiency judgments under their equity jurisdictions. Some might characterize the court's reasoning as "chicken and egg logic." The few state court decisions applying the fair value approach based on common law in the absence of a statute are states which have traditionally done so. *See, e.g.*, *Wansley v. First Nat'l Bank of Vicksburg,* 566 So. 2d 1218, 1225 (Miss. 1990) (emphasizing that every aspect of a sale must be commercially reasonable and fair); *First NH Mortg. Corp. v. Greene*, 653 A.2d 1076, 1079 (N.H. 1995) (reprimanding the mortgage company for failing to obtain a fair price); *Licursi v. Sweeney*, 594 A.2d 396, 401 (Vt. 1991) (preventing a plaintiff creditor from becoming unjustly enriched while relying on the common law).

Other courts have declined invitations to adopt the fair value approach. *See Illini Fed. Sav. & Loan Ass'n v. Doering*, 516 N.E.2d 609, 612 (Ill. App. Ct. 1987) ("Our legislature has included no such minimum price provision in the statute governing foreclosure sales, and we find no basis for reading such a provision into the statute."); *R.I. Depositors' Econ. Prot. Corp. v. Macomber*, 658 A.2d 511, 511 (R.I. 1995) ("In a series of cases this court has determined that the amount realized at a mortgagee's sale, even when bid at less than the appraised value would not be disturbed in the absence of fraud or impropriety in connection with the sale."). After first adopting the judicial fair market value standard, a subsequent decision by the Montana Supreme Court appears to require some individualized showing of unfairness before allowing testimony that the property value exceeds the foreclosure price. *See FSLIC v. Hamilton*, 786 P.2d 1190, 1193 (Mont. 1990) (pointing out the lack of facts demonstrating the price was not fair), *overruling Trs. of the Wash.-Idaho-Mont.-Carpenters-Emp'rs Ret. Trust Fund v. Galleria P'ship*, 780 P.2d 608, 619 (Mont. 1989) (requiring a fairness analysis of the price prior to approving a sale).

The effect on Mike Matheny's case of the Missouri Supreme Court's decision to forgo adoption of the fair value approach will be examined in Part IV of this chapter.

IV. Chesterfield of Dreams Meets The Anna Karenina Principle

Commercial real estate developers are obsessive visionaries and perpetual optimists. While others who gaze upon vacant Blackacre see nothing more than a farm field (except, of course, for Property professors who see a bundle of sticks), a real estate developer pictures a new housing community. A developer sees an underutilized city block and imagines a mixed-use office/retail complex. The psyche and high risk high reward lifestyle of a real estate investor were the subject of Steven Millhauser's novel *Martin Dressler: The Tale Of An American Dreamer*, which won the Pulitzer Prize for Fiction in 1997.

The very qualities essential to success in commercial real estate — ambition and audacity — are a lethal admixture during a severe economic downturn. Even a developer with the best track record for performance is at the mercy of changes in market conditions which occur in the interval between land acquisition and completion of construction. Increased citizen participation in the governmental approval process, and the growing popularity of the temporary moratorium on issuance of development permits, make it virtually impossible for even the most experienced real estate developers to predict the time and economic climate their finished product will face when it comes on the market. Besides marketplace risk, real estate development involves a myriad of temporal and transactional risks, any one of which will likely result in failure. Because of the infinite variety of unanticipated events that can and will occur, real estate development is the prototypical example of the Anna Karenina principle.

This principle describes an endeavor in which a deficit in any one of a number of factors dooms it to failure. Consequently, a successful endeavor (subject to this principle) is one where every possible deficiency has been avoided. The name of the principle derives from the opening sentence of Leo Tolstoy's 1878 masterpiece: "Happy families are all alike; every unhappy family is unhappy in its own way." Scholars and authors have extended this idea beyond families to other endeavors in which success requires avoiding many separate possible causes of failure. The principle explains why there was not a Triple Crown winner between 1978 and 2015, which we saw in chapter I.

In July 2006 Daryl Doran left MPD to start a gym. Following Doran's departure, MPD consisted of two members: Mikris Investments, LLC, an entity owned by Michael and Kristin Matheny in equal shares; and Monarch Holdings, LLC, owned by Brett Phillips and his wife. On January 4, 2007, the remaining members, Matheny and Brett Phillips, obtained a line-of-credit loan from The Business Bank of St. Louis to market, and perhaps ultimately develop, 11 acres of vacant land situated in Chesterfield, a densely populated and affluent second-ring suburb approximately 25 miles west of St. Louis. Located near the confluence of the Missouri and Mississippi Rivers, Chesterfield has become a major commercial center since the Great Flood of 1993. Once known as Gumbo Flats, the 4,000-acre Chesterfield Valley had not flooded since 1935 until the surging Missouri River breached the Monarch-Chesterfield Levee in Summer 1993, damaging 70,000 buildings and causing $12 billion in property damages. Fifty deaths were attributable to the flood. The levee that protects Chesterfield Valley has since been fortified to withstand a 500-year flood. This infrastructure improvement has been the catalyst for the region's becoming a site for office buildings and retail development on what was once submerged farmland.

The loan to Matheny and Phillips was evidenced by a promissory note in the principal sum of $6.3 million and secured by a deed of trust. On June 21, 2007, MPD signed a second promissory note in the principal sum of $5 million, also secured by a deed of trust, to evidence debt incurred to refinance a mortgage encumbering an adjacent parcel of improved property, known as the U.S. Turf Building, and to provide funds for tenant improvements. The first note matured on January 4, 2009, and the second on March 31, 2009.

An observation of the property discloses why it would have been irresistibly attractive to Matheny at the height of the bubble in real estate values. Although the 11-acre parcel remains undeveloped, the property enjoys a prime location accessible to, and visible from, a major interstate highway. It is proximate to two outlet malls that collectively house 120 stores and Chesterfield Commons, which is reported to be the largest strip mall in the nation. A levee fitness trail at the rear of the parcel enhances its value for retail or corporate use. There are no apparent topographical or site conditions that would prevent its development in a manner comparable to the neighboring property, assuming that the real estate market continues to strengthen and that lenders regain confidence. Despite nationwide calls by engineers and environmentalists to limit floodplain development after the '93 flood, its location has been marketed by the city as "Chesterfield of Dreams." Gazing upon the vacant field, Matheny likely would have envisioned a big-box retail store with acres of surrounding parking, or perhaps a health care facility.

Because MPD was a limited liability entity, Mike and Kristin Matheny were required to personally guarantee a portion of the debt in the total sum of $4.2 million. Brett Phillips and his wife, Kelly, also signed a personal guarantee. Initially, the principals had agreed to guarantee 50% of the debt. As part of an extension of the maturity date in June 2009, the Mathenys' guarantee was modified to provide that their liability was limited to $4.2 million, plus costs of enforcement. A personal guarantee of repayment, a material credit enhancement from the lender's perspective, is the most dreaded concession that a real estate developer can make. A guarantor assumes a compound triple risk of potential liability in the event of default by the principal obligor, consisting of liability on the guarantee, liability for the guarantor's own attorney's fees to defend against the creditor's claim, and liability for the creditor's attorney's fees in seeking to enforce the guarantee.

Once a developer accumulates net worth and a solid track record, institutional lenders are more willing to forego guarantees. Until then, a novice like Matheny is likely to be confronted with a demand for a guarantee that, if called and honored, could wipe out a lifetime of accumulated assets. In this sense, a personal guarantee is no different, and no less attractive, than investing one's own cash in the deal.

In the context of a loan secured by improved property already under lease, a personal guarantee may be relatively benign. To a certain extent, the location has already been proven. The property may already have a record of generating rental income sufficient to cover expenses. Yet personal liability in a loan transaction involving investment property is hardly risk-free. Even the most credit-worthy tenant can become bankrupt or engage in strategic default. Insurance proceeds may be inadequate to cover a catastrophic loss. The economic viability of a location may change.

The risks involved in development projects are exponentially greater. They include, but are not limited to, adverse environmental, geological or other site conditions; inability to obtain, or delay in obtaining, governmental permits; changes in zoning, land use regulations and building codes; delays due to severe weather or other acts of God; and the bankruptcy of the general contractor or a key subcontractor.

Matheny's downfall was the result of the inability to lease space as quickly as projected when the commercial real estate market plummeted. MPD spent three years in an unsuccessful attempt to market the property, with Brett Phillips leading the effort. St. John's Mercy Hospital and a flooring company, among others, expressed interest in leasing space. After they backed out as potential tenants, MPD's plans for the property seemed to unravel. From Matheny's deposition testimony, and consistent with his track record, MPD's plans for the property were ambiguous, and appeared to include either development or sale to a third party for a profit. There may not have been an intentional strategy to begin with. "'At the time of purchase, I don't think there was much of a plan,' Matheny said."[34]

On June 30, 2009 the parties agreed to a series of loan modifications by which the maturity date of the two promissory notes was extended to May 31, 2010. As part of a loan modification on June 30, 2009, the Mathenys complied with a demand by the lender to furnish additional collateral, consisting of a $1 million mortgage lien against their principal residence, and a pledge of a $1 million investment account maintained at the bank. During this period, Phillips filed for bankruptcy, and the lender's complaint against Phillips was returned unopened. A default judgement in the sum of approximately $5 million was entered against him on September 16, 2013.

Matheny made the last $16,000 monthly debt service payment on March 30, 2010. At a meeting with bank officers on May 3, 2010, Matheny informed the lender that he would make no further payments on the loan. On June 24, 2010 the lender filed suit against MPD in St. Louis County Circuit Court seeking to collect the unpaid balance, including interest, late charges and expenses. The Mathenys were named as defendants in their capacity as guarantors. The Business Bank foreclosed upon both properties by power-of-sale, and they were sold at auction at the St. Louis County Courthouse on July 12, 2010. The lender purchased the 11-acre parcel for $2.5 million and the U.S. Turf Building for $2 million for a total of $4.5 million, which it credited against the debt. As *St. Louis Post-Dispatch* journalist Jake Wagman described it, "The bank 'purchased' the land for $4.5 million, which is to say it took the property and credited the sale amount to Matheny's debt."[35] Although notice of the foreclosure sale was published in twenty-one consecutive issues of the *St. Louis Countian* in compliance with the Missouri power-of-sale foreclosure statute, there were no other bidders. As is typically the case in foreclosure sales, The Business Bank acquired title to the property in the name of an affiliated entity, Maryland Land Co., LLC. MPD Investments, LLC was formally dissolved on September 9, 2013, the eighth anniversary of its organization.

David Gamache, a loan officer for The Business Bank, testified during pre-trial discovery that the lender resold the U.S. Turf Building to Frisella Properties for $2,650,000 in November 2010, four months after acquiring title at the foreclosure sale for $2 million. Matheny received no credit for the $650,000 gross profit. Gamache estimated that the lender spent between $70,000 and $100,000 on tenant improvements before the sale to Frisella. In response to questioning by defense counsel, Gamache conceded that the contract of sale was signed a month after the foreclosure, and provided for a relatively short executory period, but denied that The Business Bank had any discussions with Frisella prior to the foreclosure. With regard to the 11-acre parcel, Gamache acknowledged that The Business Bank did not pay fair market value, which he estimated as "closer to $3 million." He said the lender discounted the purchase price by the broker's commission it would have to pay upon resale, and expenses it expected to incur during its ownership of the property.

The Matheny residence was sold in advance of a scheduled foreclosure for $1.9 million, of which $1 million was credited against the debt. Matheny's investment account was seized, and its $1.1 million value was credited against MPD's indebtedness. Calculated in the traditional arithmetical manner, and after receiving credit for these two items of collateral, the deficiency exceeded the $4.2 million for which the Mathenys had agreed to be personally liable. After all applicable credits, the lender claimed it was still owed a total of $4.9 million on the two notes, including unpaid principal, accrued interest, late charges and expenses. Matheny claimed that his guaranty obligation should have been credited with the proceeds from the sale of his residence and the value of his investment account, a claim that was contrary to the express language of the Mathenys' guarantees. According to court documents, "the January 4, 2007 guaranty and the guaranty executed in June, 2009 specifically provide that the Matheny Guaranty 'will only be reduced by sums actually paid by Guarantor under this Guaranty, but will not be reduced by sums from any other sources . . . .'"

The defense of a solvent guarantor involves a predictable strategy. Through exhaustive pretrial discovery and motion practice, guarantor's counsel demonstrates its ability and willingness to outwork the white-shoe law firm that typically represents an institutional lender. Besides the voluminous loan instruments following a series of modifications and extensions, documents produced through discovery include thick binders filled with underwriting and administration guidelines, which no lender ever follows without some deviation. If introduced into evidence at trial, the potential for generating confusion and sympathy will motivate the lender to settle, rather than risk trying the case to a jury of the guarantor's peers or, in Matheny's case, a jury of his fans.

A third-party guarantor has defenses that are unavailable to a principal like Matheny, such as lack of notice of extensions granted to the obligor by the lender, and loan modifications made without the guarantor's consent. Martin Bader was the Author's first client after graduating from law school in 1975 and joining the Detroit firm of Honigman Miller Schwartz & Cohn. Together with his wife, Bader had guaranteed a loan to provide working capital to his brother-in-law's snow-mobile manufacturing business. On the strength of the Baders' guarantee, but without notice to them, the lender agreed to a series of extensions and loan modifications that caused the indebtedness to balloon in size far beyond the borrower's ability to repay. When the business failed and the borrower defaulted, the lender filed suit to enforce the Baders' personal guarantee. Following months of extensive discovery, and faced with the prospect of preparing for trial, the lender offered to settle the case. At a tense meeting in Jason Honigman's office, Bader was informed of the terms of the settlement offer that would leave him considerably less wealthy, but still comfortable. The client was also told by the name partner that his case would be settled, rather than tried, for the reason that he could not afford to lose. It was an eye-opening experience that the Author has never forgotten about how decision-making in the attorney-client relationship in the practice of law differs from the version taught in law school.

The success of this defense strategy requires surviving the lender's motion for summary judgment. Conventional wisdom once held that trial courts were reluctant to grant summary judgment and, if they did, appellate courts would not uphold them. It is a relatively recent phenomenon for lenders to expect guarantees to be fully enforceable as a matter of law. The United States Supreme Court's decision in *Celotex Corp. v. Catrett*, 477 U.S. 317 (1986), helped revitalize the use of the summary judgment motion as an effective approach to litigation. In the wake of the *Celotex* decision, law students were taught that "summary judgement is properly regarded not a disfavored procedural shortcut, but rather as an integral part of the Federal Rules [of Civil Procedure] as a whole, which are designed 'to secure the just, speedy and inexpensive determination of every action.'" *Celotex* , 477 U.S. at 327. Lenders likely can expect summary judgment with a state-of-the art guarantee that is unambiguous and tightly drafted, with waivers of every conceivable defense. Reflecting a nationwide trend, Missouri trial judges have become less reluctant to grant summary judgment in cases seeking to enforce personal guarantees.

On November 1, 2011, The Business Bank filed its motion for summary judgment against the Mathenys. On November 4, 2011 Circuit Court Judge Tom W. DePriest, Jr. stayed the Matheny litigation pending the outcome of the appellate process in the case of *First Bank v. Fischer & Frichtel.* Homebuilder Fischer & Frichtel had borrowed $2,576,000 from First Bank to finance construction of a 21-lot residential subdivision in Franklin County, Missouri. Between 2000 and 2005, Fischer & Frichtel sold 12 of the 21 lots. It was never able to sell the remaining nine lots after the housing market began to deteriorate. Fischer & Frichtel ultimately defaulted, and the lender commenced foreclosure proceedings. At a public sale held in December 2008, the lender was the only bidder and acquired the nine unsold lots for $466,000.

First Bank filed suit seeking to recover a deficiency in the sum of $677,875, calculated in the traditional common law manner. First Bank sought to recover the difference between the principal due on the loan and the amount it had paid for the nine unsold lots at the foreclosure sale. At trial, in January 2010, Fischer & Frichtel presented expert testimony from an appraiser that the market value of the lots at the time of foreclosure was $918,000, double the amount of the lender's winning bid. Internal First Bank documents introduced as evidence valued the property at $1,134,000 at the time of default in September 2008. A First Bank employee testified that the bank determined the amount to bid by estimating that, in the declining real estate market, the value of the property was only $675,000, which should be discounted to $466,000 because the lender would need to sell the property in bulk rather than as individual lots.

The court instructed the jury to award the lender the difference between the balance due on the loan less the fair market value at the time of foreclosure. The jury found that the fair market value of the lots was $918,000, the value assigned by the borrower's expert, and that Fischer & Frichtel therefore owned First Bank $215,875, plus accrued interest. First Bank filed a motion for a new trial based upon improper jury instructions, which the trial court granted. Fischer & Frichtel appealed to the Missouri Court of Appeals, which transferred the case to the Missouri Supreme Court given the importance of the issue at stake.

The Missouri Supreme Court accepted transfer in order to re-examine Missouri's common law approach in light of the Restatement position, as adopted by statute in a number of other states. The court heard oral argument on January 11, 2012. It was apparent from their questions that the judges' principal concern was whether, as a matter involving the balancing of competing public policies, this was a decision better left for the legislature rather than common law development. Creditors who can rely upon the availability of an efficient method of enforcing their mortgage documents reduce their overhead by minimizing losses attributable to inefficiency in attempting to collect nonperforming loans. According to Missouri real estate law expert Tim Tryniecki, "Missouri's power of sale foreclosure statute is an extraordinary piece of legal machinery. It is theoretically possible to foreclose a major property in little more than a month. Compared with most legal remedies, this is a millisecond."[36] Assuming that creditors pass savings through to borrowers, the net result should be lower costs and increased availability of mortgage credit to a broad category of borrowers at the time of loan origination. It is unsurprising that the Missouri Supreme Court would want elected officials to determine whether the public benefit of a state's foreclosure laws outweighs the harm to individual defaulting borrowers like Matheny.

In a 6–1 decision (Judges William Ray Price, Jr. and George W. Draper did not participate) filed on April 12, 2012, the Missouri Supreme Court declined the opportunity to change long-standing Missouri law by adopting the Restatement position. According to Tryniecki, "Missouri is not one of those states that goes to great pains to protect makers and guarantors of secured obligations from deficiency judgments."[37] The court ruled that First Bank did not have to credit Fischer & Frichtel with the fair market value of the nine empty lots acquired by the bank at the foreclosure auction. The court held that the borrower was entitled only to credit for the $466,000 purchase price paid by First Bank, which left the borrower owing a deficiency of $667,000.

Chief Justice Richard B. Teitelman disagreed. In a spirited dissent, he characterized the arithmetical method of calculating deficiency judgments as an anomaly in the law of awarding damages, and inconsistent with the purpose of making an injured party whole while avoiding a windfall.

> It is plainly evident that the practical effect of calculating a foreclosure deficiency by reference to the foreclosure sale means that the secured lender benefits from an often substantial windfall by purchasing the property at a discounted from fair market value while also obtaining an inflated deficiency judgment. This windfall is subsidized by the already financially distressed debtor. *First Bank*, 364 S.W.3d at 226 (Teitelman, J., dissenting).

He described the inability to recover the debt through foreclosure in the event of default as an inherent risk of lending, and a risk for which the lender is compensated through the interest rate. Justice Teitelman noted that

> A lender compensates for risk by charging an interest rate that is set both by the financial markets and by the lender's assessment of the borrower's creditworthiness. . . . That risk of loss should not be borne solely by the borrower and then amplified by measuring the deficiency by reference to the foreclosure sale price. *Id.* at 227 n.5.

Justice Teitelman conveyed the passion of a lone appellate judge sufficiently exercised to take pen in hand and, on his own time, write in opposition to the majority. He exemplifies Justice Benjamin Cardozo's classic description of the genre: "The dissenter speaks to the future, and his voice is pitched to a key that will carry through the years."[38]

The court signaled its willingness, under different factual circumstances, to consider adopting the Restatement approach. The court found no need to modify the current approach as "nearly all of the problems that Fischer & Frichtel alleges concern *not the fairness of the deficiency determination itself but the fairness of the foreclosure sale price* due to lack of sufficient notice to obtain alternative financing or other bidders." *First Bank*, 364 S.W.3d at 217 (emphasis added). Further, the very first sentence of Judge Laura Denvir Stith's majority opinion described Fischer & Frichtel as "a sophisticated commercial debtor." *Id.* She reiterated this characterization in the penultimate paragraph of her opinion. "Here, the public policy reasons that form the basis of Fischer & Frichtel's argument for modification of the more than century-old practice of using the foreclosure sale price have no application to a sophisticated debtor such as it." *Id.* at 224. The opinion noted that, with more than six decades of experience in real estate development, Fischer & Frichtel earned revenues in the hundreds of millions of dollars, and profits in the tens of millions of dollars, from 2005 to 2008. The court implied that little rationale for modifying the current approach existed as Fischer & Frichtel was not an ordinary bidder, such as a homeowner, who often cannot secure financing as a potential bidder within the short statutory minimum time period between notice of foreclosure and the sale.

The outcome of *First Bank* was a critical set-back for Matheny. Although the Matheny litigation resumed following the decision in *First Bank*, it now had an anticlimactic quality. The court heard oral argument on The Business Bank's motion for summary judgment on October 30, 2012. By order dated January 11, 2013, Judge DePriest granted summary judgment in favor of the lender.

The court considered and rejected the defenses left to Matheny in the wake of *First Bank*. Defendants argued that The Business Bank violated the Equal Credit Opportunity Act by requiring Kristin Matheny to execute a guarantee. The court held that the statute was inapplicable, both because Kristin Matheny was a joint applicant for the loan in her capacity as a 50% owner of one of the members of MPD, and because she had waived the defense at the time of the June 2009 loan modification.

Matheny claimed that the lender was the first to materially breach the loan agreement. He argued that The Business Bank committed a material breach either of an express agreement or of the implied covenant of good faith and fair dealing by refusing to advance $75,000 of loan proceeds for needed tenant improvements at the U.S. Turf Building in Spring 2010, and by unlawfully freezing an operating account maintained by MPD at the bank, at a time when MPD was still actively negotiating with an existing tenant to lease additional space and with prospective tenants. He sought to portray these actions as part of a grand scheme by the lender to oust him from the property and profit from its sale. The court held that these actions did not constitute a breach because they occurred only after Matheny had already told the lender that he would not make any further payments.

Matheny argued that the lender should be barred from recovery under the doctrine of commercial frustration. The borrower's performance should be excused by the economic crisis in the real estate and financial markets, events which were beyond the borrower's control. The court cited the decision by the Missouri Court of Appeals in *First Bank* for the proposition that the doctrine of commercial frustration was inapplicable.

Citing the recent holding in *First Bank*, Judge DePriest summarily rejected Matheny's argument that he was entitled to credit for the fair market value of the properties acquired by the lender through foreclosure. In an otherwise conscientious opinion, Judge DePriest may be faulted for ignoring the multiple signals in Judge Stith's opinion that provided the basis for distinguishing *First Bank* in the case of an unsophisticated borrower with virtually no experience in commercial real estate.

By way of contrast, just two months after the *First Bank* decision was filed, Senior U.S. District Judge Scott O. Wright, of the Western District of Missouri, concluded that "if the Missouri Supreme Court were to address the issue today *with the right case*, it would follow the Restatement approach for valuing the deficiency amount." *M & I Marshall & Ilsley Bank v. Sunrise Farms Dev., L.L.C.*, No. 10-0627-CV-W-SOW, 2012 WL 2522671, at *8 (W.D. Mo. June 28, 2012) (emphasis added), rev'd, 737 F.3d 1198 (8th Cir. 2013). In an opinion filed on June 28, 2012, Judge Wright cited "clear evidence that the state's highest court would not uphold the prior decision," and determined that he was not bound to follow it in a diversity case. *Id.*

It would be pure speculation to consider whether Judge Stith's majority opinion was written with the pending Matheny litigation in mind. Although not a party in the case, The Business Bank had filed a 62-page amicus brief on behalf of First Bank. The appellate brief filed on behalf of Fischer & Frichtel by Robert Blitz (an experienced commercial litigator who was simultaneously representing the Mathenys) made reference to facts in the Matheny case. Specifically, the brief referenced the fact that The Business Bank had paid $2 million for property that it sold four months later for $2,650,000. The brief also noted that The Business Bank did not credit any portion of the $650,000 difference to the borrower or guarantors in its deficiency action. It is not inconceivable that, to borrow a baseball metaphor, Judge Stith attempted to give Judge DePriest a sequence of signs that he simply or intentionally missed.

It would also be pure speculation to consider whether the outcome would have been different if the Matheny case had reached the Missouri Supreme Court ahead of *First Bank.* However, it would not have been the first time that the order in which cases arrived for appellate review may have been outcome determinative. For example, corporate law expert Robert Clark argued that the U.S. Supreme Court might not have created a narrow standing doctrine for plaintiffs bringing Rule 10b-5 actions under the Securities Exchange Act of 1934 if the Court first heard the case of *Ernst & Ernst v. Hochfelder*, 425 U.S. 185 (1976), before deciding *Blue Chip Stamps v. Manor Drug Stores*, 421 U.S. 723 (1975).[39]

V. A Modest Proposal

We saw in Part III that foreclosure historically was never intended to effect a liquidation of the mortgaged property, obtain repayment of the debt, or determine the extent of the borrower's liability for a deficiency. The purpose was simply to terminate borrower's right of redemption and transfer title from the borrower in order that the lender might gain control of the property. Only then, in the case of improved property, does the lender have an opportunity to inspect the collateral to ascertain the degree to which its value has deteriorated from the effects of deferred maintenance, neglect or intentional waste, which is not uncommon. The lender must also anticipate that it may bear the real estate taxes, insurance and other carrying costs of ownership for an extended period of time before foreclosed property can be resold, as well as the broker's commission and closing costs. A foreclosing lender takes these factors into account in determining the maximum amount of its bid.

From its historical roots and by its very nature, foreclosure was not designed to generate the best possible price, or even a fair price. "A good price at a foreclosure sale is an accident."[40]

> After buying the property, the lenders take the property into their portfolios. They then can take such action as is

> necessary to obtain a fair price, such as publicizing the availability of the property in publications likely to engender interest in the property. Frequently, they hire real estate agents to locate prospective purchasers.[41]

This may be assumed to reflect legislative intent in the more than half the states that allow foreclosure by power of sale, where the statutory minimum time period between notice of foreclosure and the actual sale is often less than a month. Power-of-sale foreclosure is permitted in more than thirty jurisdictions, and notice requirements under power-of-sale foreclosure are usually significantly less rigorous than those associated with judicial foreclosure.

Given the grossly inadequate time for potential bidders to secure financing or engage in due diligence, the depressed price paid by the lender as high bidder, and often sole bidder, is an incurable structural defect of the system. The legislature in non-judicial foreclosure states may be presumed to understand that property sold at foreclosure, through a process that bears little relationship to a negotiated transaction between willing parties, is likely to yield considerably less than fair market value. In its *amicus* brief supporting the respondent in the *First Bank* case, the Missouri Bankers Association noted that "foreclosure sale, by definition, involves an unwilling seller, which is inconsistent with fair-market value," and that the foreclosure statutes that the legislature has enacted are "not structured to produce sales at fair-market value."

Because it ignores these historical and practical realities, the traditional common law method of arithmetically calculating deficiency judgments is a tool of ignorance. At the other end of the extreme, anti-deficiency legislation ignores the economic realities. Real estate investors enjoy unlimited upside potential through their ability to leverage other people's money. The Missouri Bankers Association's *amicus* brief explained that the borrower has the potential to earn returns that dwarf the maximum recovery of the lender, and that the leverage provided by a lender permits borrowers to obtain a higher return on investment than cash purchasers of real estate could obtain in the same transaction. Lenders who earn a fixed rate of return cannot be expected to bear the full burden of the risk of declining property values. Protecting defaulting borrowers against deficiencies adversely impacts a broader category of non-defaulting borrowers by increasing the cost and reducing the availability of credit.

The fair value approach seeks to thread the needle. Although well-intentioned, fair value limitations in their present form are subject to criticism for their unintended consequences, the soundness of their rationale, and especially their failure to provide clarity and guidance to triers of fact charged with giving concrete meaning to the concept of "fair value."

Some scholars argue that mortgagor protection laws may serve an insurance function and that they "may also promote economic efficiency by minimizing the risk of homebuying, leading to higher levels of individual well-being and a more optimal level of housing consumption."[42] However, the fair value approach, as with other defaulter-friendly foreclosure laws, has unintended consequences. Adjudicating fair value delays final judgment and increases lenders' foreclosure costs. The fair market value standard could require costly judicial intervention to resolve very small discrepancies between the foreclosure price and intrinsic value. Lenders predictably respond to more burdensome foreclosure laws by charging higher interest rates and reducing loan supply. For example, mortgage loans are statistically significantly smaller in states that require judicial foreclosure and limit deficiency judgments. Smaller loan sizes adversely impact real estate values. The price that buyers are willing and able to pay for property is directly related to the cost and availability of mortgage financing.

The drafters of the Restatement explicitly intended the fair value approach to prevent unjust enrichment of the mortgagee through the double recovery that would result if it purchases the property at foreclosure at a deflated price, obtains a deficiency judgment, and later resells the collateral at a profit. The problem with this rationale is that there are legitimate reasons why a mortgage lender may be unwilling to make a higher bid. The decision as to how much to bid at the foreclosure sale is a complex one for the mortgagee. The mortgagee might decide to let the property go for less if the lender believes it is worth less than the mortgage balance, or if it simply does not want the property in its portfolio for a variety of reasons. Possible explanations include the avoidance of adverse publicity, environmental liability, and the fact that the lender already has an excess of distressed property, known as "Real Estate Owned" on its books. A lender may be seeking a bad debt deduction as an offset against taxable income. Another problem is that this rationale is only applicable in situations where the mortgagee purchases at the foreclosure sale, because it may realize the amount of the debt or more upon resale. It protects mortgagors at the expense of non-purchasing mortgagees in situations where a third party purchases.

The drafters of the Restatement acknowledged *in extenso*, both in the Comments and Reporters' Notes to §§ 8.3 and 8.4, the most significant problem with their approach: the challenge courts face in adjudicating fair value, and the lack of clarity or meaningful guidance on the subject.

> The chief weakness of these statutes would appear to be that they speak in terms of 'fair value', but usually set forth no definition of 'fair value'. The determination of 'fair value' was a difficult, nebulous problem . . . . [T]here were no instructions set forth in the statutes to define and clarify the meaning of that rather vague term. And yet this was the most important problem.[43]

The inherent vagueness of fair value and its subjectivity is the fundamental flaw of the fair value concept. To acknowledge the problem but leave it unresolved is reminiscent of the conduct of subdivision developers who, in the era before courts created the implied warranty of habitability, would provide an owner's manual warning buyers of defective conditions.

On this most critical of subjects, the only common feature of fair value limitation is that the foreclosure sale price should not be determinative of the amount of the deficiency. As far as measuring the value to be credited against the debt, there are almost as many variations as there are statutes. It is a fair criticism that fair value is left to be determined on an ad hoc basis, and that the number of relevant factors to be considered is mind-boggling. Is "value" determined solely by reference to prevailing prices of comparable property at the time the sale was held? Or should the trier of fact consider potential future value based upon the eventual reversion of prices to the norm? "The essence of the rule seems to be that after all the suggested factors have been considered, they are to be combined in some mystical manner to determine the final 'value' through the exercise of judgment."[44]

It would be naïve to conclude that the vagueness and subjectivity of § 8.4 was unintentional, or an exercise in magical thinking. The Restatement is published by the prestigious American Law Institute. Professors Grant Nelson and Dale Whitman, co-authors of the leading treatise on land finance law, served as coreporters. The section seems designed to confer unlimited discretion upon triers of fact to bring their sense of intuitive fairness to bear in granting relief to their defaulting neighbors. Courts interpreting fair value statutes have acknowledged that the textbook definition of fair market value (the price a willing buyer will pay to a willing seller in an open market) is only one factor among many to be considered when determining "fair value." *Rainer Mortgage v. Silverwood, Ltd.*, 209 Cal.Rptr. 294, 300 (Cal. Ct. App. 1985). The Supreme Court of Washington held that:

> [I]n deciding upon fair value at a foreclosure sale, the court may consider the state of the economy and local economic conditions, the usefulness of the property under normal conditions, its potential and future value, the type of property involved, its unique qualities, if any, and any other characteristics and conditions affecting its marketability along with any other factors which such a bidder might consider in determining a fair bid for the mortgaged property. *National Bank v. Equity Investors*, 506 P.2d 20, 46 (Wash. 1973).

One court has candidly acknowledged that the real purpose of the fair value approach is to provide a mechanism to force lenders to "share the risk of loss if market values fall." *Fed. Land Bank*, 425 N.W.2d at 363. The court stated that "A candid recognition that the statutory requirement has been adopted as an expedient to force an equitable sharing of losses in a period of economic and financial difficulties would avoid much of the confusion . . . ."

Institutional lenders are mindful of the unfavorable dynamics of the courtroom setting in which triers of fact personally confront the victims of economic dislocation. Under these circumstances, it is foreseeable that emotional impulses may influence judgment, notwithstanding Justice

Cardozo's warning that a judge "is not to yield to spasmodic sentiment, to vague and unregulated benevolence."[45] "[J]udges, like everyone else, have two cognitive systems for making judgments — the intuitive and the deliberative — and the intuitive system appears to have a powerful impact on judges' decision making."[46] Hardship cases invoke powerful forces of human nature, such as empathy, indignation and outrage, as a pair of cases from the Great Recession illustrate.

For no apparent good reason, Miami-Dade County Circuit Court Judge Valerie Schurr in the summer of 2009 granted a request by Joseph and Blanca Doyle for continuance of Republic Federal Bank's residential mortgage foreclosure of their 8,300 square foot home with an assessed value of $2.6 million. *Republic Fed. Bank v. Doyle*, 19 So. 2d 1053, 1054 (Fla. Dist. Ct. App. 2009). " I was trying to make everybody happy," Judge Schurr explained in her opinion:

> We have so many foreclosures here and I give continuances on these sales. I just do. . . . [Y]ou know, people are having a hard time now. They are having a difficult time. Everybody knows it. Businesses are failing. People are losing money in the stock market. You know, unemployment is high. It's just everybody knows that we are in a bad time right now and I hate to see anybody lose their home.

In another case, a Long Island couple was left debt-free as a result of a Suffolk County judge's indignation after hearing testimony by the regional manager for IndyMacBank. *See IndyMac Bank v. Yano-Horoski*, 890 N.Y.S.2d 313 (N.Y. Sup. Ct. 2009). The lender's intransigent refusal to restructure the couple's sub-prime loan, or otherwise cooperate in avoiding foreclosure was, according to Judge Jeffry Spinner, not only "harsh, repugnant, shocking and repulsive," but also "inequitable, unconscionable, vexatious and opprobrious." Noting that "Suffolk County is in the yawning abyss of a deep mortgage and housing crisis with foreclosure filings at a record high rate," Judge Spinner *sua sponte* invoked his equitable jurisdiction to void the mortgage, erasing the $290,000 principal balance and an additional $235,000 in accrued interest and penalties. Judge Spinner wrote: "Thus, where a party acts in a manner that is offensive to good conscience and justice, he will be completely without recourse in a court of equity, regardless of what his legal rights may be."

Unpredictability of outcome being anathema to the institutional lender's mindset, fair value seems intentionally designed to motivate the parties to reach a settlement.

Nevada is widely considered the epicenter of the collapse in real estate values during the Great Recession. A newspaper article published in December 2011 noted that "Home prices in southern Nevada have dropped 65 percent in the past four years."[47] A recent case from the Silver State illustrates the guesswork involved in adjudicating property value in fair value states. In *Oreo Corporation v. Nielson*, Centennial Hills, LLC entered into a construction loan agreement with KeyBank National Association for $14.1 million. No. 2:10-cv-00352-PMP-VCF, 2013 WL 6384535 (D. Nev. Dec. 5, 2013). After multiple project delays and resulting extensions, the loan finally matured on November 1, 2009. After Centennial defaulted, a successor to KeyBank purchased the property for $5.3 million on March 31, 2010. As of that date, Centennial owed almost $12.3 million. KeyBank's successor sought a deficiency judgment against Centennial for the $7 million difference between the amount owed by Centennial and the purchase price paid at the foreclosure sale. Centennial claimed the fair market value of the property at the date of the foreclosure sale was $14.9 million and, accordingly, there should be no deficiency judgment.

Like other fair value states, Nevada limits deficiency judgments to the amount by which the debt exceeds the greater of the fair market value of the collateral on the date of foreclosure or the high bid at the foreclosure sale. An appraiser for KeyBank's successor testified that the fair market value of the property was $4,350,000 at the time of the foreclosure sale. Centennial's appraiser determined the fair market value on that date was $14,905,000. The parties' appraisers differed by $10,555,000 or over 70%.

What is a court to do under such circumstances? In this case, the court heard the testimony of a third appraiser who testified that the value of real property had fluctuated wildly during the real estate recession in

Southern Nevada from 2007 until the time of foreclosure in 2010. The third appraiser testified to appraisals with the following values: July 2007, $23.3 million; October 2008, $21.6 million; December 2009, $11.4 million; and March 2010, $7.8 million. In the final analysis, the court gave marginal weight to the appraisal evidence introduced by the parties for the reason that it was utterly irreconcilable. Compelled to reach a result notwithstanding such evidence, the court determined that the third appraiser's results were more reliable and determined that the fair market value of the property as of the date of foreclosure was $7.77 million. The court awarded KeyBank's successor a deficiency judgment of $4.6 million.

Adjudging property value for deficiency purposes without direction or meaningful guidance is an exercise in judicial guesswork. In remanding for further consideration a deficiency judgment determined on the basis of the arithmetical method, the Montana Supreme Court blithely wrote, "The method of determining fair market value we will leave to the District Court." *Trs. of the Wash.-Idaho-Mont. Carpenters-Emp'rs Ret. Trust Fund v. Galleria P'ship*, 780 P.2d 608, 617 (Mont. 1989). Left with little practical guidance, and faced with evidence of appraisals that ranged from $562,736 to $1,595,000, the trial court simply averaged the experts' values at $1.1 million, a result that the state supreme court affirmed. *Galleria P'ship II*, 819 P.2d 158, 163 (Mont. 1991). Because the appraisals were so disparate, the Montana Supreme Court stated that the district court "was entitled to discount [all of] the appraisals."

A provocative 1940 law review article contained an audacious proposal for reforming the mortgage foreclosure process. Describing the foreclosure sale as "a meaningless farce and an entirely unnecessary expense" for which the mortgagor is ultimately liable, the author called for a return to the practice of strict foreclosure as serving the best interests of both parties. *See* Harold C. Vaughan, *Reform of Mortgage Foreclosure Procedure — Possibilities Suggested by* Honeyman v. Jacobs, 88 U. PA. L. REV. 957, 958 (1940). The principal advantage of the proposal is that it would significantly reduce transaction costs, including auctioneer's fees and advertising that is read by no one. The proposal would create an exception for the rare situation in which the borrower believed the property was worth more than the debt and was willing to incur the risk of being wrong. In such a case, the debtor may demand a foreclosure sale, but would be personally liable for the deficiency if the price realized at sale was insufficient to discharge the debt plus expenses of sale. The proposal was not well-received. Only four states (Connecticut, Illinois, Maryland and Vermont) still permit lenders to use the strict foreclosure method and only under limited circumstances. However, it is hard to quarrel with the author's underlying assumptions about the play-acting nature of open cry auction sales.

One aspect of the proposal deserves to be revisited. If a lender wanted to preserve the ability to pursue the borrower for a deficiency, the proposal still called for strict foreclosure, but coupled strict foreclosure with appraisal of the property to determine its fair market value. This chapter proposes a variation of the appraisal mechanism as a means of solving the fundamental problem with the Restatement's approach that was identified by courts and commentators 75 years ago but remains unaddressed. Given that only about half the states have enacted fair value statutes in the decades since New York first adopted its statute in the post-Depression era, § 8.4 is less of a restatement of the law, in the plain meaning of the phrase, than it is an advocacy for law reform. It is similar in this respect to other sections of the Restatement of Property. *See, e.g.*, RESTATEMENT (THIRD) OF PROPERTY: SERVITUDES § 3.2 (2000) (eliminating the requirement that a covenant must touch and concern the land to be enforceable against subsequent owners); *Id.* § 2.4 (eliminating the horizontal privity requirement for covenants running with the land).

First Bank was a closely watched and well litigated case in the immediate aftermath of the worst economic downturn since the Great Depression, a time when the attention of thoughtful persons is likely to be focused on deficiency judgments. The opportunity to adopt § 8.4 by judicial decision was squarely presented and decisively rejected by the Missouri Supreme Court. Although the Missouri Supreme Court may once have been considered conservative, its composition has changed in the past decade, and seven of the nine judges on the current court were appointed by Democratic governors. It is possible that the court, due to its current composition, would decide differently a case similar to *First Bank*. The task of sifting through irreconcilable appraisal testimony to adjudicate the fair market value of real property may not to be something appellate court judges are willing to impose on their trial court counterparts. The direct examination of each appraiser in a fair value determination proceeding tends to last several hours. Cross-examination may be expected to take at least as long. When the results are given only marginal weight in the final determination, and when the same result can be reached through a streamlined process, it is hard to justify the commitment of judicial resources to the exercise.

Except for West Virginia and Hawaii, no state has followed the recommendation of the American Law Institute to adopt fair value by judicial decision, and it is time that it be withdrawn. In its place the National Conference of Commissioners on Uniform State Laws should propose model legislation along the lines of existing statutes in the two states that have achieved a workable solution to the problem of calculating deficiency judgments in a fair and efficient manner.

By statute in South Carolina and Louisiana, a deficiency is measured by the difference between the foreclosure sale price and the value of the property as established by professional appraisal. LA. CODE CIV. PROC. ANN. arts. 2336–37 (Westlaw through 2014 Reg. Sess.); S.C. CODE ANN. §§ 29-3-660 to 29-3-760 (Westlaw through 2014 Reg. Sess.). In these states, real estate appraisers act in a quasi-judicial capacity to make a factual determination of the value of the property. The United States Supreme Court has commented favorably upon the ability of appraisers to reconcile the difference between foreclosure sale value and fair market value. "An appraiser's reconstruction of 'fair market value' could show what similar property would be worth if it did not have to be sold within the time and manner strictures of state-prescribed foreclosure." *BFP v. Resolution Trust Corp.*, 511 U.S. 531, 539 (1994). The South Carolina and Louisiana statutes strike an appropriate balance among the legitimate interests of both the lender and borrower, and the public's interest in judicial economy and the cost of borrowing to finance the purchase and improvement of real estate.

The statutes contain significant variations. Louisiana's statute, which has existed in a variety of forms since 1805, is said to reflect a strong public policy of protecting debtors from possible abuse from the mortgagee buying the property at a price substantially less than its actual market value. The legislative intent was to avoid the injustice of a mortgagee obtaining a deficiency judgment, and later reselling the property and realizing a total recovery far in excess of the remaining balance owed. Both the debtor and creditor have a right to appoint an appraiser. If either (or both) does not timely appoint an appraiser, the sheriff appoints one for the party. If the two appraisers differ by less than $250,000, the appraised value will be the average of the two. If the difference is greater than $250,000, the sheriff appoints a third appraiser whose appraisal becomes the value.

In South Carolina the deficiency is measured by the higher of the foreclosure sale price and the appraised value. S.C. CODE ANN. § 29-3-680 (Westlaw through 2014 Reg. Sess.). The borrower has 30 days after the foreclosure sale in which to ask the court for an order of appraisal. If the borrower exercises this right, the borrower and lender each select an appraiser, and the court selects a third. § 29-3-710 specifies that the appraisers must be state-licensed and disinterested parties. Within 30 days of their appointment, all or a majority of the appraisers must agree on the value of the property as of the date of sale. The report of the appraisers is then recorded as a judgment of the court. Either party can appeal to the court. In the event of an appeal, the only discretion the court has is to order reappraisal. A South Carolina bank challenged the constitutionality of the statute claiming that due process required it have an opportunity to attend the appraisers' viewing of the property or to present evidence to the appraisers. *S.C. Nat'l Bank v. Cent. Carolina Livestock Mkt., Inc.*, 345 S.E.2d 485, 487 (S.C. 1986). The court held that the right of appeal afforded the parties sufficient opportunity to be heard.

If a majority of the appraisers is unable to agree within the prescribed time period, then yet another set of appraisers is appointed until a majority is able to reach agreement. This aspect of the statute creates the potential for unnecessary additional cost and delay. The approach recommended in this chapter would correct for that defect.

Institutional lenders responded predictably by including boilerplate waivers of appraisal rights in mortgage loan documents. The

South Carolina Supreme Court ultimately held that contractual waiver of appraisal rights was unenforceable. The court held that "We now join those jurisdictions that give effect to a debtor's statutory rights and hold the contractual waiver of appraisal rights invalid as against public policy." *SCN Mortg. Corp. v. White*, 440 S.E.2d 868, 869 (S.C. 1994), *overruling Tri-South Mortg. Investors v. Fountain*, 221 S.E.2d 861 (S.C. 1976). The South Carolina legislature responded by amending the statute in 1996 to allow waiver in commercial transactions if disclosed in a capitalized sentence that is underlined, or other prominent manner, on the signature page of one of the loan documents.

The involvement of appraisers in a quasi-judicial capacity in South Carolina and Louisiana reflects the growing trend toward alternative dispute resolution. Since its inception more than 30 years ago, alternative dispute resolution has become increasingly popular in response to what is perceived as the courts' inability to resolve disputes in the commercial context in a cost-efficient, time-effective manner. Conflicts that best lend themselves to resolution through alternative means tend to be unnecessarily costly, time-consuming, and complex if pursued through formal court proceedings. The State Bar of Michigan's Alternative Dispute Resolution Section published a study in 2011 demonstrating that the public benefits from more efficient and effective dispute resolution, which streamlines overcrowded court dockets.[48]

The approach recommended by this chapter is informed by the alternative dispute resolution regimen that is intricately woven into the long-term ground leases that are frequently used for office buildings, shopping centers, hotels and other commercial real estate projects. The concept of ground leasing dates back to the Old Testament. *See* Leviticus 25:10-24. Many of the largest metropolitan area commercial properties have long been constructed on ground-leased land. According to Missouri real estate law expert Tim Tryniecki, "many of the old commercial properties in downtown St. Louis were built on 99-year leases."[49] The New York Times reported in 1909 that "nearly all" of the "skyscrapers" in St. Louis were built on leaseholds.[50]

Because of their extended terms (typically ranging from 50 to 99 years), ground leases necessarily include provisions to adjust the rent periodically to accommodate inevitable changes in economic conditions. Ground leases frequently include an option for the tenant to purchase the fee at various intervals during the term at a purchase price determined by an appraisal mechanism that closely resembles the rent-adjustment provision. The rent-adjustment mechanism is designed to provide the lessor a reasonable return decades into the future. From the tenant's perspective, the rent must continue to bear a reasonable relationship to the income-producing capacity of the improvements over time.

There are alternative means of accomplishing the rental adjustment. For example, a ground lease may provide for adjustment of rent based upon changes in the Consumer Price Index, or other benchmark. But the most common method involves the appointment of a panel of appraisers tasked with reaching a final determination of fair rental value. As codified in California, the panel is the functional equivalent of an arbitrator whose decision is final.

Among other things, a well-drafted ground lease addresses the number of appraisers to be appointed, their qualifications, the process of appointment, and the time frame within which the process must occur. It also allocates responsibility for the payment of fees. Although a panel will necessarily be more expensive and take more time than a single appraiser, the parties are rarely willing to rely upon the determination of a single appraiser who may be biased and is surely fallible. Qualifications should include being a Member of the Appraisal Institute ("MAI"), a designation held by appraisers who are experienced in the valuation of commercial and industrial as well as residential property. The MAI designation is granted to appraisers with at least 4,500 hours of field experience who demonstrate mastery of the skills and ethical standards of the profession by completing coursework and passing a 16-hour comprehensive examination. The MAI designation is considered the gold standard appraisal accreditation. Recipients are required to maintain good moral character and complete 100 hours of continuing education every five years.

A ground lease typically contains one of three possible appraisal processes:

1. Each party selects an appraiser, and the two appraisers jointly select a third appraiser who is

charged with determining fair market rental value. The clause must address the possibility that the two appraisers are unable to agree upon a third appraiser. In such event, the parties may agree to petition the court to appoint a third appraiser, or the president of the local board of Realtors may be tasked with making the appointment. The disadvantage of this method is that one appraiser has the power to make a final determination.

2. Each party selects an appraiser, and the two jointly select a third appraiser. The first two appraisers each make a determination of value, and the third appraiser chooses between them. Because it requires multiple determinations of value, this process is more expensive and less efficient than the first. Because the third appraiser is limited in his or her discretion to a choice between the determinations of the party-appointed appraisers, this method may also produce an outcome that lies at an extreme end of the range of reasonable value.

The second approach is similar to the way salary arbitrations in Major League Baseball are conducted. The player and his team each propose salaries to a panel, and the panel decides which salary to award. There is no middle ground. Either the team or the player wins.

3. Each party selects an appraiser who makes a determination of value. If the two are unable to agree, they together choose a third appraiser who makes an independent determination of value. If a majority of the three is unable to agree, the three are averaged together. A variation is to have the middle appraisal govern. An alternative variation is to disregard any low or high appraisal that varies by more than 10% from the middle appraisal before averaging the results.

Because up to three separate appraisals may need to be conducted, the third method is likely to be the most expensive and time consuming. Nevertheless, in the Author's experience, it is the most widely used method. Parties are rarely willing to rely on the determination of a single appraiser, who may be biased and is surely fallible. And research has repeatedly shown that aggregating a number of individual judgments provides a significantly more reliable result. Case Western Reserve Law Professor Cassandra Robertson found that: "there is the advantage of probability — the idea that having more people answer a particular question can increase the probability of reaching a correct answer, even when their conclusions are independent of each other."[51]

Borrowers facing personal liability for sizeable deficiency judgments are entitled to the same kind of rigorous appraisal regimen that sophisticated parties to commercial ground leases choose for themselves when important financial consequences are at stake. The statutory proposal that follows is aimed at accomplishing this objective:

Foreclosure: Action for a Deficiency

(a) If the foreclosure price is less than the unpaid balance of the mortgage obligation, an action may be brought to recover a deficiency judgment against any person liable on the mortgage obligation in accordance with the provisions of this section.

(b) Subject to subsection (e) of this section, the deficiency judgment is for the amount by which the mortgage obligation exceeds the foreclosure sale price.

(c) Any person against whom recovery of a deficiency is sought may request in the proceeding in which the action for a deficiency is pending a determination of the appraised value of the real estate as of the date of the foreclosure sale by designating an appraiser within thirty (30) days following commencement of such action. Such designation shall be made to the clerk of the court, and a copy of such designation shall be served upon the creditor or its attorney of record. Such appraiser shall make an independent determination of value within thirty (30) days of such selection, which shall constitute the appraised value of the real estate for purposes of subsection (e), unless the party seeking a deficiency designates a second appraiser within thirty (30) days after receiving the first appraiser's determination of value. If the two appraisers thus selected are unable to agree upon the appraised value of the real estate within thirty (30) days after selection of the second appraiser, they together shall designate a third appraiser who shall make an independent determination of value within thirty (30) days after selection, in which event the middle of the three appraisers' determinations of value shall constitute the appraised value of the real estate for purposes of subsection (e). The appraised value thus determined shall be filed and recorded by the clerk as a judgment of the court.

(d) If the first two appraisers designated by the parties are unable to agree upon the appraised value of the real estate and fail to designate a third appraiser within thirty (30) days after their selection, then the court having jurisdiction of the action or any judge thereof shall appoint a third appraiser.

(e) If it is determined that the appraised value of the real estate is greater than the foreclosure sale price, any person against whom recovery of the deficiency is sought is entitled to an offset against the deficiency in the amount by which the appraised value exceeds the sale price.

(f) For purposes of this section, any appraiser (i) shall have the designation MAI; (ii) shall be state-licensed; and (iii) shall not be a party to the action, or affiliated in business with, or related by blood or marriage to, any party to the action. Each appraiser shall be compensated by the party who selected such appraiser. The costs of the third appraiser, if necessary, shall be paid one-half by the party seeking to recover the deficiency and one-half by the party or parties against whom such a recovery is sought.

The following illustration of the operation of the proposed statute is based on the facts of *Oreo Corp. v. Nielson*, No. 2:10-cv-00352-PMP-VCF, 2013 WL 6384535, at *1 (D. Nev. Dec. 5, 2013). The borrower selects Appraiser A, who values the subject property as of the date of foreclosure at $14.9 million. The lender selects Appraiser B, who values the property at $4.35 million. Because the two appraisers are unable to agree, they together select Appraiser C, who values the property at $7.8 million. As the middle appraisal of the three, Appraiser C's valuation governs, and the appraised value will be $7.8 million, which corresponds to the outcome of the case.

This model is particularly well-suited to jurisdictions that allow foreclosure by power of sale. Power-of-sale foreclosure is a simpler, faster and cheaper alternative to judicial foreclosure. Judicial foreclosure prolongs the length of time during which lenders forgo interest and incur carrying costs such as taxes and maintenance. Judicial foreclosure on average takes 148 days longer than non-judicial foreclosure. Foreclosures in the most time-consuming state (Maine) take almost 300 days longer than in the quickest state (Texas). The average time for a non-judicial foreclosure is 60 days in Missouri, a fraction of the time required in bordering states of Kansas and Illinois. By requiring judicial adjudication of value, the fair value approach is inconsistent with power-of-sale foreclosure and reduces its benefits. Power-of-sale foreclosure is intended as a streamlined process in which court intervention is rare. A foreclosure process combining power of sale with the statutory proposal best accommodates the legitimate interests of lenders and borrowers, along with the public interest in judicial efficiency and access to affordable credit.

VI. Conclusion

One of millions of borrowers affected by the 2008 economic crisis and Great Recession, Mike Matheny's story may be difficult to distinguish from so many others. According to the National Association of Realtors, there have been an estimated five million completed foreclosures nationwide since September 2008. Matheny's story is not even particularly unusual among former professional athletes. Data suggests that about 60% of former NBA players go broke within five years of retirement. Business schools have responded to recent accounts of former athletes falling into financial distress by creating specialized executive MBA programs for athletes.

Yet sometimes a story is not just a story. A detailed account from a human perspective, involving a high-visibility figure recognizable by fans of the Great American Pastime, provides a compelling narrative and framework for examining a problem in land finance law that has remained unsolved for decades. Deficiency judgments have long been recognized as the greatest obstacle to devising a mortgage foreclosure process that accommodates the legitimate interests of lenders and borrowers, along with the public interest in judicial efficiency and access to affordable credit. Sadly, but predictably, it takes a severe economic downturn like the Great Recession to focus attention to the problem of calculating deficiency judgments.

A foreclosure sale does not always make for complete justice. Most states allow a lender whose loan remains unsatisfied following foreclosure to seek recourse for the deficiency against its borrower's other assets. In a declining real estate market, overburdened debtors often find themselves on the wrong end of lawsuits seeking sizeable deficiency judgments.

The traditional common law method for calculating deficiency judgments has been criticized by courts and commentators as unjust and overdue for reform. The fair value concept is the alternative most widely adopted and recommended by the Restatement. This approach is itself subject to criticism. First, although packaged as a restatement of the law, it is in fact a proposal for law reform in fully half the states. Despite the Restatement's urging, besides West Virginia and Hawaii, no state court has decided to adopt the fair value approach through the exercise of its equity jurisdiction. Property law evolves at a glacial pace that frustrates advocates of reform. However, characterizing law reform as restatement creates uncertainty that threatens the persuasive precedential value of Restatements generally. In fairness, the American Law Institute, which has published Restatements since 1923, receives even more criticism for the perception that it is dominated by elitists and resistant to liberalization of the common law. Second, the fair value concept is hollow at its core. Proponents concede it is vague and subjective. It provides no meaningful guidance to triers of fact charged with adjudicating value. It is fair to assume that the fair value approach is designed to benefit debtors at the expense of creditors by generating uncertainty and encouraging settlement of cases that are emotionally fraught by their very nature, or by discouraging lenders from pursuing deficiency judgments entirely.

Defaulter-friendly foreclosure laws impose transaction costs that adversely impact the availability of mortgage financing and real estate values. Fair value limitations in their current form benefit certain borrowers, while a much larger category of non-defaulting borrowers may face a reduced supply of mortgage credit, and less favorable terms, at the time of loan origination.

This chapter recommends a more structured approach modeled after statutes in South Carolina and Louisiana. It would vest well-qualified real estate appraisers with the quasi-judicial function of determining value for purposes of calculating deficiency judgments. By incorporating the benefits of alternative dispute resolution and the experience of transactional practice, this approach will make the system of foreclosure more cost-effective, expeditious, and equitable to both parties.

Notes

I. WHAT'S IN A NAME: THE TALE OF LOUIS WOLFSON'S AFFIRMED

[1] KIRKPATRICK SALE, POWER SHIFT 181 (1975).

[2] Henry G. Manne, *The Original Corporate Raider,* WSJ.COM *(*Jan. 18, 2008*)*, http://online.wsj.com/article/SB120062429680899679.html; *see also* Larry E. Ribstein, IDEOBLOG (Jan. 18, 2008), http://busmovie.typepad.com/ideoblog/2008/01/who-invented-th.html.

[3] *Wolfson: Among My People,* OCALA STAR-BANNER, Dec. 1, 1978.

[4] *Derby Choice Journal 2007-28th Edition,* INNISFREE FARM, www.innisfree.org/2007.html.

[5] Daytona Beach Morning Journal, 9/25/54.

[6] Karen Read Wolfson, Pop . . . A Very Rare Man, WOLFSON CHILDS. HOSP. (Dec. 1992),

http://www.wolfsonchildrens.org/about-us/Documents/Pop.pdf.

[7] Daytona Beach Morning Journal, *supra* n. 5.

[8] Charity Begins. . ., TIME, Nov. 10, 1958, at 68, 68.

[9] DIANA B. HENRIQUES, THE WHITE SHARKS OF WALL STREET 177 (2000).

[10] ROBERT SOBEL, DANGEROUS DREAMERS 14-15 (1993).

[11] SOBEL, *supra* n. 10, at 19.

[12] *A New Day for Wards,* PLEASANT FAMILY SHOPPING (April 17, 2009), http://pleasantfamilyshopping.blogspot.com/2009/04/new-day-for-wards.html.

[13] JAMES GRANT, MONEY OF THE MIND: BORROWING AND LENDING IN AMERICA FROM THE CIVIL WAR TO MICHAEL MILKIN 28 (1994); *see also* HENRIQUES, *supra* note 9, at 151 (discussing Avery's cash accumulation strategy).

[14] Martin Weiss, United States Battles Won and Battles Lost, MARKET ORACLE (May 28, 2007, 1:50 PM), http://www.marketoracle.co.uk/Article1111.html.

[15] SOBEL, *supra* note 10, at 20.

[16] LELAND C. WHETTEN, RECENT PROXY CONTESTS: A STUDY IN MANAGEMENT-SHAREHOLDER RELATIONS 43-44 (1959).

[17] Daytona Beach Morning Journal, *supra* note 5.

[18] For images of the Wolfson family, *see There Will Never Be Another Like Lou Wolfson,* POST TIME USA (Feb. 2008), www.posttimeusa.com/Portals/16/v35%20number%202PT%20Feb%2008%20%20WOLFSON4.pdf.

[19] SOBEL, *supra* note 10, at 20.

[20] *See* PLEASANT FAMILY SHOPPING, *supra* note 12.

[21] SEC Historical Society Interview With Paul Windels Conducted on September 18, 2007 by Kenneth Durr, www.sechistorical.com/collection/oral-histories/windels_091807.pdf.

[22] SALE, *supra* note 1, at 181.

[23] Henry G. Manne, *Corporate Governance – Getting Back to Market Basics,* at 12 (2008).

[24] SOBEL, *supra* note 10, at 12.

[25] JOHN COONEY, THE AMERICAN POPE: THE LIFE AND TIMES OF FRANCIS CARDINAL SPELLMAN 314-6 (1984).

[26] ALFRED F. CONARD ET AL., ENTERPRISE ORGANIZATION 641 (4th ed. 1987).

[27] THOMAS LEE HAZEN, THE LAW OF SECURITIES REGULATIONS §4.27[5] (4th ed. 2002).

[28] CONARD, *supra* note 26.

[29] LAURA KALMAN, ABE FORTAS: A BIOGRAPHY 363 (1990).

[30] William Safire, *ON LANGUAGE; Masterful Meltdown,* NYTIMES.COM (June 5, 1994), http://www.nytimes.com/1994/06/05/magazine/on-language-masterful-meltdown.html?pagewanted=all.

[31] BRUCE ALLEN MURPHY, FORTAS: THE RISE AND RUIN OF A SUPREME COURT JUSTICE 174 (1988).

[32] *Id.* at 174–75.

[33] Murphy, *supra* note 31, at 197.

[34] *Id.*

[35] MURPHY, *supra* note 31, at 208.

[36] ROBERT SHOGAN, A QUESTION OF JUDGMENT: THE FORTAS CASE AND THE STRUGGLE FOR THE SUPREME COURT 211 (1972).

[37] JOHN W. DEAN, THE REHNQUIST CHOICE 5 (2001).

[38] BOB WOODWARD & SCOTT ARMSTRONG, THE BRETHREN: INSIDE THE SUPREME COURT 19 (1979).

[39] MURPHY, *supra* note 31, at 552.

[40] WOODWARD & ARMSTRONG, *supra* note 38, at 19

[41] KALMAN *supra* note 29, at 377.

[42] WILLIAM O. DOUGLAS, THE COURT YEARS 358 (1980).

[43] Terry Carter, *The Boss*, A.B.A. J., June 2010, at 39.

[44] WOODWARD & ARMSTRONG, *supra* note 38, at 20.

[45] DOUGLAS, *supra* note 42, at 359.

[46] GERALD R. FORD, A TIME TO HEAL 91 (1979).

[47] KALMAN, *supra* note 29, at 378.

[48] EDWARD L. BOWEN, LEGACIES OF THE TURF: A CENTURY OF GREAT THOROUGHBRED BREEDERS 208 (2004).

[49] *Horse Racing's Greatest Rivalry*, REGARDING HORSES (Feb. 25, 2009), http://www.regarding horses.com/2009/02/25/horse-racings-greatest-rivalry-affirmed-vs-alydar.

[50] John Williams, *Bench Mark Thoroughbred,* BLOODHORSE.COM (Jan. 16, 2001), http://www.bloodhorse.com/horse-racing/articles/2479/bench-mark-throughbred.

[51] Donna Campbell Smith, *I'm Rooting for Big Brown* (June 6, 2008), http://donnacampbellsmith.blogspot.com/2008_06_01_archive/html.

[52] E-mail from Edward L. Bowen (Jan. 18, 2010) (on file with the author).

[53] E-mail from Jack B. Jacobs (Jan. 20, 2010) (on file with author).

[54] E-mail from Bruce Stargatt (Jan. 25, 2010) (on file with author).

[55] A Nice, Quiet Life, TIME, May 29, 1978, at 66.

[56] E-mail from Timothy T. Capps (Jan. 26, 2010, 4:28 PM) (on file with author).

[57] Telephone interview with Michael D. Goldman, Partner, Potter, Anderson & Corroon, LLP (Jan. 19, 2010).

[58] SHOGAN, *supra* note 36, at 213–14.

[59] Wikipedia, *Louis Wolfson,* http://en.wikipedia.org/wiki/Louis_Wolfson (last visited January 21, 2011).

[60] E-mail from Timothy T. Capps, *supra* note 56.

[61] Jessie-Lynne Kerr, Millionaire Excelled in Various Endeavors, FLA. TIMES-UNION, Jan. 2, 2008,

http://jacksonville.com/tu-online/stories/010208/met_230808569.shtml.

---

[62] Esther Marr, *Affirmed Exhibit Opens at Kentucky Horse Park*, BLOODHORSE.COM (June 6, 2007), http://www.bloodhorse.com/horse-racing/articles/392541/affirmed-exhibit-opens-at-kentucky-horse-park.

[63] J.B. FAULCONER, THE NAMES THEY GIVE THEM 1 (Jim Bolus & Suzanne Bolus eds., 1998).

[64] E-mail from Timothy T. Capps, *supra* note 56.

[65] Daytona Beach Morning Journal, *supra* note 5.

[66] SEC Historical Society Interview with Paul Windels, *supra* note 21.

[67] E-mail from Timothy T. Capps, *supra* note 56.

[68] Peter Klein, *The Original Corporate Raider*, ORGANIZATIONS AND MARKETS (Feb. 3, 2008), http://organizationsandmarkets.com/2008/02/03/the-original-corporate-raider/ (last visited February 13, 2011).

[69] HENRIQUES, *supra* note 9, at 169.

[70] Manne, *supra* note 2.

[71] GRANT, *supra* note 13, at 35

[72] *See* SOBEL, supra note 10, at 11–12.

[73] Roger Ebert, *Citizen Kane (1941)*, ROGEREBERT.COM (May 24, 1998), http://rogerebert.suntimes.com/apps/pbcs/dll/article?AID=%2F19980524%2FREVIEWS08%2F401010334%2F1023.

[74] E-mail from Timothy T. Capps, *supra* note 56.

II. HENRY FORD'S WINGMAN: A PERSPECTIVE ON THE CENTENNIAL OF *DODGE v. FORD*

[1] DAVID L. LEWIS, THE PUBLIC IMAGE OF HENRY FORD 102 (1976) (quoting Raymond-Leopold Bruckberger, a French priest whose insightful reflections on the U.S. have been compared with those of Alexis de Tocqueville).

[2] Anthony Page & Robert A. Katz, *The Truth About Ben & Jerry's*, SSIR.ORG (Fall 2012), *available at* https://ssir.org/articles/entry/the-truth-about-ben-and-jerrys (citing Dodge v. Ford for the proposition that Ben & Jerry's had to accept Unilever's offer).

[3] M. Todd Henderson, *The Story of* Dodge v. Ford Motor Company: *Everything Old Is New Again, in* Corporate Law Stories 37, 45 (J. Mark Ramseyer ed., 2009).

[4] Flynn Wayne, A Master Builder of Business Efficiency, THE NATIONAL MAGAZINE (Sept. 1915), at 823, available at https://books.google.com/books?id=ieJAAQAAMAAJ&pg=PA820&lpg=PA820&dq=wayne+flynn+national+magazine+couzens&source=bl&ots=8rLIoM2Qqr&sig=GTOtZE4VJrcB5ztbBGFJSev7Les&hl=en&sa=X&ved=0ahUKEwiIrafO_fbXAhVM5oMKHfIdD7kQ6AEI

PzAE#v=onepage&q=wayne%20flynn%20national%20magazine%20couzens&f=false.

[5] Ford R. Bryan, Henry's Lieutenants 67, 69 (2003).

[6] RICHARD SNOW, I INVENTED THE MODERN AGE 128 (2013).

[7] HARRY BARNARD, INDEPENDENT MAN: THE LIFE OF SENATOR JAMES COUZENS 65 (1958).

[8] RICHARD BAK, HENRY AND EDSEL 88 (2003).

[9] Keith Sward, The Legend of the Ford 124 (1948).

[10] CHARLES E. SORENSEN, MY FORTY YEARS WITH FORD 84 (1956).

[11] Linda Kawaguchi, *Introduction to Dodge v. Ford Motor Co.: Primary Source and Commentary Material*, 17 CHAPMAN L. REV. 493, 576 (2014) (quoting trial court decision in *Dodge v. Ford*).

[12] BARNARD, *supra* note 7, at 20.

[13] Henderson, *supra* note 3, at 53.

[14] Vincent Harding, *Equality Is Not Enough,* N.Y. Times, Oct. 11, 1987, at 7 (reviewing Derrick Bell, And We Are Not Saved: The Elusive Quest For Racial Justice (1987)).

[15] Paul A. Lombardo, *Legal Archaeology: Recovering the Stories Behind the Cases,* 36 J. L. MED. & ETHICS 589 (2008).

[16] Vincent Curcio, Henry Ford 94 (2013).

[17] Curcio, *supra* note 16, at 39.

[18] Anne Jardim, The First Henry Ford: A Study in Personality and Business Leadership 52 (1970).

[19] David L. Lewis, Introduction to HARRY BARNARD, INDEPENDENT MAN: THE LIFE OF SENATOR COUZENS xv (1958; new ed. 2002).

[20] BAK, supra note 8, at 50.

[21] SORENSEN, *supra* note 10, at 40.

[22] BAK, *supra* note 8, at 69.

[23] LEWIS, THE PUBLIC IMAGE OF HENRY FORD, *supra* note 1, at 69.

[24] REYNOLD M. WIK, HENRY FORD AND GRASS-ROOTS AMERICA 5 (1972).

[25] Benson Ford, Typewritten Notes for The New Henry Ford, The James Couzens Papers [hereinafter Couzens Papers] (on file with the Library of Congress and with author). Letter from Couzens to Theodore H. Price, Sept. 22, 1916, Couzens Papers (copy on file with author).

[26] CURCIO, *supra* note 16, at 159.

[27] SWARD, *supra* note 9, at 75.

[28] XVIII THEODORE ROOSEVELT, THE WORKS OF THEODORE ROOSEVELT 271 (1926).

[29] Kawaguchi, *supra* note 11, at 517.

[30] Henderson, *supra* note 3, at 61.

[31] IRVING YOUNGER, THE IRVING YOUNGER COLLECTION: WISDOM & WIT FROM THE MASTER OF TRIAL ADVOCACY 463 (Stephen D. Easton, ed. 2010).

[32] Henderson, *supra* note 3, at 50.

[33] LEWIS, THE PUBLIC IMAGE OF HENRY FORD, *supra* note 1, at 101.

[34] Thomas Paine, The Rights of Man, Part II, at 14–15 (1792).

[35] Amity Shlaes, The Greedy Hand 181 (1999).

[36] ARTHUR HERMAN, 1917: Lenin, Wilson, and the Birth of the New World Disorder 99 (2017).

[37] HERMAN, *supra* note 36, at 149.

[38] HERMAN, *supra* note 36, at 253.

[39] Henry L. Stimson, *Introduction* to XXI Theodore Roosevelt, The Works of Theodore Roosevelt, at xiv (1926).

[40] Steven R. Weisman, The Great Tax Wars 328 (2002) (quoting Edwin R.A. Seligman).

[41] Lawrence Goldstone, Drive 100 (2016).

[42] Henderson, *supra* note 3, at 56-57.

[43] Henderson, *supra* note 3, at 56.

[44] Barnard, *supra* note 7 at 324.

[45] David Zatz, John and Horace Dodge: From Building Fords to Dodge Brothers, ALLPAR.COM, (Aug. 20, 2017), available at https:/www.allpar.com/corporate/bios/dodge-brothers.html.

[46] Steven Watts, The People's Tycoon 258 (2005).

[47] John B. Rae, Henry Ford 152 (1969).

[48] WIK, *supra* note 24, at 162.

[49] Henry L. Lewis, *Introduction* to SAMUEL S. MARQUIS, HENRY FORD: AN INTERPRETATION *xxx* (1923; new ed. 2007).

[50] Wayne Ferrens, *James J. Couzens: An Extraordinary Man,* MOTORCITIES.ORG (Jan. 4, 2017), *available at* www.motorcities.org/About+Us/James+J+Couzens+An+Extraordinary+Man-356.html.

[51] George K. Yin, *James Couzens, Andrew Mellon, the "Greatest Tax Suit in the History of the World," and the Creation of the Joint Committee on Taxation and its Staff*, 66 Tax L. Rev. 787, 819, 821 (2013).

[52] WATTS, *supra* note 46, at 189–90.

[53] CURCIO, *supra* note 16, at 270.

[54] WIK, *supra* note 24, at 6.

III. UP FROM *JAVINS*: A 50-YEAR RETROSPECTIVE ON THE IMPLIED WARRANTY OF HABITABILITY

[1] Richard H. Chused, *Saunders (a.k.a Javins) v. First National Realty Corporation 10th Anniversary Symposium Issue: Empowering the Poor and Disenfranchised: Making a Difference through Community, Advocacy, and Policy*, 11 GEO. J. ON POVERTY L. & POL'Y 191, 193 (2004). *See, also,* Mary Ann Glendon, *The Transformation of American Landlord-Tenant Law,* 23 B.C. L. REV. 503 (1982); Gerald Korngold, *Whatever Happened to Landlord-Tenant Law,* 77 NEB. L. REV. 703 (1998) (recognizing that in this era, "no area of the law was more vibrant than landlord-tenant.").

[2] Ginny Monk, *'Habitable' not in rules for state landlords,* ARK. DEMOCRAT GAZETTE (Jul. 8, 2018), https://www.arkansasonline.com/news/2018/jul/08 /habitable-not-in-rules-for-state-landlo/.

[3] Brian Gilmore, *Love You Madly: The Life and Times of the Neighborhood Legal Services Program of the District of Columbia*, 10 D.C. L. REV. 69, 95, 100 (2007) (quoting Willie Cook, Jr., managing attorney at Neighborhood Legal Services Program and a colleague of Fleming).

[4] MOLLY MCCARDLE, AMENITIES, *available at* https://mollymccardle.com/ amenities (2008).

[5] MOLLY MCCARDLE, *supra* note 5.

[6] Richard Delgado, *Storytelling for Oppositionists and Others: A Plea for Narrative,* 87 MICH. L. REV. 2411, 2415 (1989).

[7] Paul A. Lombardo, *Legal Archaeology: Recovering the Stories Behind the Cases*, 36 J.L. MED. & ETHICS 589, 589 (2008).

[8] MCCARDLE, *supra* note 5.

[9] MCCARDLE, *supra* note 5.

[10] Marisa M. Kashino, *The Reinvention of 14th Street: A History*, WASHINGTONIAN.COM (Apr. 4, 2018), https://www.washingtonian.com/ 2018/04/04/how-14th-street-came-back-reinvention-a-history/.

[11] https://www.facebook.com/ pages / category / Organization / Clifton-Terrace-University-168066489943323/.

[12] MCCARDLE, *supra* note 5.

[13] Bart Barnes, *Sidney J. Brown Dies*, WASH. POST (Dec. 13, 2000), https://www.washing

tonpost.com/archive/local/2000/12/13/sidney-j-brown-dies/226e7ccc-99ef-4619-960d-beb683cO1d5e/?utmterm=.33958af0cedf [https://perma.cc/EU52-ZNNU].

[14] Broyhill, B-168191 U.S. Dep't Hous. & Urb. Dev. 16 (Comp. Gen. Sept. 23, 1970).

[15] Les Shaver, *Making it Work*, www.multifamilyexecutive.com (June 2, 2005).

[16] The Three-Front War for URLTA (1964-1972), https://rentconfident.com/blog/1165/the-three-front-war-for-urlta-1964-1972.

[17] "The Three-Front War for URLTA," *supra* note 17.

[18] MCCARDLE, *supra* note 5.

[19] MCCARDLE, *supra* note 5.

[20] Chused, *supra* note 1, at 212 (citing a telephone interview with Fleming on May 29, 2002).

[21] Louis Michael Seidman, *J. Skelly Wright and The Limits of Liberalism* 1, *available at* https://scholarship.law.georgetown.edu/cgi/ viewcontent.cgi?article=2399&context=facpub (2014).

[22] Edward H. Rabin, *The Revolution in Landlord-Tenant Law: Causes and Consequences,* 69 CORNELL L. REV. 517, 548 n. 175 (1984).

[23] Anthony Downs, *Introduction: Why Rental Housing is the Neglected Child of American Shelter, in* REVISITING RENTAL HOUSING (Nicolas P. Resinas and Eric S. Belsky, eds. 2008) 1.

[24] David A. Super, *The Rise and Fall of the Implied Warranty of Habitability*, 99 Cal. L. Rev. 389, 407 (2011).

[25] Zachary Best, *Landlord-Tenant Work is Empathy in Action*, WASHINGTON LAWYER, Dec. 2018, at 43–44.

[26] Best, *supra* note 26.

[27] N.R. Kleinfield, *Unsheltered: Where Brooklyn Tenants Plead the Case for Keeping Their Homes*, N.Y.TIMES (May 20, 2018), https://www.nytimes.com/interactive/2018/05/20/nyregion/landlord-tenant-disputes-housing-court.html.

[28] Andrew Scherer, *The Right to Counsel for Tenants Who Face Eviction* (Feb. 20, 2018), https://www.citylandnyc.org/the-right-to-counsel-for-tenant-who-face-eviction/.

[29] Order in the Matter of the Adoption of New APR 28—Limited Practice Rule for Limited License Legal Technicians, No. 25700-A-1005, at 5-6 (Wash. 2013).

[30] Kashino, *supra* note 11.

[31] Shaver, *supra* note 16.

[32] Cynthia Gray, *When Judges Speak Up*, American Judicature Society (1998) (quoting *New Jersey Guidelines for Extrajudicial Activities,* III.A.2b), https://www.ncsc.org/~/media/Files/PDF/Topics/Center%20for%20Judicial%20E

thics/Publications/When-Judges-Speak-Up-Study-Materials.ashx; *see also* William C. Vickrey, *et al.*, "Opinions as the Voice of the Court," *Court Review: The Journal of the American Judges Association*, http://digitalcommons.unl.edu/ajacourtreview/396 (2012).

[33] Richard A. Posner, *Judicial Opinions and Appellate Advocacy in Federal Courts – One Judge's Views,* 51 DUQUESNE L. REV. 3 (2013).

[34] Rabin, *supra* note 23, at 548.

IV. FOREVER YOUNG: *TEXAS GULF SULPHUR* RULES AT FIFTY

[1] Clay Calvert and Robert D. Richards, *Defending the First and the Ninth: Judge Alex Kozinski and the Freedoms of Speech and the Press,* 23 LOY. L. A. ENT. L. REV. 259, 287.

[2] Ronald K. L. Collins, *The Judge & Company – Questions for Judge Posner from Judges, Law Professors & a Journalist,* CONCURRING OP.'S (Dec. 3, 2014), https://concurringopinions.com/archives/2014/12/the-judge-company-questions-for-judge-posner-from-judges-law-professors-a-journalist.html.

[3] Alan Adelson, *Texas Gulf Sulphur, Top Officers Broke Disclosure Law On Firm's Mineral Find in Canada, Appeals Court Rules*, WALL ST. J., Aug. 14, 1968, at 3.

[4] *Fair to All People: The SEC and the Regulation of Insider Trading,* SEC HIST. SOC'Y, *http://www.sechistorical.org/museum/galleries/it/takeCommand_c.php* (last visited August 1, 2020) (describing *Texas Gulf Sulphur* as a landmark decision). Legal commentators have echoed this characterization. *See, e.g.,* ROBERT C. CLARK, CORPORATE LAW 328 (1986); Michael P. Dooley, *Enforcement of Insider Trading Restrictions,* 66 VA. L. REV. 1, 1 (1980); Thomas Lee Hazen *Corporate Insider Trading: Reawakening the Common Law,* 39 WASH. & LEE L. REV. 845, 849 (1982). It appears not only in Securities Regulation casebooks, but also in casebooks for courses in Corporations and Business Associations. *See, e.g.*, ROBERT W. HAMILTON, CASES AND MATERIALS ON CORPORATIONS 837 (11th ed. 2010); CHARLES R.T. O'KELLEY & ROBERT B. THOMPSON, CORPORATIONS AND OTHER BUSINESS ASSOCIATIONS 1126 (2010); THOMAS L. HAZEN & JERRY W. MARKHAM, CORPORATIONS AND OTHER BUSINESS ENTERPRISES 902 (3rd ed. 2009); JESSE H. CHOPER, *et al.,* CASES AND MATERIALS ON CORPORATIONS 373 (5th ed. 2000).

[5] Paul A. Lombardo, *Legal Archaeology: Recovering the Stories Behind the Cases*, 36 J. L. MED. & ETHICS 589, 589 (2008).

[6] Sarah Furchner, *30 Images Proving that Northeastern Ontario is the Most Beautiful Place on Earth,* NORTHERN ONT. TRAVEL (May 13, 2015),

http://www. northernontario.travel/northeastern-ontario/a-photographers-perspective-of-northeastern-ontario; www.thecanadianencyclopedia.ca/en/article/ontario/.

[7] A.E. Alpine, *Timmins Yesterday and Today*, NORTHERN MINER (Mar. 23, 1994).

[8] *RC Archbishop Recalls Importance of Kidd Find,* MINING LIFE & EXPLORATION NEWS OFFICIAL 50TH ANNIVERSARY KIDD OPERATIONS SOUVENIR ISSUE, at 28 [hereinafter "50th Anniversary Issue"].

[9] *Treasure Hunt at Timmins,* NEWSWEEK, May 4, 1964 at 73.

[10] Harold B. Kline, Remarks at Vanderbilt University Law School (1980), *available at* http://www.sechistorical.org/museum/film-radio-television/videoplayer.php?vid=1426245440001 &title=Harold+Klein,+former +General +Counsel+of+Texas+Gulf+Sulphur,+at+Washington+University+School+of+Law. Contrary to the caption on the SEC's website, in which Kline's name is misspelled, his recorded comments were made at a law school class at Vanderbilt University in 1980 and not at Washington University. E-mail from Carla L. Rosati, Executive Director of the Securities and Exchange Commission Historical Society, to author (Oct. 20, 2016, 14:16 PM CST) (on file with author).

[11] John Brooks, Business Adventures 139–142 (1959).

[12] Kline, *supra* note 10.

[13] Len Gillis, *50 Years Ago: Discovery of Kidd Mine,* SUDBURY STAR.COM (Nov. 10, 2013), http://www.thesudburystar.com/2013/11/10/discover-of-a-mine-timmins-kidd.

[14] Frank Kaplan, FINANCIAL POST (TORONTO) (Nov. 9, 1968).

[15] See, e.g., CHARLES FRIED, CONTRACT AS PROMISE 177 n.17 (2nd ed. 2015); Robert Heidt, Maintaining Incentives for Bioprospecting: The Occasional Need for a Right to Lie, 13 BERKELY TECH. L. J. 667, 675 (1998).

[16] Alan M. Weinberger, *O'Hagan Decision Bodes Ill for Enforcement of Insider-Trading Laws,* STAR-TRIBUNE (MINNEAPOLIS) (Sept. 12, 1996), at A23.

[17] Alan M. Weinberger, *Preventing Insider Trading Violations: A Survey of Corporate Compliance Programs*, 18 SECURITIES REGULATION L. J. 180, 182-83 (1990).

[18] Weinberger, *supra* note 16.

[19] *See* 2 JAMES KENT, COMMENTARIES ON AMERICAN COMMON LAW 490-91 (Oliver Wendell Holmes Jr. ed., 12th ed. 1896).

[20] John E. Moye, *Legal and Ethical Aspects of Negotiations – Duties of Disclosure and the Right to Maintain Confidentiality in Natural Resources Transactions,* 42 ROCKY MTN. MIN. L. INST 1, 19 (1996).

[21] E-mail from Mary Frontczak, formerly general counsel for Peabody Energy, to author (Nov. 17, 2016, 14:48 PM CST) (on file with author).

[22] E-mail from John Lowe, George W. Hutchinson Professor of Energy Law at SMU Dedman School of Law, to author (Oct. 15, 2016, 15:31 PM CST) (on file with author); e-mail from Bruce Kramer, Jack F. Maddox Professor of Law Emeritus at Texas Tech University School of Law, to author (Oct. 15, 2016, 19:52 PM CST) (on file with author); e-mail from James M. King, adjunct professor of natural resources transactional law at Sturm College of Law at the University of Denver, to author (Oct. 17, 2016, 12:18 PM CST) (on file with author).

[23] Eisenberg, Disclosure in Contract Law, 91 CAL. L. REV. 1645, 1681, 1687 (2003).

[24] Frank H. Easterbrook, *Insider Trading, Secret Agents, Evidentiary Privilege, and the Production of Information,* 1981 SUP. CT. REV. 309, 328.

[25] *See, e.g., Grynberg v. City of Northglenn,* 739 P.2d 230 (Colo. 1989); *Tinsley v. Seismic Explorations*, 117 So.2d 897 (La. 1960); *Wilson v. Texas Co.*, 237 S.W.2d 649 (Tex. Civ. App. 1951); *Ready v. Texaco, Inc.*, 410 P.2d 983 (Wyo. 1966); *Mallon Oil Co. v. Bowen/Edwards Assoc.*, 940 P.2d 1055 (Colo. App. 1996) (dictum). *See, also,* Note, *Oil and Gas: Improper Geophysical Exploration,* 32 OKLA. L. REV. 903 (1979); Earl A. Brown, *Geophysical Trespass,* 3 ROCKY MTN. MIN. L. INST. 57, 62-63 (1957); Wex S. Malone, *Ruminations on a New Tort: Angelloz v. Humble Oil & Refining Company,* 1 LA. L. REV. 309 (1942).

[26] Modernization of Property Disclosures for Mining Registrants, https://www.sec.gov/rules/proposed/2016/33-10098.pdf.

[27] Len Gillis, *In 15 years, Shania Twain Centre Went from Idea to Reality to Rubble*, TORONTO SUN (Dec. 5, 2014, 10:15 AM), http://www.torontosun.com/2014/12/05/in-15-years-shania-twain-centre-went-from-idea-to-reality-to-rubble.

V. IMMACULATE DEFAMATION

[1] Editorial, *Don Weber wants to change the courthouse climate in Madison County,* THE MADISON-ST. CLAIR REC. (Jan. 28, 2012), http://madisonrecord.com/arguments/241298-don-weber-wants-to-change-the-courthouse-climate-in-madison-county.

[2] Stewart McBride, Is it libel if it's never printed? (June 25, 1981), http://www.csmonitor.com/1981/0625/062563.html.

[3] Paul A. Lombardo, *Legal Archaeology: Recovering the Stories Behind the Cases*, 36 J. L. MED. & ETHICS 589, 589 (2008).

[4] KRISTIE C. WOLFERMAN, THE INDOMINABLE MARY EASTON SIBLEY: PIONEER OF WOMEN'S EDUCATION IN MISSOURI 33, 45 (2008).

[5] B. CLAY SHANNON, STILL CASTING SHADOWS: A SHARED MOSAIC OF U.S. HISTORY 201 (2006).

[6] Wolferman, *supra* note 4, at 45.

[7] SHANNON, *supra* note 5, at 202.

[8] Judy Hoffman, *"If I fall, my grave shall be made in Alton": Elijah Lovejoy, Martyr for Abolition,* GATEWAY: THE QUARTERLY (Spring 2005).

[9] John Quincy Adams, *Introduction to* JOSEPH C. LOVEJOY AND OWEN LOVEJOY, MEMOIR OF THE REV. ELIJAH P. LOVEJOY 12 (1838).

[10] Letter from Professor Iver Bernstein, Washington University in St. Louis (Oct. 12, 2009) (on file with author).

[11] Former President Herbert Hoover, Centennial Observance of Martyrdom of Elijah Parish Lovejoy Address at Colby College (Nov. 8, 1937) (transcript available at http://www.colby.edu/lovejoy/recipients/hoover_r.shtml).

[12] Hoffman, *supra* note 8.

[13] W.R. BRINK, HISTORY OF MADISON COUNTY, ILLINOIS 389 (1882).

[14] CONRAD C. FINK, STRATEGIC NEWSPAPER MANAGEMENT 308 (1995).

[15] PETER E. KANE, ERRORS, LIES AND LIBEL 113 (1992).

[16] McBride, *supra* note 2.

[17] THOMAS B. LITTLEWOOD, COALS OF FIRE 148 (1988).

[18] E-mail from Rex Carr (Jul. 3, 2013, 12:43 p.m.) (on file with author).

[19] McBride, *supra* note 2.

[20] McBride, *supra* note 2.

[21] JOHN A. JENKINS, THE LITIGATORS 372 (1989).

[22] E-mail from Rex Carr, *supra* note 18.

[23] E-mail from Rex Carr, *supra* note 18.

[24] Brief of Appellants at 32, James C. Green v. Alton Telegraph Printing Co., 438 N.E.2d 203 (No. 80-602) (App. Ct. Ill. Jul. 28, 1981).

[25] Appellants' Brief, *supra* note 24, at 99.

[26] Gary A. Parazino, The Future of Libel Law and Independent Appellate Review, 71 CORNELL L. REV. 477, 483 (1985).

[27] Richard Salant, Libel Speeches and Articles, NEW CANAAN LIBRARY DIGITAL COLLECTIONS, http://newcanaanlibrary.info/omeka/items/show/8.

[28] E-mail from Rex Carr, *supra* note 18.

[29] FINK, *supra* note 14.

[30] John Curley, How Libel Suit Sapped the Crusading Spirit of a Small Newspaper, WALL ST. J., Sept. 29, 1983, at 1.

[31] Salant, *supra* note 27.

[32] Sam Zagoria, Time to Review Use of Libel Litigation, COURIER, Dec. 14, 1984, at 4A.

[33] Cassandra Burke Robertson, The Right to Appeal, 91 N.C. L. REV. 1219, 1263 (2013).

[34] Chris Guthrie, *et al., Blinking on the Bench: How Judges Decide Cases,* 93 CORNELL L. REV. 1, 43 (2007).

[35] Salant, *supra* note 27.

[36] Doug Rendleman, *A Cap on the Defendant's Appeal Bond?: Punitive Damage Tort Reform,* 39 AKRON L. REV. 1089, 1091 (2006).

[37] For a summary of the appeal bond requirements in all 50 states, *see* Arizona Chamber Foundation Policy Brief (Jan. 2011), *available at* www.azchamber.com/assets/files/Foundation/RegReform/Bonds.Appeals.pdf (Exhibit #1).

[38] Many states have caps that are set at such high levels as to be virtually meaningless. *See, e.g.,* ARK. CODE ANN. § 16-55-214 (2003) ($25 million); COLO. REV. STAT. § 13-16-125 (2003) ($25 million); FLA. STAT. ANN. § 45.045 (1) (2013) ($50 million); GA. CODE ANN. § 5-6-46 (2004) ($25 million); IND. CODE § 34-49-5-3 (A), (B) (1), (2) (2013) ($25 million); IOWA CODE ANN. § 625A.9(2) (B) (West 2013) ($100 million); KY. REV. STAT. ANN. § 411.187(1) (West 2012) ($100 million); MICH. COMP. LAWS ANN. §600.2607 (1) (West 2013) ($25 million); MO. REV. STAT. § 512.099 (1) (West 2012) ($50 million); M.R.A.P. Rule 8(b) (2), (c) (2013) ($100 million); N.C. GEN. STAT. ANN. § 1-289 (B) (West 2013) ($25 million); N.D. CENT. CODE ANN. § 28-21-25 (1) (West 2011) ($25 million); OHIO REV. CODE ANN. § 2505.09 (West 2013-2014) ($50 million); OKLA. STAT. ANN. tit. 12, § 990.4 (B) (1) (C) (West 2013) ($25 million); R.I. GEN. LAWS § 42-133-11.1(A) (2012) ($50 million); S.D. CODIFIED LAWS §15-26a-26 (2013) ($25 million); TENN. CODE ANN. § 27-1-124 (A), (B) (West 2013) ($25 million); VA. CODE ANN. §8.01-676.1(J) (West 2013) ($25 million); W.VA. CODE ANN. § 58-5-14(B), (D) (West 2013) ($50 million); WIS. STAT. ANN. § 808.07 (2M) (a) (West 2013) ($100 million).

[39] K.S.A. § 60-2103 (d) (1) (2012).

[40] A.R.C.A.P. Rule 7(a) (2) (A) (B) (C) (2013); NEB. REV. STAT. § 25-1916(1) (A). (B), (C) (2012); TX Rules App. Proc. Rule 24.2 (a) (1) (A), (B) (2013).

[41] HAW. REV. STAT. § 607-26 (A) (1) (2013) ($1 million); WYO. STAT. ANN. § 1-17-201(A) (West 2013) ($2 million).

[42] Elaine A. Carlson, *Mandatory Supersedeas Bond Requirements – A Denial of Due Process Rights?,* 3 BAYLOR L. REV. 29, 39 (1987).

[43] G. MICHAEL KILLENBERG, PUBLIC AFFAIRS REPORTING NOW: NEWS OF, BY AND FOR THE PEOPLE xv (2008).

VI. THE ART OF BREAKING THE DEAL: THE CASE OF THE PENTHOUSE CASINO

[1] ROBIN MALLOY & JAMES SMITH, REAL ESTATE TRANSACTIONS: PROBLEMS, CASES AND MATERIALS 522, 538 (3d ed. 2007).

[2] Patricia Bosworth, *The X-Rated Emperor,* VANITYFAIR.COM, Feb. 2005, http://www.vanityfair.com/culture/features/2005/02/guccione200502.

[3] Mike Pritchard, *Guccione Left His Mark on Atlantic City,* ATLANTIC CITY WEEKLY.COM, Oct. 21, 2010, http://www.atlanticcityweekly.com/news-and-views/Guccione-Left-His-Mark-On-Atlantic-City-105441273.html.

[4] Jonah Lehrer, *Royal Flush,* THE NEW YORKER, Mar. 26, 1969, at 69.

[5] JOHN HEIDENRY, WHAT WILD ECSTASY 204 (2007).

[6] RODNEY A. SMOLLA, SUING THE PRESS 161–62 (1986).

[7] Bosworth, *supra* note 2.

[8] HEIDENRY, *supra* note 5 at 239, 304.

[9] E-mail from Philip M. Horowitz (June 1, 2012, 6:56 AM) (on file with author).

[10] E-mail from Philip Horowitz, *supra* note 9.

[11] JOSEPH W. BARTLETT, 1 EQUITY FINANCE: VENTURE CAPITAL, BUYOUTS, RESTRUCTURINGS AND REORGANIZATIONS 188 n.9 (2d ed. 1995).

[12] Michael A. Berch, *We've Only Just Begun: The Impact of Remand Orders from Higher to Lower Courts on American Jurisprudence*, 36 ARIZ. ST. L. J. 493, 498 (2004).

[13] CHARLES B. KATZENSTEIN, THE LAW OF MORTGAGE COMMITMENTS §6.06[1] (1992).

[14] Berch, *supra* n. 12, at 499 (emphasis added).

[15] Fowler V. Harper and George C. Pratt, *What the Supreme Court Did Not Do During the 1951 Term*, 101 U. PA. L. REV. 439, 440 (1953).

[16] Harold Hongju Koh, *Unveiling Justice Blackmun*, 72 BROOKLYN L. REV. 9, 10–11 (2006).

[17] Lee Epstein, Jeffrey A. Segal & Harold J. Spaeth, THE DIGITAL ARCHIVE OF THE PAPERS OF JUSTICE HARRY A. BLACKMUN (2007), available at: http://epstein.wustl.edu/research/BlackmunArchive.html.

[18] Laura Kalman, *'Becoming Justice Blackmun': Deconstructing Harry*, N.Y. TIMES (May 8, 2005) §7, at 9.

[19] Daniel Schechter, *Second Circuit Throws Out $128 Million Judgement in Penthouse Suit Against S&L*, 51 BANKING REP. (BNA), at 477 (Sep. 12, 1988).

[20] Stephen L. Pepper, *Counseling at the Limits of the Law: An Exercise in the Jurisprudence and Ethics of Lawyering*, 104 YALE L. J. 1545, 1550 (1995).

[21] E. ALLAN FARNSWORTH, CHANGING YOUR MIND: THE LAW OF REGRETTED DECISIONS 110, 112 (1998) (quoting Oliver Wendell Holmes, *The Path of the Law*, 10 HAV. L. REV. 457, 462 (1897)).

[22] CHARLES FRIED, CONTRACT AS PROMISE: A THEORY OF CONTRACTUAL OBLIGATION 127 (1981).

[23] Pepper, *supra* n. 20.

[24] Thomas D. Morgan & Robert W. Tuttle, *Legal Representation in a Pluralist Society*, 63 GEO. WASH. L. REV. 984, 1023 (1995) (emphasis added).

[25] KATZENSTEIN, *supra* n. 13, §12A.02[5] n.2.

[26] Daniel Bogart, *Games Lawyers Play: Waivers of the Automatic Stay in Bankruptcy and the Single Asset Loan Workout*, 43 UCLA L. REV. 1117, 1118–19 (1996).

[27] Paul A. Lombardo, *Legal Archaeology: Recovering the Stories Behind the Cases,* 36 J.L. MED. & ETHICS 179 (2008).

[28] Music Copyright Infringement Resource, George Washington University Law School, https://blogs.law.gwu.edu/mcir/case/grand-upright-v-warner/.

[29] Dean Calbreath, *Melrod Redman: Old-fashioned Innovation*, WASH. BUS. J., May 7, 1990, at 14.

VII. TOOLS OF IGNORANCE: AN APPRAISAL OF DEFICIENCY JUDGMENTS

[1] Dan McGrath, *Tough and Smart and Behind the Plate*, N.Y. TIMES (May 8, 2010), https://www.nytimes.com/2010/05/09/sports/09cnccatchers.html (last visited Nov. 1, 2020).

[2] Vi-An Nguyen, *All-Star Catcher Jason Kendall Reveals Major League Secrets in Throwback*, CONDE NAST (July 12, 2014), http://parade.condenast.com/313825/viannguyen/all-star-catcher-jason-kendall-reveals-major-league-secrets-in-throwback/.

[3] Joe Strauss, *Matheny Says Financial Woes Helped Him Grow*, ST. LOUIS POST-DISPATCH (Mar. 28, 2014), http://www.stltoday.com/sports/columns/joestrauss/strauss-matheny-says-financial-woes-helped-him-grow/articlec7c0635aa679-5ea3-bOb2-121294d15e28.html.

[4] David Hunn, *Financial Trials Hurt Matheny, But Also Brought Him Back to Cardinals*, ST. LOUIS POST-DISPATCH (Jan. 21, 2013), https://www.stltoday.com/sports/baseball/professional/financial-trials-hurt-matheny-but-also-brought-him-back-to-cardinals/article_7b3bd867-93b5-5c3e-99f4-bf18e7e03ce7.html.

[5] Paul A. Lombardo, *Legal Archaeology: Recovering the Stories Behind the Cases*, 36 J.L. MED. & ETHICS 179 (2008).

[6] Jean C. Love, Commentary, *The Value of Narrative in Legal Scholarship and Teaching*, 2 J. GENDER RACE & JUST. 87, 88, 92 (1998).

[7] FEDERAL HOUSING FINANCE AGENCY OFF. OF INSPECTOR GEN., AUD-2013-001, FHFA'S OVERSIGHT OF THE ENTERPRISES' EFFORTS TO RECOVER LOSSES FROM FORECLOSURE SALES 15 (2012), http://fhfaoig.gov/Content/Files/AUD-2013-001.pdf.

[8] KATALINA M. BIANCO, CCH, THE SUBPRIME LENDING CRISIS: CAUSES AND EFFECTS OF THE MORTGAGE MELTDOWN 8–9 (2008).

[9] Basil H. Mattingly, *The Shift From Power to Process: A Functional Approach to Foreclosure Law*, 80 MARQ. L. REV. 77, 79 n.9 (1996) (quoting Steven Wechsler, *Through the Looking Glass: Foreclosure by Sale as De Facto Strict Foreclosure-An Empirical Study of Mortgage Foreclosure and Subsequent Resale*, 70 CORNELL L. REV. 850, 887 (1985)).

[10] Mattingly, *supra* note 9, at 106.

[11] THE QUAD, Southern Methodist University (Fall 2008).

[12] Joshua Cooley, *Matheny's Mission*, FELLOWSHIP OF CHRISTIAN ATHLETES (May 1, 2014), https://www.fca.org/magazine-story/2014/05/01/mathenys-mission (last visited Nov. 10, 2020).

[13] *Michigan mentor: Bill Freehan prepared Mike Matheny,* RETROSIMBA.COM (June 19, 2012), http://retrosimba.com/2012/06/19/michigan-mentor-bill-freehan-prepared-mike-matheny/.

[14] Strauss, *supra* note 3.

[15] Cooley, *supra* note 11.

[16] Jake Wagman and Jennifer Mann, *Matheny lost his home in legal fight with bank over business debt*, ST. LOUIS POST-DISPATCH (Nov. 20, 2011), https://www.stltoday.com/sports/baseball/professional/matheny-lost-his-home-in-legal-fight-with-bank-over-business-debt/article_5c9087aa-c1e7-5fb9-bc25-9f93f8e313c9.html.

[17] Jenifer Langosch, *Matheny's Selfless Approach A Perfect Fit For Cardinals*, MLB.COM (Sept. 29, 2013), https://www.mlb.com/cardinals/news/st-louis-manager-mike-matheny-has-made-a-point-to-put-his-players-ahead-of-himself-and-theyve-responded/c-62025156.

[18] Tim McKernan, *Mike Matheny: From InsideSTL to Cardinal Manager*, INSIDESTL.COM (Nov. 14, 2011), http://insidestl.com/mike-matheny-from-insidestl-to-cardinal-manager-2/1938452.

[19] Cooley, *supra* note 11.

[20] Langosch, *supra* note 15.

---

[21] Jayson Stark, *Mike Matheny wishes he'd done more*, ESPN.COM (March 15, 2014), http://espn.go.com/mlb/story/_/id/10614171/mike-matheny-st-louis-cardinals-manager-glad-baseball-trying-eliminate-home-plate-collisions.

[22] Strauss, *supra* note 3.

[23] Posting by Gary Becker to The Becker-Posner Blog (Dec. 23, 2007), http://www.becker-posner-blog.com/archives/2007/12.

[24] Strauss, *supra* note 3.

[25] 4 JAMES KENT, COMMENTARIES ON AMERICAN COMMON LAW 159 (Oliver Wendell Holmes Jr. ed., 12th ed. 1896).

[26] John L. Tierney, *"Fair" Value and the Deficiency Judgment*, 16 J. LAND & PUB. UTIL. ECON. 181, 181 (1940).

[27] 9 JOHN S. GRIMES, COMMENTARIES ON THE MODERN LAW OF REAL PROPERTY 693 (1958).

[28] THOMAS LITTLETON, LITTLETON ON MORTGAGES § 332, quoted in THEODORE F.T. PLUCKNETT, A CONCISE HISTORY OF THE COMMON LAW 606 (5th ed. 1956).

[29] *See* Alan M. Weinberger, *Neither an Early Nor a Late Payor Be—Presuming to Question the Presumption Against Mortgage Prepayment*, 35 WAYNE L. REV. 1, 6 (1988).

[30] JESSE DUKEMINIER, ET AL., PROPERTY 618 (7th ed. 2010).

[31] Robert H. Skilton, *Assessing the Mortgage Debtor's Personal Liability*, 90 U. PA. L. REV. 440, 443 (1942).

[32] *See generally* ARIZ. REV. STAT. ANN. § 33-814 (Westlaw through 2015); ARK. CODE ANN. § 18-50-112 (West, Westlaw through 2014 2d. Ex. Sess.); CAL. CIV. PROC. CODE § 580(b) (West, Westlaw through 2014 Reg. Sess.); COLO. REV. STAT. ANN. § 38-38-106(6) (West, Westlaw through 2014 2d. Reg. Sess.); CONN. GEN. STAT. § 49-14(a) (West, Westlaw through 2014 Sess.); GA. CODE ANN. § 44-14-161 (West, Westlaw through 2014 Reg. Sess.); IDAHO CODE ANN. § 6-108 (West, Westlaw through 2014 2d. Reg. Sess.); KAN. STAT. ANN. § 60-2415(b) (West, Westlaw through 2014 Reg. Sess.); LA. CIV. CODE ANN. arts. 2723, 2771 (Westlaw through 2014 Reg. Sess.); ME. REV. STAT. tit. 14, § 6324 (Westlaw through 2013 2d. Reg. Sess.); MICH. COMP. LAWS ANN. § 600.3280 (West, Westlaw through 2014 Reg. Sess.); MINN. STAT. ANN. § 582.30 (West, Westlaw through 2015 Reg. Sess.); NEB. STAT. REV. ANN. § 76-1013 (LexisNexis, LEXIS through 2014 2d. Sess.); NEV. REV. STAT. ANN. § 40.459 (West, Westlaw through 2014 Spec. Sess.); N.J. STAT. ANN. § 2A:50-3 (West, Westlaw through 2014 Legis. Sess.); N.Y. REAL PROP. ACTS. LAW § 1371(2) (McKinney, Westlaw through 2014 Legis. Sess.); N.C. GEN. STAT. ANN. § 45-21.36 (West, Westlaw through 2014 Reg. Sess.); N.D. CENT. CODE ANN. § 32-19-03 (West, Westlaw through 2013 Reg. Sess.); OHIO REV. CODE ANN. §§ 2329.17, 2329.20 (West, Westlaw though 2013–2014 Legis. Sess.); OKLA. STAT. ANN. tit. 12, § 686 (Westlaw through 2014 Sec. Sess.); 42 PA. CONS. STAT. ANN. § 8103 (West,

Westlaw through 2014 Reg. Sess.); S.C. CODE ANN. § 29-3-700 (Westlaw through 2014 Reg. Sess.); S.D. CODIFIED LAWS § 21-47-16 (Westlaw through 2014 Reg. Sess.); TENN. CODE ANN. § 35-5-118 (West, Westlaw through 2014 Reg. Sess.); TEX. PROP. CODE ANN. § 51.003 (West, Westlaw through 2013 3d. Sess.); UTAH CODE ANN. § 57-1-32 (West, Westlaw through 2014 Gen. Sess.); VT. R. CIV. P. 80.1; WASH REV. CODE. ANN. § 61.12.060 (West, Westlaw through ch. 1-3 2015 Reg. Sess.); WIS. STAT. ANN. § 846.165 (West, Westlaw through 2013 Act 380).

[33] GRANT S. NELSON & DALE A. WHITMAN, REAL ESTATE FINANCE LAW § 8.3, at 945 (5th ed. 2007).

[34] Wagman & Mann, *supra* note 16.

[35] Jake Wagman, *Missouri Supreme Court Decision Could Hit Matheny in the Wallet*, ST. LOUIS POST-DISPATCH (Apr. 18, 2012), http://www.stltoday.com/news/local/govt-and-politics/political-fix/missourisupreme-court-decision-could-hit-matheny-in-the-wallet/articlec34069aa-88d1-11e1-92b5-0019bb30f31 a.html.

[36] TIMOTHY J. TRYNIECKI, 18A MISSOURI PRACTICE SERIES, REAL ESTATE LAW-TRANSACTIONS AND DISPUTES § 58:1 (3d ed. 2006).

[37] TRYNIECKI, *supra* note 36, § 61:7.

[38] BENJAMIN N. CARDOZO, *Law And Literature*, *in* LAW AND LITERATURE AND OTHER ESSAYS AND ADDRESSES 36 (1931).

[39] ROBERT C. CLARK, CORPORATE LAW 320 (1986).

[40] Mattingly, *supra* note 9, at 95.

[41] Maury B. Poscover, *A Commercially Reasonable Sale Under Article 9: Commercial, Reasonable, and Fair to All Involved*, 28 LOYLA L. REV. 235, 246 (1994) (drawing an unfavorable comparison between personal property foreclosures and real property foreclosures).

[42] Michael H. Schill, *An Economic Analysis of Mortgagor Protection Laws*, 77 VA. L. REV. 489, 500 (1991).

[43] Skilton, *supra* note 31, at 451.

[44] Tierney, *supra* note 26, at 187.

[45] BENJAMIN CARDOZO, THE NATURE OF THE JUDICIAL PROCESS 141 (1921).

[46] Chris Guthrie et al., *Blinking on the Bench: How Judges Decide Cases*, 93 CORNELL L. REV. 1, 43 (2007).

[47] Mark Roth, *Las Vegas is Ground Zero for America's Housing Collapse*, PITTSBURGH POST-GAZETTE (Dec. 4, 2011), http://www.postgazette.com/businessfbusinessnews/2011/12/04/Las-Vegas-is-ground-zero-for-America-s-housing-collapse/stories/201112040240.

[48] STATE BAR OF MICH., ALT. DISPUTE RESOLUTION SECTION, ALTERNATIVE DISPUTE RESOLUTION COMPENDIUM (2011), https://courts.michigan.gov/

Administration/SCAO/OfficesPrograms/ODR/odr-cdrp-admin-site/ReportsStats OtherDocs/7-ADR_Cost_Study_2011.pdf [perma.cc/7SQY-N54X].

[49] TRYNIECKI, *supra* note 36, § 15.2.

[50] *St. Louis Thriving on Leasehold Idea*, N.Y. TIMES, Oct. 10, 1909.

[51] Cassandra Burke Robertson, *The Right to Appeal*, 91 N.C. L. REV. 1219, 1264 (2013).

Index

S

T

W